Praise for *Digging through History*

"Richard Freund takes readers on a fascinating trek through a vast archaeological landscape that spans three continents and details over two decades of his own research and active participation in excavations. From the lost cities of Atlantis and Tarshish to the dusty caves of Qumran to the horrors of the Sobibor death camp, Freund connects history, material remains, and texts as he expertly unravels some of the most vexing questions associated with these and other sites. Engaging, informative, and written in a style that will appeal to both lay readers and scholars alike, *Digging through History* is a rare gem." —**T. J. Wray, Salve Regina University, author of *What the Bible Really Tells Us***

"*Digging through History* is a fascinating glimpse into how archaeologists collect data—not only from a variety of sites but also across an expansive temporal range. Richard Freund imaginatively and intelligently explores how data transform to story, and the crucial roles that archaeology and the scientific method play in that process." —**Jerome Hall, University of San Diego**

"For scholars and the general public alike, a great deal of what is known—or what we think we know—concerning persons and events from antiquity to the mid-twentieth century derives from a complex intermingling of material culture and history. *Digging through History* offers an extraordinarily illuminating series of studies on the relationship between archaeology and history. Richard Freund's approach, which is both deeply personal and scholarly, makes the book an engaging read, bridging disparate academic disciplines and a vast chronological sweep. While respectful of religious beliefs and traditions, it rigorously challenges a number of seminal myths concerning monumental historical remains and watershed events. Given the breathtaking range of Freund's investigations on the historical mediation of archaeology—from the ocean floor to arid caves holding the Dead Sea Scrolls to Nazi killing grounds in Poland—readers will be tremendously enriched through the fascinating insights of *Digging through History*." —**Michael Berkowitz, University College London**

DIGGING THROUGH HISTORY

Archaeology and Religion
from Atlantis to the Holocaust

RICHARD A. FREUND

Come to Excavate!

Richard

ROWMAN & LITTLEFIELD
Lanham • Boulder • New York • London

Published by Rowman & Littlefield Publishers, Inc.
A wholly owned subsidiary of The Rowman & Littlefield Publishing Group, Inc.
4501 Forbes Boulevard, Suite 200, Lanham, Maryland 20706
www.rowman.com

Unit A, Whitacre Mews, 26-34 Stannary Street, London SE11 4AB

Copyright © 2012 by Rowman & Littlefield Publishers, Inc.
First paperback edition 2017

All rights reserved. No part of this book may be reproduced in any form or by any
electronic or mechanical means, including information storage and retrieval systems,
without written permission from the publisher, except by a reviewer who may quote
passages in a review.

British Library Cataloguing in Publication Information Available

Library of Congress Cataloging-in-Publication Data

The hardback edition of this book was previously cataloged by the Library of Congress as
follows:

Freund, Richard A.
  Digging through history : archaeology and religion from Atlantis to the Holocaust /
Richard A. Freund.
      p. cm.
  Includes bibliographical references and index.
  1. Archaeology and religion. 2. Excavations (Archaeology) 3. Antiquities.
  4. Mysteries, Religious—History. I. Title.
  BL65.A72F74 2012
  200.9—dc23   2012023525

ISBN 978-1-4422-0883-4 (pbk. : alk. paper)
ISBN 978-1-4422-0882-7 (cloth : alk. paper)
ISBN 978-1-4422-0884-1 (electronic)

∞™ The paper used in this publication meets the minimum requirements of American
National Standard for Information Sciences—Permanence of Paper for Printed Library
Materials, ANSI/NISO Z39.48-1992.

Printed in the United States of America

This book is dedicated to

Judy Freund
Howard Berkowitz
Beatrice Freund
Aaron Stovitz

CONTENTS

A Short Chronology

5500–4500 BCE	The Neolithic (Stone) Age (pottery was introduced)
4500–3200 BCE	The Chalcolithic (Copper) Age (copper and flint were used; writing was developed in Mesopotamia and Egypt) The Rise of Atlantis
3200–1200 BCE	Bronze Age (Early, Middle, and Late) The End of Atlantis The Exodus from Egypt
3000–2700 BCE	First and Second Dynasties of the Egyptian Kingdom
1200–586 BCE	Iron Age (from the exodus from Egypt until the destruction of the First Temple by the Babylonians in 586 BCE) Hebrew Bible Written Down The Rise of the Phoenicians and the Sea Peoples
586–539 BCE	The Babylonian Exile of the Judeans from Israel
546–333 BCE	The Persian Period and the Rise of Classical Greece: Socrates, Plato, and Aristotle Story of Atlantis Written Down
332–63 BCE	The Greek Period: The Rise of Alexander the Great Rise of the Dead Sea Scrolls Community at Qumran
63 BCE–325 CE	The Roman Period in the Ancient Middle East Dead Sea Scrolls Community Ends
325–638 CE	The Byzantine Period: The Rise of Christian Rome
638–1096 CE	The Early Muslim Period: The Golden Age of Spain
1100–1200 CE	Crusader Period

1200–1517 CE	Middle Muslim Period, Spain, North Africa, Middle East
	Reconquista in Spain and Expulsion from Spain
1517–1917 CE	Ottoman Empire Period in Mediterranean
	Enlightenment
	The Cairo Geniza is discovered
	World War I
1917–1948 CE	British Mandate Period in Israel
1933–1945 CE	Rise of Nazism in Germany, World War II, the Holocaust
1947 CE	Discovery of the Dead Sea Scrolls
1948 CE–Present	Modern State of Israel

Divine Footprints
Digging through History

Courtesy of Richard Freund, University of Hartford

Figure 1.1.   Champagne Castle, Drakensberg, KwaZulu-Natal, South Africa

Your way was through the sea and Your path through the mighty waters; but Your footsteps left no prints.

—PSALMS 77:20

T HIS IS A BOOK ABOUT SOME OF THE WORLD'S great mysteries of religion and how archaeology has helped us understand the meaning of these mysteries. I have been using chapters of this book in my courses at the University of Hartford for the past decade. This book is intended for students and for the general public who often struggle with many of the mysteries of religion and wonder if archaeology has produced answers to help resolve some of the most fundamental questions of history. Writing a book called *Digging through History* is a daunting task, but it started because I could not find a single book that utilized archaeology to encompass the full sweep of history, from the ancient period to the modern period, for my survey course. Even this book is not comprehensive. It is episodic history that extends from the ancient period to the modern period, focusing on critical junctures or events that illustrate great principles of history. Out of this, *Digging through History* was born.

But history is very long, so the question is this: Where do you begin? Human history is much older than the period from Atlantis to the Holocaust, which is the main thrust of this book. This book covers perhaps only six thousand years of human history, and my focus is on how this history played itself out in the life and times of the ancient Israelites and later the Jews. This is all a small part of the vast human history that has existed on the planet. Geologists write about a history of the earth using a framework of billions and millions of years. Paleontologists use the gauge of millions and hundreds of thousands of years. This book covers only a small fraction of the much shorter human history, focused upon a few illuminating subjects, areas of the world, and peoples who inhabit the earth.

I was in South Africa while I was finishing this book, and it gave me a perspective on just how difficult it is to look at human history. The caves around Drakensberg, South Africa, contain cave paintings that the locals say go back thousands of years. These early artistic renderings by ancient peoples tell us something about who they were and what their lives were like, but we have no texts about their lives that we can compare the paintings to. In this book, I compared how textual information and material culture together help us understand events in history. Although the cave paintings are attempts to create and transmit human culture, it is nearly impossible to know what they were trying to say since we do not have any textual information to compare it to.

I have been involved in excavations that have textual information associated with them. This is both good and bad. It is good because we can compare and contrast the textual information with the material culture. It is bad because we inherently never know if the site we have chosen is indeed the site associated with the text. I have tried to connect texts with the different sites discussed in this book so that readers can see how you can take the text seriously as a source to help understand the past, even while you are not reading it literally.

People are often struck by what appears to be serendipity in archaeology—how random the preservation patterns were from site to site, and how one site is excavated and another is not. I am still pleasantly surprised to see what has been preserved of human history and saddened by what has not. An excavation site is for many archaeologists a "planned accident." Some start in one place, set up a grid, monitor everything that comes from each square, clean the finds, mark them, photograph them, attempt to reassemble (restore) the broken pieces, reconstruct the architecture, and then repeat in an adjacent square—or, alternatively, move around searching for a spot that will yield enough information to actually restore/reconstruct. In the end, everything must fit into an analysis, and a theory must be posited about the nature of the settlement and the finds, since they are inevitably fragmentary. Some of the best archaeologists I know have a sense of the historical ebb and flow of the site and are able to weave the finds into the mesh of regional and international events that surrounded them, with grandiose theories of culture, religion, and society as their guide. These archaeologists are engaged in the process of interpretation in order to understand what happened at a single location, a single stratum, and yet they are concerned about how their finds fit into the larger context of the area. How the story of a place emerges from the disparate finds is not apparent to those who work in the excavation day to day.

In this book, I have an overarching theory of how the material culture of human beings has created a history of civilization that can be traced from the earliest literary attempts at capturing civilization in the Bible and Plato's *Timaeus* and *Critias* to the Nazi attempts at a Final Solution in the extermination camps of Europe. It is a history of events that define different ages and cultural developments, and although there are many points of history that are not included, the examples discussed throughout the book are all connected with my own work on excavations associated with different ages of history.

But as I sat writing *Digging through the Bible* over the past three years, in the comfort of my university office, and attempted to see how all of the different excavations fit into the process of history, I realized just how remarkable the entire process of the writing of history is and why it is both good and bad to personally reflect upon events from the past through the lens of material culture. As you are working in the field, you cannot plan how or if the elements will fit together. Yet, eventually, you must make sense out of material culture that you find, and you are often faced with elements that just do not seem to fit together.

The best scholars I have known are able to take the evidence, both textual and material culture, and create a hypothesis about how the historical events unfolded. Take, for example, Egyptologists who have created an understanding of the long history of Egypt despite the fact that there are so many missing pieces. Standing in the shadow of the Sphinx, I have listened to guides and scholars explain how the Sphinx and the pyramids nearby came to be and who created them. They wonder at the enormity of the task, and despite efforts to re-create in miniature versions of the monumental creations, usually they admit that they are unable to figure out exactly how it was done. In the end, the theory that fits the largest amount of evidence is considered the "winner." Most of the time archaeologists and historians are missing major pieces in the reconstruction of a historical person, place, or event, and yet they can extrapolate or fill in all of the missing pieces by comparing it with other people, places, and events that have almost nothing to do with their work and have taken place half a world away. Sometimes one wonders whether it is the creativity of the human mind that allows us to reconstruct an event or site or whether the event is reconstructed because it is the only way to put all of the distinct pieces together.

The thesis of this book is that history and the reconstruction of history (especially using archaeology and material culture as a guide) are not as straightforward as many books present. History is, for lack of a better term, "messy." It is not a straight line that leads from one period to another, even in the same location. My aim in writing this book was to look carefully at the "unseen hands" of history and see whether there were any patterns. Some archaeologists think that what makes archaeology scientific is good methodology, good planning, and a good measure of old-fashioned luck.

As I went around the world lecturing on topics found in *Digging through the Bible*, I discovered that people were interested in why archaeologists chose to excavate one site and not another. The number one answer I gave to this question was funding (some projects were just more interesting and fundable), but the number two answer was what the site could tell us about the larger questions of the region and the discipline. Often, people would ask me if the decision to excavate a site was directed by some higher power or insight, especially when I was working on sites that are mentioned or associated with the Bible. In reality, it was a series of issues (sometimes logistical and sometimes strategic) that governed whether we could or could not work on a site.

All of the sites we worked on in this book were licensed by national bodies of archaeology, and our work was often documented in films, articles, and books by others. I do not claim to have the last word on any of these sites. Most of the sites are still under excavation, and I am not always still involved with the excavations. I can only comment on my period of involvement and the conclusions that I reached. When I decided to work on the projects in Spain, Israel, and Poland that appear in this book, it ultimately was based upon whether or not the people I would be working with were passionate about the site and had a larger question they were trying to resolve, as well as whether or not the site was from a critical historical period that would be better understood by the work. I did not plan to excavate in chronological order sites from the ancient period to the modern period, but as my work emerged, I started to see patterns. Religion did play a part. I was specifically interested in how the ancient world, and particularly the ancient biblical world of the Middle East, spread through Judaism, Christianity, and Islam up until the modern period. I was interested in Atlantis because I saw it (and the related ancient site of Tarshish) as connected to the spread of Middle Eastern ideas to the farthest end of the Mediterranean. I was interested in why the Dead Sea Scrolls were important for ancient and modern Judaism and Christianity. Ancient religious art and the spread of distinctive characteristics and motifs from the Middle East to Judaism, Christianity, and Islam gave me a way of transcending different sites and texts with a question about what art does for civilization. In Spain, I wanted to see how the Jews left the Middle East and became a part of the most important enterprise of the Middle Ages, the so-called Golden Age of Spain. In a few centuries, Jews, Christians, and Muslims had found a way to coexist, yet in a few more centuries the tolerance and coexistence was lost. Finally, I was interested in how the Holocaust could happen.

The sites and the historical episodes discussed in this book are far from exhaustive. I spent a decade of my life exploring these sites, and the events surrounding them connected themselves in a way that I never could have planned.

Footprints

As I spoke to groups about *Digging through the Bible*, I told them that each artifact, each site, each spade in the ground is in many ways a search for the clues to the divine message in the world. In fact, it is this idea that motivated me to begin writing this book. Human history goes far beyond the confines of the Bible, and I am happy to have the opportunity to use the techniques that I learned in biblical archaeology to reveal the meaning behind other places, times, people, and written testimonies in history. One of the earliest memories I have about this connection between archaeology and human history was when I saw the fossilized footprints of two hominids that were discovered by Mary Leakey in Africa in 1976. I was a graduate student in Israel at the time, and I remember how it affected my understanding of the world. I always wondered why these particular 3.5-million-year-old footprints were preserved and not others. Who were these people? Why were only their footprints preserved? Why not many others from the same time period? It occurred to me that the idea of "footprints" was a way of looking at not only these early hominids but also every single piece of evidence from the ancient period. The quote from the Psalms that I cited in the beginning of the chapter is an example of how a psalmist thousands of years ago was asking that same question. *Where were the divine footprints?*

The term "footprints" is used to discuss a number of different types of activity. There is a lot of talk today about our carbon footprint and how it affects the world in which we live. This is usually meant to describe how we use the limited resources of the planet, but it has come to mean much more: an intergenerational and transcendent impression that connects us in unimagined ways. When I was researching the Atlantis project in Spain in March 2009, a Spanish Roman Catholic archaeologist who knew that I was Jewish asked me what I thought about the recent study that showed that there was a large genetic footprint of Jews in Spain. Scientists researching the Y chromosome of more than eleven hundred non-Jewish males from Spain in Portugal concluded that there was an extraordinary connection between modern-day Spaniards and the Jews who lived in Spain for nearly a thousand years, before they were expelled in 1492. The study, which appeared in the *American Journal of Human Genetics* on December 4, 2008, pointed out that perhaps as many as 20 percent of all Spaniards living today are linked to Jewish origins. These are very different uses of the term "footprints." I began to look at many different types of artifacts and religious ideas that I refer to as "divine footprints" because they go beyond a single individual.

In this book, I will trace some of the most famous mysteries of archaeology that I have been involved in and show how often these excavations reveal much about both the people who created the civilizations and the archaeologists involved in recovering this lost history. Some were mysteries of a single or multiple faith communities, while some were exclusively mysteries of archaeology, and some were mysteries of both. This first chapter is called "Divine Footprints" because I see a connection between the discovery of divine footprints (and handprints) and the messages that these ancestors were trying to send to us in the future. Some of these footprints were produced by the faithful in antiquity as artifacts to inspire other people in antiquity. Some are just natural formations that look like footprints and became objects of veneration by the faithful over time. Archaeologists who discovered them in the modern period puzzle over their meaning. Divine footprints are not necessarily real footprints, and they are not necessarily made by a divinity. A "footprint," in this book, can be a literary text, an artifact, or a site that points to something beyond itself.

Artifacts as Divine Footprints

I was on a radio show on NPR whose express topic was "Religion and Archaeology." They had assembled experts on the Shroud of Turin; scholars of the Olmec, Maya, and Aztec; and me. We spoke about the types of artifacts that have become symbols of religious veneration. I spoke about relics that I knew from Judaism, Christianity, and Islam. We discussed an amazing array of issues that included the head of John the Baptist (five different heads are found in major locations), pieces of the cross (found in many locations), and the famous Shroud of Turin (Jesus's burial shroud), as well as objects and tombs from India, China, Latin America, and the Middle East. I realized as we spoke to the host that each one of these objects is important because they are considered physical reminders of the divine in the world. I call all of them divine footprints.

The importance of these footprints has become evident to me in the past twenty-five years as we excavated Bethsaida, a village on the Sea of Galilee. The excavations were closely followed by many in the Roman Catholic Church, and thanks to Father Bargil Pixner, news of our discoveries reached the Vatican. We were excavating a site on the north shore of the Sea of Galilee that was associated with the beginnings of Christianity. Bethsaida (literally, "House of the Fisherman") was, according to early Christianity, home to many of the apostles and the place where many of the major miracles of the New Testament occurred. Despite how important the site was for Christianity, it could not be found by the faithful pilgrims and Church officials who so desperately wanted to uncover it. No one seemed to be able to locate this important site, and it was one of the great mysteries of faith and archaeology through the twentieth century. In 1987, thanks to the instincts of Father Pixner and Israeli archaeologist Dr. Rami Arav, we began to do systematic excavations. Father Pixner told me about twenty years ago how he found the site. He said that he first saw this mound, located some two miles back from the Sea of Galilee, after the 1967 war. The site, which had been in use as a Syrian army base, was surrounded by land mines, and he could not understand exactly how to safely reach the summit of the mound. Then he began to observe the cows of a local farmer as they grazed in the field, and he followed the cows' footprints through the minefields and made it to the top. He (and some other scholars from the nineteenth and twentieth centuries) speculated that the site of Bethsaida was located in this location, but it was only in 1987, when Dr. Rami Arav began the systematic excavations at the site, that the issue could be decided. Father Pixner felt that he had been led to the site by the footprints of those cows. The mix of religion and archaeology always permeated his work. He was a good archaeologist but also paid attention to the "footprints" that he saw on the ground.

In the twenty-five years that we spent on our Bethsaida Excavations Project, we were finally able to learn the ancient city's secrets. We uncovered the largest fishermen's village ever discovered on the Sea of Galilee. This discovery has been hailed worldwide because it recovered a missing part of the history of the early movement of Christianity. Each artifact we found helped unlock the history of what became Christianity; the faithful followed our progress with interest because the artifacts recall the events of the New Testament. At the same time, the project revealed the entire history of King David's family, from the same city, going back some three thousand years. Together, the artifacts we found tell us more about the New Testament and the Hebrew Bible than was known before.

Almost every single artifact discovered in the fishermen's village began to take on transcendental importance for Jews and Christians when the Roman Catholic Church recognized the site as Bethsaida. (It didn't necessarily take on such significance for us excavating, but certainly for people following our work!) One artifact in particular became important enough to catch the attention of the Vatican: an iron door key that was found near the large fisherman's house on the acropolis of the site. In 1999, as Pope John Paul II's historic visit to Israel was taking shape in negotiations with the State of Israel, we were contacted about whether Bethsaida could be a part of the pope's itinerary and if one artifact in particular could be a part of our audience with him. Dr. Rami Arav and I (along with all of the leaders of some of our university partners involved in the excavations) were deeply honored to be included in the delegation that met with Pope John Paul II during his visit. We were asked to make a presentation of this artifact to the pope during our audience with him, and we were surprised to learn that out of the hundreds of thousands of artifacts found during our excavating at Bethsaida, it was the iron door key found near the fisherman's house that had caught his attention. Weathered and broken (where it would have been worn on a rope belt), it was not as aesthetically pleasing as many other artifacts that we had found over the years, but the papal request was honored. Indeed, its symbolic importance was far more than the confines of archaeology. We realized that this iron door key, from this door, in this particular location (and perhaps in this particular condition) had much more symbolic meaning than any of the other more beautiful artifacts that we had uncovered. The key is similar to the key found on the Vatican flag and is also similar to the depictions of the key worn on the rope belt of Saint Peter. The keys on the flag and on Saint Peter's belt are identified by Roman Catholics as the key to the Kingdom of Heaven. The iron door key that we found is dated to a first-century context, but it became much more than the sum of its parts; to the pope, it symbolized Peter's key.

I told the complete story of the presentation of the replica of the key in *Digging through the Bible*. Many people wrote to me about this story (which I encourage you to read in that book) and told me that they thought it was one of the most meaningful parts of the narrative (although other people criticized me for seemingly agreeing with the pope's words "the key of Peter," knowing full well that it was a replica and that even the original could never be scientifically described as the key of Peter). To me it was emblematic of the power of artifacts and how this particular artifact brought new life to an aged pontiff at the end of an exhausting day in Israel.

Many years after the presentation, a student asked me if there was anything remarkable about the key, which for years was on display at the University of Hartford in our archaeology section of the museum. "No," I told the student, "there is nothing remarkable about this particular artifact, except perhaps that it survived in this climate at all!" For all intents and purposes, it is not an aesthetically beautiful artifact. It is not altogether unusual to find ancient door keys from the Roman period in warm and dry parts of Israel (in the south and desert caves, for example), but given the weather extremes of Galilee (wet and cold in winter, hot and humid in summer), it is unusual that the artifact lasted at all. I have seen iron and

Courtesy, of the Bethsaida Excavations Project

Figure 1.2.   The first-century door key

bronze debris from other Galilean sites that are only a few hundred years old and have nearly disintegrated. The recovery of this iron door key at Bethsaida is similar to the recovery of the ancient wooden boat in the mud near Kibbutz Ginosar, the so-called "Jesus boat." It is remarkable first that these artifacts (the boat and the key are from the same time period) survived, since wood and iron would disintegrate under similar conditions elsewhere. The fact that these artifacts endured and were able to be recovered and preserved for viewing (the key and the boat were both restored by the same person, Orna Cohen) is really an amazing tale unto itself. Galilee's winters and summer weather can be unforgiving. This wreaks havoc on artifacts—wood and metals especially. I believe the unusual coupling of chemicals in the water and in the soil/mud created a good preservative medium for the substances. For many of the faithful, there is much more to it. Our key doubled as a door handle, and its unique shape is easily identifiable for those with a trained eye. Although its design does not exactly match the one on the Vatican flag or in the many medieval depictions of Saint Peter's keys, it is similar. It illuminates not only the story of Peter and the Kingdom of Heaven but also a history of the Church, which searched for meaningful symbols for the faithful in the daily lives of the followers. A key is just a simple piece of metal—except when it comes from a specific time and place, and when it becomes a way of focusing the eyes of the faithful on the larger message—that is, salvation.

Unfortunately, in the end, we were not allowed to present the original artifact to the pope when we visited with him. The archaeological protocol in most countries around the world is that excavated artifacts should remain in their country of origin. We had a replica made, which did not seem to dim his interest in the artifact or its history. I often think back on that Friday in March 2000, when I met the pope and presented the history of the key to him at the Tabgha Monastery on the Sea of Galilee, and I think of how history is made up of moments such as this when faith and archaeology suddenly come together with unanticipated consequences. I therefore call artifacts that have this type of transcendent meaning divine footprints, not because they are made by God, but because they allow us a window into the understanding of a divine presence in the world.

Holy Sites as Divine Footprints

The divine footprints that I refer to in this book are found in our world but border on otherworldliness because of the importance that the faithful put in physical symbols of events that shape their religious identity. It is intriguing to think that through the centuries, people in all corners of the globe have actually considered the question of their own footprints and tried to capture their moments of encounter with the divine by creating an artifact that would live beyond their own years. When we observe the earliest pieces of human activity on the planet, they inevitably involve a depiction of a handprint or footprint of the artist, left on a cave wall or building. Leaving a remnant of oneself for others to witness is one facet of these handprints and footprints.

I decided to call this book *Digging through History: Archaeology and Religion from Atlantis to the Holocaust* because every place that I excavated, visited, and researched seemed to be much more than just a simple area where people were born, lived, worked, and died. The places or events that I write about have had a significant impact upon the religious or cultural life of the world. I chose places that have been enshrined as holy places or that commemorate a significant event. Of course, significant events have happened every place in the world. What made the events, places, and people that I will highlight so important is that they are mentioned in literary texts (and oral testimonies) that were preserved and venerated. I chose particular discoveries and sites in archaeology that have had a long-term impact upon civilization and that I was able to experience for myself. I tried to address a number of questions in my work at each place, questions such as these:

- What is the correlation between the archaeology and the texts?

- What is it about this particular place, event, or person that made it worthy of remembrance?

- What makes a place or an artifact holy?

Why a certain site is called "holy" and another is not is one of the ideas that this book discusses, but I certainly recognize that there are ecclesiastical bodies that have made designations over time. I do not intend to write about this procedure but instead to focus on a process that is much more popular and is the result of people anointing a place with their own devotion. At the ecclesiastical level, leaders of a particular religion will debate the merits of whether a site or an artifact should indeed be invested with an official designation based on testimonies by their reliable envoys. This book, however, discusses a process that does not originate with an ecclesiastical group or denomination but is an authentic expression of people's devotion. I have seen it at sites associated with Princess Diana of England on the anniversary of her death, at the gravesite of a sainted rabbi in Morocco or Brooklyn, and at Arlington National Cemetery in Virginia on Memorial Day. Archaeological sites may undergo the same sense of "popular religion," finding an expression as they are being excavated, restored, and finally open to the many visitors who come and sense the importance of the site. I have seen the devoted fall to their knees looking at a grinding stone at Bethsaida, and people struggle through the cold water of the Siloam water channel in Jerusalem just to walk in the footsteps of a biblical figure associated with this place. During the medieval period, this popular interest often resulted in official ecclesiastical bodies taking notice and later sanctifying a location.

I remember a particular insight that I received one evening some twenty years ago when I interviewed a local bedouin leader at his home. (I did the interview in conjunction with public television for a documentary my team and I worked on, called *The Lost City of Bethsaida*, and produced by University of Nebraska at Omaha Television at the site that we had recently begun to excavate on the northeastern shore of the Sea of Galilee.) The bedouin elder we interviewed (who was in his nineties) knew about local traditions; since we had discovered bedouin burial grounds around the site, I thought it would be appropriate to ask him what he remembered of the burials. Bedouins are indigenous, heterodox Muslims who generally do not stay in one place too long and continually migrate with the seasons. In the present-day period, many bedouins in modern states with borders are assigned to specific places, but their burial places in the premodern period were generally tied to the people's migration patterns. Collecting testimonies from indigenous peoples is a regular part of archaeological excavations, when there are indigenous peoples who still exist in close proximity to a site. I asked the elder simply, "Why did the local bedouin choose to bury their dead at this site?" In one magical moment, he looked at me and answered plainly and directly: "Because it was a holy place!" If we had not captured the moment for television, I do not think I would have believed it. It is a moment when religion and science collide. When I asked him why it was a holy place, he said because holy people had been there. He then proceeded to relate an oral tradition that went back nearly three thousand years in history.

I did this interview nearly twenty years ago, and I remember it so well because it gave me a new and healthy respect for the medium of oral traditions. I was a graduate student when the television miniseries *Roots* premiered. It was based on the book *Roots: A Saga of an American Family*, by Alex Haley (1976), which included how ancient African oral traditions were passed down by African storytellers. I remember how impressed I was by this way of handing down stories from generation to generation. The viewing public also was introduced to a vehicle of human communication that was foreign to the literary-oriented Western traditions. I remember watching all of the series (and again showing it to my classes to teach the importance of oral tradition), but also thinking how difficult it was to believe that an oral tradition could be faithfully maintained for thousands of years by hundreds of different generations of individuals. I thought this despite the fact that, according to Judaism, the oral traditions of the Jews were faithfully maintained by "human books" for thousands of years, and I had studied with professors who knew the equivalent of thousands of pages of text by heart and possessed instant recall for discussion. The ancient tale that this bedouin elder produced on that evening spanned some three thousand years, from King David to Jesus to the modern bedouin. The information that he related to us that evening had taken us nearly twenty years and thousands of hours of excavations and research to recover evidence that backs up that same oral tradition.

I was not the only one who was amazed that his oral tradition could have survived the centuries and that here we had a living book of an ancient tradition with "staying power." The elder's son was sitting and translating for us that evening, and even he was surprised. He asked his father why he had never told him this story before. The bedouin elder responded with the type of wisdom that one can only have in the modern family. He answered very directly: "You never asked!"

Many of the places and artifacts that we will investigate in this book were built by people to create a lasting reminder of their lives on earth. The idea of successive civilizations building on top of one another in the same place is a well-known archaeological phenomenon. I was reminded recently of this fact by a student in my "Introduction to World Religions" course at the University of Hartford. She asked me a simple question about the Taj Mahal in India, which made me rethink my understanding of this holy place. I always teach students that the Taj Mahal is not a Hindu site, but rather a Muslim site, which reflects Muslim architecture and the Islamic concept of style and reverence for the dead. The question was this: "Why did the Muslim leader build the Taj Mahal at that location?" The student was asking a foundational question about holiness; she wanted to know whether there was something special about the location that made the Muslim leader who built it choose that location over another. Indeed, she was right to ask. This site was built over an earlier Hindu holy site. One of the principles I have learned in faith and archaeology is that one holy site breeds another—the holiness that one group experiences at a site is transferable to other groups. In some of the most holy shrines around the world, from Mecca to Jerusalem to Rome, the idea of layer upon layer of holiness can be found. It is difficult to pinpoint the moment in history in which a particular place took on the characteristic of holiness, but it is clear that whatever it was, it continued to be meaningful to others outside of the original group.

A divine footprint or holy site that was reused by different religions points to something other than just a single event. It usually points to multiple events and parallel histories, and rarely do all the groups celebrate simultaneously at the same site—but the idea that it is a holy site remains for all to believe. In this book, I will look at why people rebuild at the same location over and over, why a certain site that originally was not holy became holy, and why burial places, in particular, became places venerated as a symbol not only of death but also of the meaning of how to lead one's life.

The ancient cities and shrines that ancient peoples built were in a specific location because of geology and geography, and often because of astrology and astronomy. It is sometimes difficult to know why a place was important because of subtle or catastrophic changes in the geography and geology; even the placement of the stars and constellations has changed over thousands of years. The original reasons were frequently determined by the most rudimentary issues of access to roads, water, large tracts of fields, ethnic backgrounds, and even the existence of populations (or lack thereof). The reasons why the ancients built in one place over another may not always be attached to any of these arguments and may not be discernible even with the best theories. Often an ancient location, though very important, has been forgotten, covered over with dirt or sand, and abandoned. Its later rediscovery causes it to suddenly have importance in a much later period. Not all inhabited cities and places have been continuously populated. And while a place may have great importance in the ancient period, this may be fleeting. It is impossible to know why a particular site survived and why another did not, but each one of the holy sites that survived can be considered divine footprints.

Divine Footprints as
Footprints of a Divine Leader

There are bona fide divine footprints that have been discovered at many archaeological sites as well: actual footprints that according to religious traditions were left by gods or founding figures of religions, which today are associated with an archaeological or pilgrimage site. In fact, the footprints of Jesus are found in many different places. At the Chapel of the Ascension in Jerusalem, there is a pair of footprints of Jesus that were made at the time of his ascension to heaven. The Church of Saint Sebastian outside the Walls, located in Rome, has a stone that bears the footprints of Jesus from when he appeared to the Apostle Peter on the Appian Way. A copy of these footprints is preserved in Rome in the Church of Domine Quo Vadis, the chapel marking the spot where Jesus appeared to Peter. In Kashmir, there is a tomb/shrine that has the footprints of Jesus, and even Henry III of England placed a copy of the footprints of Jesus, which Jesus had left for the apostles after his ascension, in Westminster Abbey. There are footprints of Mary in Wales and in the Ukraine. The list of such artifacts is long and impressive. Are they all "pious frauds" or footprints that were created to give the faithful a physical image they could focus (or meditate) on in their devotions? Almost none of these footprints can easily be evaluated to place them in a specific time period or to specifically relate them to a single person. They are validated only by the individual group's traditions.

According to written and oral sources of Islam, Abraham's footprints are near the Kaaba (the holiest shrine in Islam) in Mecca. It is believed that the prophet Muhammad left imprints of his bare feet on a number of stones in different places. Some of these footprints are preserved *in situ* (meaning in "the original location"), but other footprints were moved and later saved in mosques, shrines, and tombs of prominent Muslim figures. Some of Muhammad's footprints were collected and are now housed in the Topkopi Museum in Istanbul. Muhammad's footprints are found in the Dome of the Rock in Jerusalem; in Damascus, Syria; and in mosques in West Bengal and Gudjarat (both in India) and in Bangladesh. Shiite Muslims also have stones with the footprint of the venerated Ali (the fourth caliph; according to Shiite tradition Ali, the son-in-law and cousin of Muhammad, was from the authentic line of the caliphs, early leaders of Islam). In fact, there are many such sites with footprints and handprints of human beings, religious figures, and even gods from around the world.

I first wrote about divine footprints in *Digging through the Bible*. I refer to them there as relics (artifacts that purport to be of a foundational person or god but cannot be fully or scientifically studied), after I learned of the footprints of Abraham, Jesus, and even Muhammad in Jerusalem:

> In the fourth century CE Christians pilgrims began to visit a site called "the footprints of Jesus," a column nearby where pilgrims were shown the place that Jesus grasped a column as he was whipped. . . . Later Muhammad's footprints came to be shown to pilgrims when they visited the rock as well as the imprint of the saddle and even the place where Gabriel flattened the rock for his ascent. Some Islamic traditions establish a host of other pilgrimage sites in the area, and many of the Meccan traditions were performed on the Temple Mount in the two mosques. Jacob's "ladder" had been there, according to Jews and now the Muslim tradition vs "ladder" as well; the sacrifice of Abraham's son and his footprints had been there according to the Jews and the Muslims. (pages 139, 142)

I do not want to mislead people into thinking that when I use the word "relic" it refers to a thoroughly modern fake, created to deceive the pious. Relics are real, usually ancient artifacts, although the claims of the artifact cannot always be fully and scientifically examined for authenticity. Sometimes the relics are old, but the problem is that it is nearly impossible to know if they are as old as the event or person they are related to. Sometimes I suspect that the real artifact may have actually been there in an earlier period, and it either disappeared or was replaced as it wore out. The keepers of the relic saw nothing wrong with this since it had originally been there. They were just restoring an existing tradition for future generations. Relics can be made from anything, and we have textile, stone, bone, metal, or pottery relics. The authentication process for an ancient relic is different than the authentication process of an original artifact *in situ* because the religious organization or group that has preserved and cared for it does not always need or want to have it authenticated by an outside "expert" in order to consider it valid for the group's purposes. Often the vox populi ("voice of the people") is enough, even if it is not authenticated by a governing ecclesiastical body. The relic has a power all its own that often is the focus of intense pious devotion and special religious attention. A psychologist of religion would say that the intense devotion and piety exhibited around and for the artifact is a form of self-prophecy. There are entire sites that are relics. These sites are presented as significant and holy locations that have little or no scientific evidence to support the claim being made about them. Yet people come to be near the stones, express their deepest devotion in the presence of others, and use these sites to help them through enormous personal challenges. You must judge relics by comparing them to other relics in other religions, rather than judging them as archaeological artifacts or sites. In *Digging through the Bible*, I identified a number of relics that are pointers, or footprints, because they point to something beyond what they really are to a grander and more significant message. Archaeologists often begin with the claims of relic artifacts as a jumping-off point for the study of a site. Often it is simply not possible to fully investigate an artifact or site that has become "holy" because the site has attained a level of devotion that the faithful do not think needs further investigation. At that point, the relic will remain just a relic, and any pronouncements about the artifact must remain in the realm of speculation.

Archaeologism: The Search for Meaning

I have searched for a vocabulary to understand the common experience that archaeologists and pilgrims have when they are visiting a sacred or venerated site. Archaeologists and pilgrims go through a similar set of steps when taking in a site. Most archaeologists begin with a site survey and move around the site looking for clues about the extent of the village. A pilgrim circumambulates the holy site in search of the different aspects of the site that they have come to know. Archaeologists use architecture, stratification, and pottery reading as primary methods for dating and reconstructing a site. They realize that the piece of pottery they are examining is something more than just clay, water, fire, effort, and use. The pilgrim usually takes away from the religious site a series of interactions with the buildings, the ambience, and religious paraphernalia (either sold or brought with them) as ways of interacting with the site. For the archaeologist, a piece of pottery, often its style, color, and composition, the time period when it was produced, the decoration, and a whole host of elements points to a whole series of ideas: the ethnic identity of the potter, the location of the clay, the potter, the use of the vessel in the time period it was made. Even the smallest decoration can have an important meaning for the interpretation and understanding of the vessel. The symbols that the pilgrim encounters at a holy site are as meaningful to him or her as any of the symbolic renderings on the pottery shards. For some archaeologists and certain sites, the site itself creates meaning for the artifact that the artifact would not have at another site.

I have been asked about the single most important artifact that I have seen. It is a simple broken piece of pottery no bigger than a couple of inches, but its interpretation makes it one of the most significant artifacts in Jewish history. It is an inscribed potshard (a fragment of pottery) from Masada (in Israel) marked with the name "ben Yair." This potshard, however, is a time capsule of sorts, since it encapsulates an entire moment in history that brought Yigael Yadin, archaeologist and chief excavator of Masada, to the very moment of the mass suicides of the Jews that took place during the Roman siege of Masada in 73 CE. The final chapter of the desperate Zealots who escaped the Roman destruction of Jerusalem in 70 CE was at Masada. Eleazar ben Yair, the leader of the Masada Zealots, exhorted them not to allow themselves to fall into the hands of the Romans and become slaves, but rather offered them the opportunity to die by the hands of the hand-picked Jewish fighters before the Romans could get them. Josephus Flavius, the first-century Jewish historian (and the only historian to record this event), mentions in his book the *Jewish Antiquities* that it was at Masada that Eleazar ben Yair "chose ten men by lot to slay all the rest." For Yadin, this was ben Yair's potshard used in this fateful choosing of lots. While it remains a single potshard marked in ink, it is a powerful symbol of what motivates archaeologists into the field: a simple object that signifies an entire historical event. In many ways, archaeologists have and create their own form of relics that are akin to religious relics. In reality, it is nearly impossible to know if this is the same "ben Yair" potshard used for the final drawing of lots between the Zealot fighters. It is possible that it was another ben Yair, or that it was a piece used in food allocations or other transactions at Masada. But the explanation that Yadin gave to this shard has always stood out for me. It is what I remember when I remember what happened on that fateful day in 73 CE at Masada, and I have continued to discuss it in my "Bible and Archaeology" class over the past thirty years. I find that this artifact is as significant as any religious relic, and the veneration that many archaeologists have for a single artifact like this one borders on religious faith.

The idea that an artifact (or a site) can transcend itself and bring "added value" meaning to both the religious and the archaeologist is what I call "archaeologism." It is one of the mysteries of how religion and archaeology are interwoven in the interpretation of artifacts and sites. In the early days of the State of Israel, Israelis were asked what the religion of modern Israel is, and the half-serious answer was: "archaeology." While you might expect the standard answer—Judaism, Christianity, or Islam—in fact, most Israelis are secular, and archaeology provided a link back to the past without the rigors of religious traditions. Even if Israelis did have a religious identity, it would not always fit neatly into the categories of the past. Archaeology and its interpretation allowed for greater flexibility in the discovery of what the culture of ancient Israel meant in any one period.

I find that some people are surprised by how many religions have relics (both physical artifacts and sites) that are venerated without any critical investigation. One of the biggest problems in biblical archaeology is whether an object or place is really from the ancient period that it purports to represent, or whether it was created by later religious leaders to give pilgrims a reminder of an important religious event (even though the artifact itself may not be from that time period). It is like an American flag that is venerated, even though it's not the original flag. Another example is when people visit Epcot Center in Orlando or Las Vegas and feel that they are in Paris, London, Egypt, or New York while still being in Orlando or Las Vegas.

We all have had the experience of going to a significant location in American history—such as the Statue of Liberty—and bringing back a souvenir such as a small version of the statue or perhaps a loose piece of brick or metal that was picked up on the visit. We all realize that this is not really the Statue of Liberty in our possession, but merely a reminder of the experience. In antiquity, as people began to make pilgrimages to the site of a significant biblical event or to the site of an important person's life or death, the pilgrims would often gather a concrete piece of something they were told was connected to the event.

The faithful frequently came back from pilgrimages transformed, and they would then create miniature versions of the place they visited. Many of my students who were interested in Buddhism made pilgrimages to places where the Buddha lived, died, or meditated, and brought back a leaf that had fallen to the ground from a tree identified as the tree under which

Siddartha Gautama had had his famous revelation. In the centuries after the Byzantines had turned Israel into the Holy Land, Christian pilgrims there would bring back a sliver of the wood they were told came from the cross or a bone of an apostle or saint, and a site would be established to house it so others (who could not afford to go on pilgrimage) could come and in a vicarious fashion experience the pilgrimage. Churches became venerable storehouses for artifacts. I often wonder if this was one of the origins of museums: miniature versions of an ancient site visited and remembered by a pilgrim who was moved by the past.

A visit to a sacred site can have lasting impact: the smells, the tastes, the overall impression that it leaves serve as reminders of the place. The scent of the incense burning in the Coptic church that I visited in Cairo has stayed with me until today. Santa Barbara, the church where Jesus and the Holy Family stayed when they went down to Egypt (according to the Gospel of Luke), has that effect upon people. The blackened sign of burnt candles and the moldy smell of the tunnel next to the Western Wall in Jerusalem forever stick in my brain, especially reminding me of the summer hours spent there with the hundreds of worshippers trying to touch the holy stones and stay out of the hot sun. The taste and the smell of the salt (actually more like a foul smell of spoiled eggs) that you experience as you walk along the Dead Sea reminds me of the millions of people who have passed along this road that leads from Africa to Asia. It is a connection that you feel whenever you are there. When I show slides of my work in the caves of the Dead Sea (where the Dead Sea Scrolls were found in the 1940s and 1950s), I am immediately reminded of the sight and the smell of the hundreds of thousands of bats (and their dung) that inhabit these caves and the hours I spent in the shower trying to remove the sediments from my skin.

The feeling of a pilgrim at most of these places is not dissimilar to that of an archaeologist. The pilgrim is in search of the meaningful; so is the archaeologist. The pilgrim draws or photographs the site of pilgrimage and perhaps removes a meaningful stone or artifact from there; this is very similar to the documentation process of the archaeologist. After the pilgrimage, the pilgrim prays and meditates upon the experience in the solace of a house of worship. The archaeologist spends time examining and thinking about the artifacts under investigation in the lab. Often an archaeologist will find comparative photos and artifacts that match what has been found at one site and spend hours studying these comparative photos and artifacts. It is very similar to the experience of a pilgrim, who purchases something at a holy site and takes it home in order to remember the experience and understand its meaning. I am not talking about people who create religious objects just for the enhancement of the pilgrim experience (such as the aesthetically beautiful icons or art in a church), or those who create copies of relics for profit at holy sites, or even those who attempt to deceive people into thinking they are purchasing an ancient artifact when in fact it is a fake. Every holy site is an attempt to take a physical space and turn it into a place for spiritual reflection and meditation. There is sometimes a crossover of archaeological and holy sites. When I take students to see the Church of the Annunciation in Nazareth and they see that in the center of the basilica is a limestone cave that resembles the limestone caves they have visited in other locations, it immediately gives them the sense of authenticity. They realize that this cave is different from the other caves because the tradition of the Roman Catholics associates it with the Holy Family. It is in the center of the basilica because it is the focus of the faithful who visit and can envision the Holy Family gathering in the cave; it brings them to understand the deeper meaning of what these figures mean to them. Could they experience this in another cave? Perhaps, but the faithful I have spoken to say that having that historical connection gives them a different level of satisfaction than visiting another nearby cave around Nazareth.

Recently when I was working in Nazareth I realized how the local people were very connected to almost every area of Nazareth—as if it had been a chosen site from the beginnings of human history. When we met with the mayor of Nazareth, Ramiz Jaraisy, he spoke to me passionately not about the Church of the Annunciation but of a cave that showed just how important Nazareth was throughout all human history. Nazareth is filled with caves. One of the caves near Nazareth contains one of the most ancient burials ever discovered. The Qafzeh Cave can be dated to almost a hundred thousand years ago, and some of the people buried inside were intact. It did not become a religious shrine, but because it is so ancient and because the bodies inside were so well preserved, the mayor (and the archaeologists) took the preservation and discovery of the bodies as a sign of the importance of Nazareth throughout history.

Relics: Jesus, John the Baptist, Buddha, Genghis Khan, and the Nazca Lines

Sometimes, to be sure, religious leaders often did associate a specific artifact with a specific place, event, or person and attempted to give the faithful more certitude about its authenticity by scientifically examining the artifact, with varying results. Often, like the Shroud of Turin, it is an artifact that is associated with a person, an event, and a specific moment in history (the burial shroud of Jesus), signifying that it is something more than just any other burial shroud in Italy. Some assert that this is specifically *the* burial shroud of *the* Jesus at *the* moment that he was taken from *the* cross. Jesus was wrapped in it for burial. The head of John the Baptist is another example. Although there are different relic burials for the head of John the Baptist, each location states that it has *the* head of *the* John the Baptist, which was cut off in *the* specific moment mentioned in the New Testament. John the Baptist could not have had more than one head, so it is bewildering to think how the faithful in each location can invest so much of their faith in an object that is often scientifically untested but affirmed by popular faith. When I point this out to the faithful, they usually answer me with a simple and pithy "But that is the mystery!" A very dissatisfying answer when one is seeking to bridge the gap between religion and science, but for the faithful the mystery is that they cannot understand every single detail of how the world works.

The idea of creating relics is common not only to Judaism, Christianity, and Islam, but also to almost every single religion and group on earth. Relics associated with burial sites provide the local populations with a sense of connectedness that is not easily displaced, even when religion is no longer the issue. In China, for example, the site of the mausoleum of Genghis Khan, the Mongolian leader of the twelfth to thirteenth centuries CE, has been established and built up in Inner Mongolia, despite the fact that the burial place of Genghis Khan has never been found. The site is a memorial for the local Mongolians and visitors to experience the pride they feel about their great leader. The burial site brings with it ethnic pride that borders on religious veneration of a holy site for a saint.

When I was in Peru with students a few years ago, the students asked me what I thought were the meanings of the Nazca Lines that are incised on the ground there. Spanning fifty miles, massive geoglyphs (symbols etched in the earth) are scratched into the ground; they extend between the villages of Nazca and Palpa. The designs can only be fully understood from high altitudes (although you can see the lines running on the surface), and they are reminders of what the Nazca culture thought was important. But the idea of a distinct Nazca culture is derived from the fact that the lines are close to the city of Nazca, and we really only know about what we call "Nazca culture" from the artifacts that they left behind. The lines are an excellent example of a divine footprint. Although some look at them as landing strips for aliens, the faithful in Peru see

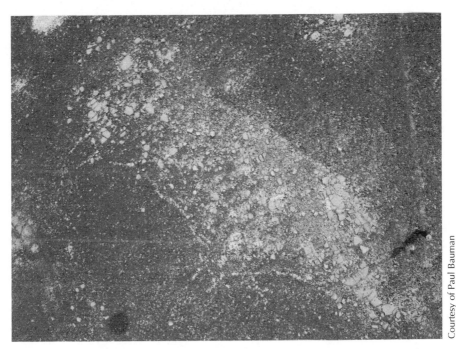

Courtesy of Paul Bauman

Figure 1.3.   A bull geoglyph at Har Karkom, Israel

them as designed by and for the divine. For almost a thousand years in this isolated desert, the Nazca people drew the images of animals, fish, spiders, and other forms of life. I tell my students that the Nazca Lines appear to be attempts by ancients to approximate on earth the enormity of the universe that they saw above them—they are a reflection of the contours of the world and the heavens. The Nazca people created these divine footprints not necessarily only for the divine, but also for themselves. When we discovered geoglyphs on top of a mountain in the southern Negev of Israel at a site that is thought to be the real Mount Sinai (according to the Bible, the place where Moses received the Ten Commandments), I realized that this was a common way for ancient peoples to connect with the Creator of the universe without creating a small standing statue or figurine. It was a reflection of the divine and of the enormity of the universe. Finding geoglyphs and discerning their meaning led me to rethink what I thought about the meaning of these divine footprints throughout the world.

From Prehistoric to Historic Times

The mud and the resulting cooling stone from various lava flows around
the world left a series of very ancient impressions that have recently
been discovered. The millions of years of pressure that was caused by
the flows created the footprints (in volcanic ash) of hominids (early man)
from three to four million years ago in Egypt at places like the Siwa
Oasis in Western Egypt and in Laetoli (in modern Tanzania in volcanic
ash). For me, these ancient footprints can be called near-divine—first for
their preservation, which is amazing, and second for their rediscovery
in the modern period. There are footprints that were found in modern-
day South Africa (called the "Eve" footprints) that are over a hundred
thousand years old and are the oldest and closest to a human-like being
that has ever been discovered. Premodern man's footprints from five
thousand to six thousand years ago are preserved in volcanic ash, mud,
and even clay in Africa and areas from Central America to Wales. In
the Peche Merle caves formed millions of years ago in France, there are
what appear to be footprints of children from at least twenty-five thousand years ago in the hardened clay of the cave floor. The footprints of
ancients were used for many different types of ceremonies. Kings and
leaders from England to Asia had to fit their feet into carved or naturally
occurring footprints. It is really not so unusual. Tourists who visit Los
Angeles often make a stop at the famous Walk of Fame, which has the
footprints and handprints of the Hollywood stars.

Ancient footprints and handprints are usually associated with sites that
archaeologists have uncovered, so they are relevant to the study of archaeology. Most of the archaeologists I know who visit these sites do not think
the footprints they find actually belong to a famous holy figure, but they
realize that the prints are a part of some ancient ceremony or experience.
It may have started with ancient people coming to a location as pilgrims,
but today people go to these places in order to walk in the footsteps of
these holy individuals and to walk the path of an ancient pilgrim. We
would probably categorize most of these footprints as relics, although it is
hard to say whether they are natural bumps in the stone or were artificially
created by an artist. The reasons why a physical footprint is important in
religions (such as Hinduism and Buddhism, for example) have more to do
with teaching people to use the footprints as objects of meditation that allow the mind to move from the physical to the metaphysical, rather than
as real objects of worship. It is similar to the role of the many gods and
goddesses of Hinduism and the clay figurines that pilgrims pick up at holy
sites all over India.

When I tell students that the Hindus have almost three hundred million gods and that they are represented by clay figurines and statuettes that are found throughout India in temples devoted to these gods and goddesses, most of the students are confused about the number of Hindu deities and question whether Hindus really believe that a clay figurine is a powerful god or whether it stands as just a symbol of the power of this god. When I asked a professor of Hinduism how the figurines and statuettes used in the devotion to a god such as Ganesha, for example, she showed me a small figurine that she kept on her desk. She explained that a practitioner of Hinduism knows that the painted elephant-headed clay figurine is not really Ganesha but is intended as a sort of learning prop for the faithful to focus their attention on when they go on the massive pilgrimages in each region. The figurine, which represents the qualities of education, wisdom, wealth, and success, is supposed to give the individual pilgrim the means for his or her own intimate journey and to help personalize the pilgrim's encounter with Ganesha when visiting the Ganesha shrine. The figurine is also supposed to embody the characteristics associated with Ganesha, which can be personalized for the participant as a search for a good grade on an exam or success in a new business endeavor. The divine footprint in almost all religions is like the sites and artifacts that we have been looking at in this chapter: they are targets for our energies, but not necessarily actual footprints.

The footprint of the Buddha found in many locations in Asia is an excellent example of this phenomenon. Despite the fact that Buddhism does not see the value of gods and goddesses in the ultimate redemption of the individual, massive statues of Buddha are found throughout the Buddhist world. Buddhists tell me that the size of the Buddha gives them insight into the ultimate size of the spirit that they aspire to, in much the same way that Christians were inspired by the vaulting ceilings of cathedrals in Europe at the same time that they lived in abject poverty. The immense spaces allowed the heart and the mind to stir. In Asia, sometimes a monastery or shrine will contain only a footprint of the Buddha rather than a statue of the complete being. The footprint itself will be immense and unusually decorated. If you asked a local Buddhist monk if he thinks that the historical Buddha who lived in India 2,500 years ago made the footprint, he would probably not understand the question. The footprint is not intended to really be the Buddha's; it is intended to point to what the Buddha stood for: contemplative and focused inner development.

There are an estimated three hundred footprints of the Buddha in Japan and over a thousand in Sri Lanka. Some footprints are in places where the historical Buddha never set foot, but they also appear in other places where the Buddha is more than just a single, historical person. He is seen (by some Buddhists at least) as a multitude of figures who became enlightened and were designated as Buddha by the people. The Buddha inspired individual Buddhists to think that they, too, could be enlightened, just like the "original" Buddha. Interestingly enough, one of the Buddha's footprints in Sri Lanka is attributed by Muslims (who arrived there later) to be the footprint of Adam. These footprints are therefore recycled by different religions because they all have been popularly ordained as sacred. When Buddhists identify the footprints of the Buddha in different locations, it can be one or both of his feet. The individual Buddha footprints have become a part of local Buddhist meditation rituals at shrines that involve the practitioner standing in the footprints of the Buddha and contemplating what the Buddha experienced and how he was enlightened. I often think about how children borrow their parents' shoes and put their own feet in them at an early age. Their hope is usually to be like their parents, and the shoes that are way too big for them are just a symbol of their inner hopes and desires to be more.

The footprints of the Buddha come in two different forms: natural impressions in rock and artificial chiseled footprints. Most Buddhists will recognize that these are not the actual footprints of the Buddha (they are often immense footprints—much the same as the enormous statues of the Buddha that dot the landscape where Buddhists roamed) but are a physical manifestation of the size of the spirit of the Buddha. While it is true that there are different types of Buddhists—some venerate the historical Buddha; others see the Buddha inside of every person—when I ask Buddhists what they make of these footprints, they often just smile and answer, "It is a place to meditate on the teachings of the Buddha." In general, this is what I feel is the importance of most archaeological sites. It is much the same way that I admire the Shroud of Turin—even though I know that scientific evaluation of the fabric and markings places it in the Middle Ages, I can understand how it has provided generations of the faithful with a physical manifestation they can meditate on and experience Jesus. These relics are not just a place for scientists to apply a certain archaeological method. It is a place where regular people can commune with events, people, and periods that have religious and historical significance. I think that's what motivates people to make treks to Jerusalem, Petra, Ephesus, the Parthenon, the Coliseum, the pyramids, and the Taj Mahal. They are all searching for physical connections with that which defines them religiously. This is a universal experience and does not need to be learned or literate; it is simply an act of devotion that anyone of any age can experience.

The Middle East has its own versions of footprints. The temple at Ain Dara, Syria, has two large "Yeti"-sized footprints that lead into the main sanctuary. The large size of the footprints adds to the impressiveness that a pilgrim experiences. This is not a human-like footprint. The prints are chiseled into the outer threshold of the temple porch; a single left footprint is carved on one slab at the threshold of the antechamber, while a single right footprint is carved on the threshold from the antechamber to the main hall. This indicates that the enormous step of a divine character has been there. It is, I think, an attempt to make this place a location where the divine walked. You could walk in the footprints of the divine and be like God, but no human could make that step—it is quite impressive. This is one of the reasons why archaeological sites have a mystery all their own. They are places that many people feel are where we excavate God. If there was only one set of divine footprints in antiquity, they might be dismissed as insignificant relics of a lost religious idea. The fact that so many ancient sites in antiquity have footprints shows us that the symbolic meaning was universal.

In addition to the footprints, ancient sites also have handprints. Divine handprints seem to express a similar meaning as footprints, but I have come to understand that the symbol has persisted right into the modern period. I see people today wearing a hand dangling from a chain around their neck (and generally not a foot) in much the same way that people would wear a crucifix or star of David. Handprints are reminders of the same elements as the divine footprints.

From the Bible to the Rabbis: All Those Divine Handprints

I remember distinctly the first time that I saw a divine handprint. Actually, it was not a full handprint—it was just a finger. I was no more than five years old and in the synagogue as they lifted the scroll of the Torah from the reader's lectern. The person holding the scroll opened it for everyone to see, and then all the people stuck their pinky finger in the air and sketched the movement of the writing of the text from right to left. Some lifted the corners of their prayer shawls (a *talit*) with the pinky finger in tow. I remember asking an adult member of the congregation what the finger in the air was all about. His answer has stuck with me all of these years. He said that it is not just the motion of the finger—one does not just point up in the air with the pinky finger. He told me that he had been taught to move his finger from right to left as they raise the holy text in the air. As you see the parchment of the Torah lifted in front of you, you should say "By the finger of God" this was written. You participate in the divine act of writing the Torah scroll as was originally done when God actually gave the word to humanity (as it says about the Ten Command-ments, written by the "finger of God" on the stone tablets): to look at the letters and words on the parchment (which clearly is not the original Ten Commandments stone tablets) and to transfer that experience to the mo-ment of looking at the physical parchment scrolls. When people look at the (physical) scroll of the Torah, they really "see" God. The faithful affirm that these scrolls are the same as if they were written by the finger of God.

Exodus 24:9 is one of the few clear descriptions in the Bible of the divine by the leaders of the Israelites. This description includes the "hand" and "feet" of the divine together with a comparison to material culture (of pavement and sapphire color) that would have been readily understood by the readers of the Bible. Only four chapters after the Ten Commandments in Exodus 20 warned against the excesses of idol worship, Moses and his colleagues described God in very physical ("idol-like") terms. It gave me an insight into the way that the faith and archaeology work together. In this chapter I wanted to show many different examples of how the divine is depicted in the material cultures of different places in different periods of history. I think that the Israelites were never afraid to find a way of understanding their God in very concrete terms, and hands and feet were seen as extensions of an acting and personal God. The Egyptians, of course, had a similar expression. In chapter 25 of the proverbs of Amenemope, dating from approximately 1000 BCE, we find the divine hand as a symbol of divine favor: "Man is clay and straw and God is his potter; He over-throws and builds daily; He impoverishes a thousand if He wishes. . . . How fortunate is he who reaches the West; When he is safe in the hand of God."

Who Can See the Hand of God?

There is one image that stands out among the artistic renderings of hand-prints that have found their way into synagogue art and burial stones for Jews over the past one thousand years. This image can be regularly seen in cemetery and synagogue art today. It is two hands, with outstretched palms and fingers. Each hand is split in the middle, with three fingers on each hand extending one way and two fingers extending the other (the thumb, pointer, and middle finger extend in one direction, while the ring and pinky finger extend in the other, similar to the *Star Trek* Vulcan greeting). This image was connected with the priestly blessing of the people. In Judaism, this action was to be done only by the priests (the sons of Aaron) in Temple times (up until the first century CE) and by no others. Since the priests (called "kohanim" in Hebrew) were the representatives of God in the Temple, the hand gesture was a sign of their divine connection. It was generally used with the famous priestly blessing of Numbers 6: "May the Lord bless you and keep you! May the Lord deal kindly and graciously with you! May the Lord shine the Divine countenance upon you and grant you peace!" This blessing, which was conveyed for centuries in the Temple service as a blessing for the people visiting the Temple and is still repeated in countless synagogues worldwide, has made such an impression that it is truly another example of divine footprints. When a small, silver, seventh-century BCE scroll with these words inscribed on it was found in excavations in Jerusalem, it was seen as one of the most important examples of the connection between the biblical text and the divine favor.

The image is so well known that when the character Spock in *Star Trek* needed a universal symbol that would be used to symbolize the Vulcan motto of "live long and prosper," the (Jewish) actor Leonard Nimoy employed the symbol of the priestly hands separated in the middle to give it a depth that the words just could not embody. I remember watching Spock make this motion and thought how a single hand gesture embodied the religious values that I had been brought up with. The artistic rendering of the two hands is a symbol of God and his power.

Real divine handprints, like divine footprints, have been found at excavations. I think they demonstrate how a worshipper prepared for an encounter with the divine. Handprints are found in some of the most ancient sites on the planet. They are in caves in France, Spain, Argentina, Australia, North Africa, and the Middle East. Some seem to be an ancient form of identification at storage facilities where people left their belongings—when they returned from a trip to reclaim their items, they knew where they had left them because they had carved or painted their hand on the rock nearby. The presence of these handprints later became much more than just identification signs.

But there are other ancient handprints that point in another direction. These are found at burial sites that indicate an attempt to connect the identity of the dead with something eternal. The symbol of the hand appears to have been a universal symbol of comfort and good luck. We know today about the uniqueness of people's fingerprints—it is clear that in antiquity people thought the unique lines and wrinkles of the hand were entwined with the meaning of one's destiny. People today still have their palms read by fortune-tellers. Both Jews and Muslims sometimes have amulets they wear to ward off evil and for good luck, and the hand symbol, called *hamsa* (Arabic for "five"), is found on jewelry, pottery, and tapestries. (Sometimes it is called the "hand of Fatima" by Muslims. Fatima was Muhammad's daughter, and she was seen in Islam as particularly able to ward off evil.) The most famous handprint that I ever saw was found at the eighth-century BCE burial cave Khirbet el-Qom near Hebron in Israel. It is exceptional because the inscription is so unusual. It says "Uriyahu, the Governor wrote this, May Uriyahu be blessed by YHWH [the *tetragrammaton*, or holy name of God in the Bible] and from his enemies O Asherah save him." This is significant since it implies that the deity of ancient Israel, YHWH, had a consort or female goddess (Asherah) associated with his name. (Another inscription, found at Kuntillet `Arjud, a site in the Sinai Peninsula, confirms this notion that for some believers in YHWH, the God of ancient Israel had a female "assistant" as part of the workings of the universe.) There is an additional handprint located underneath the Khirbet el-Qom inscription. One wonders if this sunken handprint is intended to be the hand of Uriyahu, hoping to identify himself to the divine in the world to come or to have the print act as another divine marker for others.

The "Right and the Left" Hands of God in Post-Biblical Archaeology

I remember how confused I was the first time that I saw the handprint of the God of ancient Israel in an archaeological site. It was presented by a lecturer over forty years ago, and it was done in such a matter-of-fact way that I barely knew how to react. We were standing in the ancient Bet Alpha Synagogue in Galilee. The lecturer asked us simply to look at the mosaic on the fifth-century CE synagogue floor and tell us something that was unusual. I thought it was the zodiac on the floor (which was unusual, but, as we shall see in the coming chapters, actually a well-known feature of synagogues of this period). In fact, after looking at the mosaic floor many times I was surprised to see that the most famous story of Genesis, the so-called "binding of Isaac" in Genesis 22, was being retold in pictures on the mosaic floor. I knew that the story was one of the seminal stories for Jews, Christians, and Muslims, but I did not realize that it had been chosen by Jews for illustration purposes because it was seen as the great test

Courtesy of the Bethsaida Excavations Project

Figure 1.4. Bet Alpha Synagogue

for the faithful. What would one do in the name of faith? Would someone make the ultimate sacrifice of a child in the name of religion? The image of the binding of Isaac was and is used by illustrators in the traditions of Judaism, Christianity, and Islam (in different ways) to tell the essential truth of the importance of the divine demands of creation. As I looked at the mosaic at Bet Alpha, I saw I was looking at a clever re-telling of the story. I saw how the artist depicted God's intervention at the top register of the border of the mosaic floor. There is clearly a divine hand reaching down from heaven to stop Abraham. Unfortunately, in the text of Genesis 22 it is not God but an *angel* that stops Abraham's hand. The artist has gone out of his way to show the right hand of God reaching out of heaven to stop Abraham. The artist wanted to make sure that all of the people who sat in that synagogue were indeed "seeing" God when they looked at that divine hand emerging from heaven.

The figures are even identified with names so that no one would mistake who was who. It was shocking when I saw it, but it turns out I was looking at a tradition that had emerged even earlier in Greek and Roman culture and that had found its way naturally into other religious traditions of the West. If the Bible says that God brought the children of Israel out of Egypt with a "strong arm and an outstretched hand," one has the right to expect that people are going to look for the arm and hand even in a religion that did not stress corporeality of God.

The idea of the right hand of God versus the left hand is also one of those small details that are lost on most people when they look at the language of the Bible. Some scholars hold that God heals or saves with the right hand and kills with the left hand. This thought is found in the early Roman period interpretation by Targum Pseudo-Jonathan (a name for the western translation of the Torah) of the scene on the night of the killing of the firstborn of Egypt in Exodus 12:42, which holds that the ancient Israelites were saved by the right hand of God and the Egyptian firstborn sons were killed by his left hand. There are references in the book of Isaiah 48:13 ("Surely my [left] hand founded the earth and my right hand stretched out the heavens") and in the book of Psalms 89:14 ("Your left hand is triumphant; your right hand raised in victory"). By the first century CE, it is clear that the right hand of God is the saving power that even the ancient historian Josephus Flavius uses to describe the speech of Herod to the troops in his book *Wars* 1.20.4 after the earthquake of 31 BCE, where he specifically says that the "people will not escape [God's] great eye nor his invincible right hand." Josephus's version of the giving of the Ten Commandments in his book *Antiquities* 3.5.8 is different from what is literally written in Exodus 31:18 (which says, "finger of God"). Josephus states, "and the writing was by the hand of God." But it is clearly the right hand of God that Josephus believes holds the power of salvation. He put the details of a prayer in the mouth of the prophet Samuel that is not even found in the book of 1 Samuel 7:9 (*Antiquities* 6.2.2: "and he cried out to God to extend his right hand over them when they fight with the Philistines"). Despite the fact that other Jewish Roman period writers (such as Philo in Alexandria, for example) fought the idea of any anthropomorphic terminology to describe God, it is clear that other Jews saw the divine in the world in many more specific ways.

This tradition of the right hand of God being extended from heaven to protect and save us is what we regularly see when we look at the mosaics and drawings. While working on the famed Dura Europos murals in Syria, I remember how surprised I was when I saw for the first time the hands-of-God drawing of the story in Ezekiel 37 about God gathering the "dry bones" (about a prophecy of Israel's spiritual dryness being restored by God). I realized that this use of multiple hands of God reaching out to raise up the dead (together with a group of angel helpers!) was not just an isolated act of an artist in Galilee but also a well-known tradition that was found in many different places (with slight differences) and accepted as a way of defining the power of God in the world to resurrect the dead. The idea is repeated on the synagogue wall, when in the mural about the Exodus from Egypt the artist showed how God had indeed extended the hand and arm to the Israelites and brought them through on dry land. There were even two divine arms and hands reaching out from heaven, apparently to make sure that the Egyptians were stopped and the Israelites were safe. Later I saw the motif of the hand of God on amulets from the Geonic Period (eighth and ninth centuries CE) and realized that the tradition, which began in Greece with the arms of Zeus and the other gods reaching out in their *deus ex machina* way to help the Greeks in their wars and individual tasks, had found new expression in Judaism. Handprints of God show us just how important it was for the ancients to see that God had physical manifestations.

Archaeological Sites as Divine Footprints: From Atlantis to the Holocaust

In this book, I will not necessarily be searching for physical divine (or human) footprints or handprints but rather reporting about places, artifacts, and texts that have influenced history in small and large ways. The "ripple effect" created by their discovery has affected the way that we understand the world in the modern period, even though many of them were from antiquity. I call them divine footprints because they are so influential in history and they guided many people throughout the past four thousand years. In chapter 2, I begin my study with Atlantis, because it has become so iconic for the search for the beginnings of civilization. Chapter 3 discusses how a small area on the Dead Sea produced material culture in the Dead Sea Scrolls that influenced society into our own time. In chapter 4, we will see how archaeology reveals one of the most inspiring periods of interactions between Jews, Christians, and Muslims in Spain, only to turn into one of the most disgraceful periods of medieval history. Finally, chapter 5 ends with an exploration of how archaeology at a twentieth-century extermination camp can deepen our understanding of our own period of human history.

I have spent the past thirty years in search of the reasons why these particular places have inspired so many. I will take you on the same archaeological trek that I went on. Many of these locations do not have literal footprints of gods or famous figures. They are unique places that have inspired humanity in literary accounts, but they could not always be found. I discuss the lost cities of Atlantis and Tarshish, for example, which persisted in Western imagination for 2,500 years and pushed writers and poets to construct literature about a place that no one could locate.

This book is an archaeological walk that travels to Asia, Africa, and Europe and involves archaeological work that I personally participated in. I was able to find remains that archaeologists will puzzle over for years to come in far-flung locations from southern and northern Israel, northern Spain, and eastern Poland. From approximately 2000 BCE through the twenty-first century, spanning over four thousand years of human history, this book details an archaeological journey that took the better part of two decades and involved a search for evidence in holy temples and tabernacles, churches and synagogues, ancient baths and burials, ancient cities and villages, and swamps and underwater. It was a search that started with the beginnings of human history in the investigation of the location of Atlantis and ends with the near collapse of humanity in the Holocaust.

Mysteries of Religion and Archaeology in the Search for Atlantis and Tarshish   2

Figure 2.1. The CGI version of Atlantis in the center of the ancient Tartessos Bay, from *Finding Atlantis*

Courtesy of Associated Producers

> *Bordering on the [Mediterranean] Sea and extending through the center of the whole island there was a plain . . . and to make the hill whereon she [Cleito] dwelt impregnable he [Poseidon] broke [the plain] off all around it and he made circular belts of sea and land enclosing one another alternately, some greater, some smaller, two being of land and three of sea, which he carved as it were out of the midst of the island and these belts were at even distances on all sides.*

—PLATO, *CRITIAS* 113D

The Rediscovery of the Lost Atlantis, Tarshish, or Both

AS I WAS FINISHING THIS BOOK, marine archaeologists were searching the ocean floor for more pieces of evidence of what we think came from the ancient city of either Atlantis, Tarshish, or both. One might ask why we did not wait a few more years to report on the findings in order to wait to see what the next discovery might yield. I have found that it is better to report on findings while they are still fresh because it often offers more transparent and well-documented results. Over the past twenty years I have tried to publish as much as we know about a certain site as soon as we know it. The evidence that we find may combine with unpublished research that others have done and continue the dialogue. Much of what I am writing about is a compilation of the work of many different groups and represents my own understanding of what can be learned about Atlantis and Tarshish from these different groups' research in southern Spain and in central Spain.

Five separate research teams contributed to the 2009–2010 Atlantis project that I was involved with (for accuracy's sake, the project was named the "Hinojos Project" after the name of the spot the Spaniards were working in the Doña Ana Park). Two teams were from different universities and research institutions in Spain, two teams were from the United States, and one was from Canada. They were assembled over the past three years to investigate the hypotheses of other researchers from other countries (specifically Germany) about whether there was evidence of an ancient lost city buried near or on the coast of southern Spain. We were brought together because a production company, Associated Producers (working on a documentary for *National Geographic*), had already begun working with the Spaniards on filming their project and sensed that our team could help the efforts of the Spanish team. I was involved with all of the separate teams and investigated most of these hypotheses and speculation of the different researchers (even one from nearly ninety years ago) for myself. In this chapter, I report my own findings and share what I think about the different hypotheses. I do not claim to have found Atlantis or Tarshish (or both) in the same way that the RMS *Titanic* was discovered on the bottom of the ocean or in the way that King Tutankhamen's tomb was found in Egypt. This discussion is more about how science solves archaeological mysteries by testing hypotheses and accumulating evidence. For now, there is more evidence to suggest that Atlantis and/or Tarshish were located in southern Spain than at any other site worldwide. Figure 2.1 is a computer-generated satellite photograph of the research areas in southern Spain in the Doña Ana Park, with the original city in the ancient bay.

Atlantis and Tarshish Research and the First Clue: Where Atlantis Was *Not* Located

This is certainly not the first expedition to look for Atlantis. Other expeditions have had this as their raison d'être—but not this project. Our project was specifically geared to solving a very specific problem in a very specific location. The documentary of *National Geographic* was called *Finding Atlantis*, but each of the different teams and projects was focused on pieces of information that ultimately led in this direction.

The problem of Atlantis has always boiled down to where to look and what to look for. People have speculated for over a thousand years about the location of Atlantis. Plato wrote about Atlantis over 2,400 years ago, and since he was from Greece, many people thought that he was actually writing about a location near Greece, not at the very ends of the known world. Many ancient writers after Plato were interested in Atlantis, and they began writing about its location. The Jewish philosopher Philo, who lived in Alexandria, Egypt, in the first century CE, mentions it as a part of his understanding of the beginnings of the civilization. So the search for Atlantis starts with the unique nature of the description of the city and a specific location. According to Plato, the city was built on an island and appeared as three concentric circles, one within the other (Plato calls them "three belts of water and two of land"), and it was located beyond the Pillars of Hercules. The Pillars of Hercules were known by most ancient writers to be located at what today we call the Straits of Gibraltar, near Spain. Plato also specifically states that Atlantis disappeared suddenly after a major environmental catastrophe. This description of the disappearance of the city is also very unusual and requires a set of circumstances that are not found everywhere in antiquity.

The searches for an Atlantis with these concentric circles on an island that disappeared under these types of circumstances have included Italy, Sicily, Malta, Morocco, Egypt, Sardinia, Crete, Cyprus, and the depths of the Aegean Sea. Most researchers assumed that since Plato lived in Greece he might be writing about events that took place near Greece, where he lived (but far from the Pillars of Hercules), and that he simply moved an ancient story that happened nearby to a location far from his own location to avoid complaints or to give the story greater mystery by placing it in an exotic, faraway location. Some scholars moved the Pillars of Hercules to a location closer to Greece in the time of Plato, but generally most of the theories about Atlantis have to deal with this very specific location.

With the beginnings of systematic archaeology at the end of the nineteenth century, many ancient mysteries were investigated using archaeological methods in the twentieth century. Atlantis was at the top of the list. After work began at a site thought to be ancient Troy, Atlanteologists looked for Atlantis in and around Troy or in the bottom of the Black Sea. Plato's descriptions of the technological advances of Atlantis seemed miraculous in the ancient world, so some speculated that Atlantis might have been located near the site of other miracle stories in Egypt and the Sinai Peninsula. Since Plato places Atlantis at the end of the known world, other researchers began placing possible locations in the far-flung reaches of the world.

Some scholars located a potential site for Atlantis off the coast of India or Indonesia, where the environmental conditions described by Plato were more common. In these locations, tsunamis and volcanoes regularly crushed cities and submerged whole islands. There were researchers who took Plato's writings seriously (but not literally). In the twentieth century, some marine archaeologists placed Atlantis off the coasts of the Iberian Peninsula, especially in southern Spain and Portugal, where the remnants of ancient landmasses could be found on the ocean floor, near the Pillars of Hercules. But others speculated that Atlantis may have sunk off the coast of northern Spain, or in the Irish Sea, the North Sea, the Mediterranean Sea, or even in the Atlantic Ocean. Speculation in the twentieth century placed Atlantis in the Bahamas, Cuba, Mexico, and even land-locked Bolivia. Many Europeans placed Atlantis in areas in and around Denmark, Finland, Sweden, Greenland, Iceland, and even Antarctica. In short, for some, the location of Atlantis could be anywhere. I have been working with ancient texts for most of my adult life, and I was shocked that most of the researchers who placed Atlantis elsewhere did not take Plato seriously. I think that we need to take ancient texts seriously (but not literally) and that when we do we can achieve much more than by just simply discounting or slavishly following an ancient text. I think that we need to take this reference in Plato to the Pillars of Hercules seriously—and that would place Atlantis in southern Spain. I even considered that Plato, like the biblical writers, had "collapsed" several ancient destructions into one "Atlantis."

Who Were the Atlanteans?

In order to find Atlantis, it is not sufficient to just find architecture in a single location. In order to assign the location to Atlantis, one needs to assess the type of culture found in that location and compare the material cultural finds to determine whether this is indeed Atlantis and not just an unknown ancient site. In this chapter, that is what I will do. I will summarize what I have learned about this site in southern Spain and why it seems to fit the description of Atlantis found in Plato. Most important, I will assess what I think happened to Atlantis and to the Atlanteans.

As I began my research I was struck by the fascination with the entire history of Atlantis. Atlantis has inspired films, tens of thousands of articles, and books, and on the Internet one can find hundreds of thousands of musings in blogs, citations, and even music. I think Atlantis holds our fascination because Plato's story is really about the great-grandmother of all ancient civilizations. Plato clearly states that the story was passed down by the Egyptians, and he acknowledges that his own Greek civilization came after Atlantis. This acknowledgment of earlier cultures shows me that Plato had an appreciation of non-Athenian/Greek culture even though he knew that this was a little bit heretical. I think that the Atlantis account was inspirational even for Plato.

Akin to the biblical story of the Garden of Eden and the Buddhist story of Shangri-La, the story of Atlantis has achieved iconic and mythic status in Western civilization over the past 2,400 years because Plato tells us that Atlantis was more ancient and more grandiose than anything else that we have ever read about from antiquity. Plato's account of Atlantis may have inspired other Hellenistic and Roman authors, such as Euhemerus of Messene, who wrote in the fourth century BCE about Panchaea, and Diodorus Siculus in the first century CE, whose writings preserve a part of the story of Iambulos's travels. Although the technological advances of Atlantis may not have been as extensive as they are portrayed in Francis Bacon's seventeenth-century book *New Atlantis* or in the twenty-first-century Disney movie *Atlantis: The Lost Empire*, Plato's account still possesses the power to inspire awe in modern readers. By most calculations (depending on how you read the manuscripts of Plato's *Timaeus* and *Critias*), Plato places Atlantis's founding in a period that could be designated as the Stone Age—thousands of years before the rest of the ancient world had shipping and elaborate architecture as described by Plato. More important, Plato tells us that the Atlanteans had built a series of interconnected small islands with tunnels and canals that required engineering abilities not seen until the work of the Dutch and the Venetians after the Renaissance.

The idea that there was indeed such a wonderfully advanced civilization that existed so far back in human history and was destroyed by a cataclysmic environmental disaster has roots in many societies. The Hindus believe that civilizations have risen and fallen in succession over millions of years and that this is the way the universe functions. It is similar to the way that some note the disappearance of the high culture and engineering prowess possessed by the ancient Egyptians, who built the Sphinx and the pyramids in the Bronze Age. Unlike Egypt's pyramids, Atlantis's technology cannot be seen and evaluated. It existed and then suddenly disappeared.

What would the rediscovery of Atlantis prove? First, it would attest that Plato was not just a fiction writer of ancient myth. In the past century we have moved in academe from seeing the books of the ancient world as 100 percent accurate to a point where we view them with great skepticism. In this book, I analyze the ancient literary accounts together with material culture as two pieces of the same puzzle of antiquity. Material culture means artifacts such as pottery, steles, statues, figurines, writing, glass, metal, stonework, walls, wood, leather, and so on, which can be compared and contrasted with other material culture from other societies in antiquity. The evidence of what an ancient text says about a society and what the material culture from that place shows can be compared and contrasted. Unfortunately, the material culture and a literary source do not always agree. Is the text correct or is the material culture correct? In fact, both can be correct in their own way. Plato is not "true" because everyone has read him throughout the generations. He is "true" because many of the ideas he raises can be validated by a number of different sources. If we find that Plato is accurate in some things, it does not mean that he is accurate in everything. But if he is accurate in some things, then it means that we have to look seriously at what he says about everything. Since Plato was so specific in his description of where Atlantis was located (and he knew that everyone in antiquity would know where he was describing), it was natural to look in southern Spain for Atlantis.

The disappearance of Atlantis has a dark side. If there is anything that modern people fear more than the future, it is the past. The concern that we shall experience (again) the destruction and devastation that is mentioned in the pages of the Bible and in the writings of Plato keeps people reading the ancient accounts of the Flood, the details of the book of Revelation, and the Atlantis story. The possibility that we can figure out what went wrong and make sure it does not happen again (or be ready for a repeat of a past cataclysmic event) drives many researchers. The story of a technologically advanced civilization that disappeared in a blink of an eye intrigues us in the modern period because we worry that our own civilization might suffer a similar fate. The story of Atlantis represents the deepest and darkest fear of the modern period. If we could find Atlantis and evaluate what went wrong, we might be able to avoid the same fate for ourselves.

The Second Clue: Finding Atlantis in Plato's Writings

Plato was an Athenian who wrote in classical Greek in the fourth century BCE and is thought by many to be one of the greatest writers in antiquity, on par with any of the biblical writers. One of the most valuable parts of my graduate school education was spent studying ancient languages, especially Greek. It involved the study not only of the language but also of the manuscript traditions and the transmission of the text. It is important to understand ancient texts in the same way that you understand ancient material culture because both are necessary to analyze an issue in the ancient world. Studying Plato means understanding him in his original language and context. But Plato himself is something of a mystery. His birth and his death are not exactly known (but his birth is assumed to be around 428–427 BCE and his death was around 348–347 BCE). Scholarship suggests that his name may not have been Plato at all. "Plato" may have been a Greek nickname (meaning "broad-shouldered one") and his given name was Aristocles, suggesting an aristocratic lineage. Thirty-six dialogues and thirteen letters have been attributed to Plato, although it is difficult to know if he wrote all of the works credited to him. In all of the dialogues, Plato does not speak in his own voice. We know that he traveled around the ancient world and collected materials from Egypt, Italy, and Cyrene, and that he may have started formal study in Athens at the rather advanced age of forty. Plato fancied himself an enthusiastic follower of Socrates.

Since we do not have anything written by Socrates, it is only through the eyes of his students that we learn about this great man.

What most of my students know about Plato is his famous allegory of the cave. It is said to encapsulate much of Socrates's (and Plato's own) view of the world. This allegory, found in Plato's *Republic*, imagines a group of people who have lived as prisoners since birth, chained (frontward) to a wall, where the only images they ever see are shadows that are projected onto the wall as people and things pass in front of a fire in the cave. They never know any other reality but those shadows. Only the philosopher, says Plato, can come to understand that the shadows are not the reality. Plato's greatness is that he was able to produce a body of literature about the meaning of people, places, and events that no one else in antiquity was able to capture. In fact, Plato himself was a bit of a mystery, and so to understand him is to understand more about where Atlantis might be. The next step to unraveling the story of Atlantis is understanding who Plato was and the intricacies of his writing.

Plato's Atlantis in the *Timaeus* and the *Critias*

The works in which the story of Atlantis appears (the *Timaeus* and the *Critias*) have been assigned stylistically to the later period of Plato's writing activity. The *Timaeus* is a dialogue with four major speakers: Socrates, Timaeus from Locri, Hermocrates, and Critias. Socrates has already described the perfect state and now sets out to tell them about other ancient states. Critias tells Socrates about the journey of the lawmaker Solon (seventh to sixth century BCE) to ancient Egypt, where he heard the ancient story of Atlantis. In the *Timaeus*, Critias also mentions how Athens waged war against Atlantis (presumably a long time after Atlantis existed). The text of the *Timaeus* then moves on to even more ancient issues such as the origins of the world. In the *Critias*, the topic of Atlantis and the uniqueness and advanced nature of Atlantean society is picked up again as a theme in order to illustrate how Atlantis waged war against Athens. We do not have the full text of the *Critias*, but the one that has come down to us shows us that Plato had a specific interest in presenting information on Atlantis. According to Plato, Atlantis was "an island situated in front of the straits which are by you called the Pillars of Hercules" (*Timaeus* 23a ff.). Almost all of the ancient Greek writers, geographers, and historians located the Pillars of Hercules at the present-day Straits of Gibraltar. The rock and country of Gibraltar (just east of today's Spain) is really a remarkable place even today. It is located at the southern edge of the Iberian Peninsula and extends into the Mediterranean. It is the only place in Europe that has wild monkeys (even today), and its unique climate and location made it a well-known place for sailors for thousands of years. By placing Atlantis at the Pillars of Hercules, Plato was giving a very specific location.

The Pillars of Hercules as the Ancient "Twin Towers"

It is hard for me to imagine how many serious researchers put Atlantis in different places around the world given that it is so clearly identified in antiquity in one very well-known spot: the Straits of Gibraltar. However, I know that there are many people who do not read ancient written sources as authentic or serious historical documents. I attempt to do so whenever I can, unless there is a reason to suspect they have been doctored. Even if I conclude they have been doctored, knowing how and why they are doctored helps me use them as a piece of a larger puzzle in reconstructing the history of a place or event.

Plato's *Timaeus* and the *Critias* are essentially literary works, and Plato clearly knows how to make his point using drama. The work is infused with Greek values and was clearly written to inspire Greeks by presenting a dramatic counterpart to Greek society. According to Plato in the *Critias*, the people of Atlantis fell prey to ambition and vice, and what happened to them was a form of punishment. He writes that the island "disappeared in the depths of the sea. For which reason the sea in those parts is impassable and impenetrable, because there is a shoal of mud."

There are actually two variant readings found in the extant manuscripts of what happened to Atlantis. One says, "It disappeared *kapta batheos* ('captured in the depths')," and another manuscript reading states, "It disappeared *kata brachaeos* ('[became] as part of the mud') in the way; and this was caused by the subsidence of the island." Now it is clear that Plato connected the consequences of the "ambition and vice" of the Atlanteans to an environmental catastrophe that befell the island. This was a very common ancient view of sin and punishment. The way Plato describes the catastrophic environmental events that destroyed Atlantis, it seems that an earthquake struck the area or a tsunami, or both, causing it to disappear. This was a common theme that ancient writers used—seeing ancient environmental cataclysms as a form of divine punishment for the actions of the people. It is similar to the Bible's Sodom and Gomorrah or the Flood in the time of Noah. People suffer because of their evil ways. So Plato's Atlantis is a moral tale, but it was not just a moral tale.

The Third Clue: From the Disappearance of Atlantis to the Disappearance of Tarshish

My own interest in the ancient city of Atlantis is connected to my interest in ancient texts about other ancient port cities that have mysteriously disappeared. I have spent the past twenty-five years investigating a lost ancient port (Bethsaida) with two names in antiquity (Livia-Julia and Bethsaida) located on the Sea of Galilee in ancient Israel that confounded modern archaeologists for a century. Atlantis seemed like a similar case. There is another ancient port city at the edge of the Mediterranean, Tarshish, that also disappeared mysteriously in antiquity. I have always thought that the two might be different incarnations of the same city. Many researchers have speculated where Tarshish (like Atlantis) was located. Some have put it in India along the Indian Ocean, off of Africa in the Aegean, but some have placed it in southern Spain—just like Atlantis. The fact that two very similar ancient port cities went missing in a similar location led me to speculate that perhaps we may not be talking about two totally different cities, but either one city with two names in different periods or two cities that were built in similar locations, one after the other, that served a series of ancient peoples in southern Spain. The more I examined the history of Tarshish, the more it sounded like the history of Atlantis. The clue of Tarshish ultimately led me back to what happened to Atlantis.

Again, to understand the history of Tarshish, one has to study carefully the text that records what we know about it. Tarshish is found primarily in the Bible, although it looks like the city was known to other ancient Near Eastern writers and also to Greek writers, geographers, and historians. The careful study of the Bible over the past century has revealed that there were different writers who wrote down various sections of the Bible in different periods. A final editor, like Plato for the writings of Socrates, finally placed all of the ancient pieces together, but in the case of the Bible one has to pay attention to the different literary strata. Sometimes these literary strata reveal important pieces of ancient information that would often be lost if we read the Bible like a newspaper. After researching Tarshish throughout the Bible, I have discovered that different writers preserve different Tarshish traditions. When placed in their proper sequence they reveal a history of an ancient port city and where it was originally located.

First, the term "Tarshish" is given great antiquity by the writers of the Bible. It is placed at the earliest stratum of the biblical text (in the prehistory of the Abrahamic families right after creation—a similar placement to the story of Atlantis in Plato's *Timaeus*). In the book of Genesis, the people who live in Tarshish are said to be of the sons of Javan (who lived a few generations after Noah and the infamous Flood): "Elishah, and Tarshish, Kittim, and Dodanim." The section of Genesis that discusses these men, which is attributed to the priestly writers, would have been written down in the sixth century BCE, a time just before the Greek historian Herodotus was writing his history. Although the four names are supposed to be proper names of people, they are assumed to represent the ancient peoples and places of antiquity that were still known in the period of the writer. The names, which are placed in a specific order, are assumed by scholars to represent the entire Mediterranean world. Moving from the closest to the coast of ancient Israel (where the writers lived) to the farthest reaches of the known world in the west, they are a travel guide to the way that the ancient Israelites saw the world. From east to west, *Elishah* is understood by scholars to be the island of Cyprus. *"R"odanim* (usually written incorrectly in most manuscripts and translations as *"D"odanim*—because the letters "D" and "R" in Hebrew look very similar) is taken to be the people who occupy the island of Rhodes. *Kittim* is understood to be one of the Greek or Aegean islands (thought to be the Minoans), and, finally, we have the ancient place *Tarshish*—last and farthest from the coast of ancient Israel. Tarshish was still known to the Levite Jeremiah (book of Jeremiah 10:9), who wrote in the sixth century BCE, and it was also known to another sixth-century priest and prophet, Ezekiel (book of Ezekiel 27:12, 27:25, and 38:13). There are biblical references to the early commerce of the Davidic family associated with this unknown place, Tarshish, and the long-distance ships that brought the commerce back and forth. In 1 Kings 9:26–27, 1 Kings 10:22, 1 Kings 22:48, and 2 Chronicles 9:22, it is stated that the trips were made for trade in gold, silver, and precious stones. These traditions extend from the so-called priestly writers through the biblical literary strata known as the Deuteronomistic writers of the sixth century BCE into the Chronicles traditions of the late fifth century BCE.

"Tarshish" as a proper name is preserved in the book of Chronicles. The name, although unusual in the Bible, is also given to the great-great-grandson of Jacob from the family of Benjamin in the 1 Chronicles 7:10 tradition. In what is an unusual use of the name, one of the Persian princes listed in the book of Esther 1:14 is also named Tarshish. The book of Esther, set in the fifth-century BCE kingdom of Persia, shows us that the name of this famous location persisted throughout the fifth century. The main references to Tarshish in the book of Esther are also about the Tarshish stones (either the name of the stone or the name of the location where they were from), showing that even during the Persian period,

Tarshish was well known. These stones appear in Exodus 28:20 and 39:13, in the priestly literary descriptions for the making of the Tabernacle and the vestments for the high priest, Aaron. In his writings (*Antiquities of the Jews*, written in Greek in the first century CE), Jewish historian Josephus Flavius preserves an unusual interpretation of this section of the Bible. Josephus translates the Hebrew "Tarshish" into the Greek word *chyrsolite* (Greek for "golden stone"). I have always wondered how Josephus knew that the Tarshish stone was the chyrsolite. It is important to note that Josephus had access to Greek and Roman records of his time period. In the first century CE, Josephus is referring to a well-known precious stone from outside the Land of Israel, and he translated the Hebrew word Tarshish with the name of a famous stone from his own time period *that was known to come from southern Spain*. In antiquity, the first-century CE Greek natural historian Pliny, in his *Natural History* 37.43, notes that this greenish translucent stone, *chyrsolite*, is found in southern Spain. Did Josephus know in the first century that the stone came from Tarshish and that Tarshish was in southern Spain, or was it just a coincidence that he had a tradition of translating this stone this way? I think Tarshish was still remembered in the Greek period as being in southern Spain. From our careful reading of the Bible, we learn that almost all of the major writing traditions and strata of the Bible knew and venerated the ancient site of Tarshish and attributed to it great antiquity, wealth, and distance from the ancient kingdom of Israel through the Persian period—and then suddenly it disappeared.

By the Greek period (the fourth century BCE), the exact location of Tarshish was lost but not forgotten. The Greeks conquered the ancient Near East in the period of Alexander the Great in the fourth century BCE, and the Judeans were transformed by the Greek conquest into a vassal state using Greek as an important language of commerce and knowledge of the world. In the Greek Septuagint translation of the biblical book of Ezekiel 27:12, the Greek translator goes out of his way to translate the Hebrew name Tarshish as Carthage. Scholars think that the third-century BCE translator of Ezekiel changed Tarshish to Carthage because by then it was the largest ancient port that he knew on the coast of North Africa. The original location of Tarshish was lost but not totally forgotten by the third century BCE.

Every Monday morning for most of my adult life I have been in search of the missing city of Tarshish. Every Monday I read a psalm that has been chosen for the Jewish morning liturgy that contains an unusual reference to Tarshish. Psalm 48 was probably written after one of the ancient sieges of Jerusalem (according to the Hebrew Bible, Jerusalem was besieged and ultimately sacked in the tenth, eighth, and twice in the sixth century BCE) by a psalmist worried about the safety of the holy city. To express his fear about the precarious fate of Jerusalem, he created a number of parallel metaphors about how precarious life is and how risky our daily movements can be. In one of those comparisons he cites the fate of the Tarshish crews as an example. These metaphors have perplexed me for the better part of my adult life. The Psalmist in chapter 48:5–8 writes, "The kings conspired and advanced, but when they saw her [Jerusalem] they were awestruck. Panic set in and they fled in fright, seized [as they were] with trembling like a woman in labor, as the boats of Tarshish [and their crews] must feel when battered by the east wind."

When the psalmist wrote his metaphor about the "boats of Tarshish," he assumed that everyone reading that psalm (in his own time and probably into the future) would know that this was one of the great ports of antiquity, and that the boats that traveled there were on a risky and scary journey to the ends of the earth. But, I wondered, where exactly was Tarshish? The fact that the boats of Tarshish were battered by the east wind tells me that the boats may have been coming from the west, and they were being battered by the winds as they came to port in the east (i.e., ancient Israel, where the psalmist resided). The "boats of Tarshish" must have been a well-known and extremely powerful image for the ancient Israelites. But like the Twin Towers in New York City (which I also remember seeing in my youth), one wonders who will know what they were a thousand years from now. As writers, we create metaphors that we think everyone will understand and that will stand the test of time. Very few do. Unfortunately, metaphors usually have a shelf life of a few hundred years in ancient literature. Here I am living in the United States in 2010, invoking the name of Tarshish every Monday. It brought me to ask the question of how risky and how far was that journey of the "boats of Tarshish" from the shores of ancient Israel. This is how my own journey began: trying to unravel simple daily mysteries of faith by looking for the ancient archaeological trail and to see if indeed Tarshish existed in history or was it just the figment of the rich imagination of an ancient writer.

Tarshish was for the Bible what Atlantis was for the Greek writers. It was the famous "end-of-the-known-world" port city from which great goods and new technological advances emerged. One of the unique questions that our research group posed as we began our search for Atlantis was whether the disappearance of Atlantis and the disappearance of Tarshish were somehow connected. The ancient city of Tartessos, a Greek version of the Semitic name Tarshish, was located at the Pillars of Hercules (what we call today the Straits of Gibraltar). Almost every ancient navigator knew this point of reference. The ancient city of Atlantis was located at the Pillars of Hercules. Methodologically, I thought that if I could identify Tarshish, I could identify Atlantis. I soon found out that I was methodologically in good company.

From East to West or West to East? Atlanteans, Phoenicians, and the Sea Peoples

I have always wondered how the most famous mariners of the ancient Near East are connected with Atlantis and Tarshish. We know that these ports of Atlantis and Tarshish may not have existed in exactly the same time period, but we know that they probably were both connected by the most ancient sailing group of the Mediterranean Sea: the Phoenicians. The question for me was whether Atlantis, Tarshish, and the Phoenicians were somehow culturally connected. The traditional view of the Phoenicians is that they started in the east and they slowly spread throughout the Mediterranean over a thousand years. There are again similarities between the specifics of Plato's account and the biblical account and the material culture of the Phoenicians. The Phoenicians built many of their most famous ports not on the coast but on islands just off the coast. I remember learning about an island/port for the first time in Israel at a place called Atlit, off the coast of Israel. The Phoenicians found that building a deepwater port on an island off a coast made it possible to bring in very large ships without the hazards of a coastal port. Marine archaeologists have found these islands/ ports off the coast of Sicily, in the Gulf of Eilat, and off the coast of Tyre and Sidon. Most people assume that the Phoenicians learned to build their deepwater ports on an existing island so that they could avoid all of the coastal harbor problems. The question is this: Where did the Phoenicians learn this technique? Did the Phoenicians originate this technique of a deepwater port on an island in the Middle East, or did they learn it from another, more ancient people—the Atlanteans?

We know that the technological advancement of shipbuilding and war chariots was connected to the Atlanteans, the Tarshishites, and the Phoenicians. According to Plato, "The Atlanteans had chariots pulled by horses . . . and 1200 warships" (*Critias* 119a–b). The existence of chariots and the number of warships is one of the great problems for archaeologists and historians when they discuss the antiquity of Atlantis. Chariots are known as a Bronze Age innovation, as are great warships. The fact that the Atlanteans have both chariots and warships in a period which is supposed to be before the Bronze Age immediately raises serious problems. It would mean that either the Atlanteans existed in the Bronze Age or that they originated these technological advances in a period before the Bronze Age. The staggering number of twelve hundred warships is almost unimaginable, because twelve hundred warships would have been the equivalent of one of the greatest navies ever assembled in antiquity. Only one people was known to possess such a large fleet of ships in antiquity: the Phoenicians. It is for this reason that the seafaring traders, the Phoenicians, are usually linked to the Atlanteans (and to a more mysterious group called simply the Sea Peoples): because they were all known to have great numbers of ships and were active in the Bronze Age.

The mystery of the Phoenicians and the Sea Peoples has never been properly resolved. There are a number of theories, and some of those theories connect the Sea Peoples with the Phoenicians while others do not. Archaeologists are really not even sure who the Phoenicians were. We trace them to the Middle East, but the evidence of their influence is so widespread in the Mediterranean Sea culture that it is impossible to place them in one specific location. The origins of Phoenicia before it was conquered by Thutmoses III of Egypt around 1500 BCE are unknown. Were the Phoenicians just an indigenous people of the Middle East linked by their love of the sea, who just happened to coalesce as a people in port cities? Or were they, as we suspect from what remains of their material culture all over the Mediterranean, a hybrid people who collected cultural aspects from each of their regional ports of call? Most scholars of ancient Spanish history suspect that a group they call "Spanish Phoenicians" origi- nated in the east and came to the west. But it is also possible that a mariner brand of very ancient proto-Phoenicians began in Spain (in Atlantis) and spread forth and then back to Spain. If so, the original Spanish Phoenicians were not from the East, but from Spain. The term "Phoenician" works best when we refer to the ancient people who came to Spain and created a totally different culture connected with sea trade. I call the earliest people of Spain for which we have evidence in the Bronze Age "proto-Phoeni- cians," because they are different from the Phoenicians of the Middle East and yet in many ways they were innovating on the style of the Phoeni- cians. They may be from a common, more ancient mariner culture that formed in both the Middle East and in Spain. But they are linked together with many of the cultural aspects (such as language/alphabet and religious iconography) that we found in Spain, so it is possible to refer to them as "Spanish Phoenicians." The Greeks just call this amorphous group of sea- farers that they came to know in trade as "Phoenicians." What made them

Phoenicians for the classical Greeks? The fact is that they were seafaring traders and they were not Greeks! The fifth-century BCE Greek historian, Herodotus, put the Phoenicians into his *Histories*, Book I, 1–2:

> The Phoenicians, who had formerly dwelt on the shores of the Persian Gulf, having migrated to the Mediterranean and settled in the parts which they now inhabit, began at once, *they say, to adventure on long voyages, freighting their vessels with the wares of Egypt and Assyria.* They landed at many places on the coast, and among the rest at Argos, which was then pre-eminent above all the states included now under the common name of Hellas [Greece].

Neither Homer, Herodotus, nor even Plato saw the different groups they were describing as linked together. But, when looking at the sources today, it is clear that they are all talking about the similar groups of seafaring peoples. If Plato had our perspective, I think he would have realized that the Atlanteans he was describing were the beginnings of Phoenician culture, or proto-Phoenicians. Although the word "Phoenicians" does not appear in the Bible (it is a Greek word meaning either "trader" or a textile coloring agent "purple," which many ancient sea-traders sold), the footprints of Phoenician culture appear all over the Bible in one form or another (coming from two major centers of Phoenician culture in Tyre and Sidon), and they are mainly identified by their unique material culture (mainly pottery and architecture). I have always been intrigued by the Phoenicians. Arguably one of the most important influences on biblical religion and the development of early Israelite language, practice, and ideas, they are probably the group that we know the least about, while archaeological evidence of their influence abounds in ancient Israelite sites. The location of their cultural influence is limited to a very specific geographic space in ancient Israel, while the Phoenicians are found almost everywhere else in the Mediterranean. The Phoenicians came to ancient Israel somewhere after the sixteenth and into the fifteenth centuries BCE (judging from the finds identified in Bronze Age Israel with comparisons elsewhere in the same period). Judging from the Bible, their influence is assumed to have come from Tyre, the great coastal city north of Israel in today's Lebanon, which is considered a great Phoenician location. By the tenth century BCE, the relationship between Lebanon and Israel was so close that Solomon ceded twenty towns in Galilee to Tyre in exchange for the massive amounts of cedar wood (and help) he needed in the building of the Solomonic Temple of Jerusalem. Although the Phoenicians are close with the Israelites and they are located in that region in the sixteenth century BCE, scholars have not been able to pinpoint the exact origin of the Phoenicians.

As I read the accounts of Atlantis and looked at the evidence of the Phoenicians in ancient Spain, I began to speculate that perhaps it was possible to think about this problem from a different perspective. The Phoenicians (or the proto-Phoenicians) may have begun in the west and then moved to the east, where they became Phoenicians. This would make the Atlanteans the predecessors of the Phoenicians and would explain much about how the Phoenicians suddenly arrived on the scene with so many advanced seafaring techniques, architecture, and pottery. If the Phoenicians were the mother of ancient Near Eastern seafaring civilization, the Atlanteans were the grandmother of this civilization. One more piece points to this scenario: The group in the ancient Near East simply called the Sea Peoples mysteriously emerge in the Bronze Age, take on the navy of the Egyptians, and then suddenly disappear. They are similar to the Phoenicians but not the Phoenicians. The first mention of this group is found in the twentieth to nineteenth centuries BCE, or in the Early Bronze Age. By the fourteenth and into the thirteenth centuries BCE, the group was known to have warships and fought Rameses II. The ships of the Sea Peoples entered the Nile delta in the thirteenth to twelfth centuries BCE and destroyed a variety of defenders of Egypt before being turned away. Four letters from Ugarit, on the northern Lebanese coast, speak about how the Sea Peoples have devastated their cities in the eleventh century BCE. From these letters, we assume that the Sea Peoples are not from the Ugarit region (where the Phoenicians were located). So, the Sea Peoples appear to be different from the Phoenicians, but since the origins of the Phoenicians and the Sea Peoples are so ancient and unknown it is possible that they both were refugees from a similar background. It is not a stretch to think that they may have come from the west and spread to the east in an early part of the Bronze Age. The next step to learning the identity of the Atlanteans and the location of Atlantis was to see that these different seafaring people may have come from an even more ancient seafaring people: the Atlanteans.

The Fourth Clue: Archaeological Comparisons to Another Ancient "Holy" Island/City

As you read the description of Atlantis in the writings of Plato you discover that he is talking about a central holy shrine in the innermost part of the concentric-circle canals. More than just being a deepwater port and an advanced civilization, the innermost part of the concentric-circle canals led to a holy shrine in the center of the island, which was the most important place on Atlantis. I do not know that there was such a shrine at Tarshish, but ancient islands of the Phoenician ports probably had shrines associated with their ancient gods. As we began our work in search of Atlantis (and I continued to think about the connection to Tarshish), I wondered whether other modern archaeological searches had uncovered great islands/cities that had disappeared. The idea of a great island/city is not so unusual in archaeology; the recovery of other ancient islands/cities was a clue to solving the mystery of where to look for Atlantis. Comparison is one of the first rules of archaeology. When you want to know about an artifact, a design, a site plan, or an architectural feature, you look for comparisons from other archaeological sites to provide additional ideas. Here is what I knew and what I was looking for in another archaeological site comparison:

1. Atlantis was a sophisticated island/city that was located near the Mediterranean Sea just beyond the Straits of Gibraltar (called the Pillars of Hercules in antiquity).

2. It was a deepwater island/city port built with a type of canals of concentric bands of water and sea, and it had a temple in the center part of the island with only one entrance and exit into and out of the inner island canals.

3. It had a sophisticated army and navy with a large number of warships and chariots, indicating access to raw materials of great quality to provide wood and metal. Artisans of all kinds and various professions, from metal workers to horse handlers and trainers, were necessary.

4. Atlantis was built before the rise of Athens, but the Atlanteans still existed in the time of Athens and even waged war with the city. The time of the city's existence may have been very long, but the final period coincided with a historical period that dates back to the nexus between what was known as the Bronze Age and the Iron Age.

5. It had a high culture and civilization equal to that which would later develop in Athens, including a sophisticated form of government.

6. It was destroyed by a cataclysmic environmental catastrophe (and not by war).

Another step in discovering where Atlantis might be located was to compare it with the archaeology from other ancient submerged cities that had been recovered. I looked for a good comparison of an ancient island/city that had been destroyed in a cataclysmic environmental catastrophe. I did not have to look too far. I had recently visited the excavations of ancient (medieval) Mexico City and saw firsthand how an ancient Aztec city had been built on an island; thanks to the destruction of the water sources, the entire city is now buried beneath the modern cityscape. The comparisons were intriguing. The capital of the Aztecs, called Tenochtitlan, was for nearly three hundred years a floating island/city built by damming the rivers. According to archaeologists (who have datable materials), the city was founded in 1325 CE and at its height probably had as many as two hundred thousand people living and working in its environs. At the center of the island/city sat a holy shrine, which was the center of the rituals and traditions that governed the people. It was destroyed by a human environmental catastrophe. The Spaniards (*conquistadores*) besieged the city, broke the dams, and caused the silt to fill the artificial canals that had been dug. The final destruction of the city took place in August 1521 and is well chronicled by historians. The city was slowly buried in silt and mud and only recently has been rediscovered under the convents, streets, churches, and residences that were built afterward by the Spaniards. Archaeologists knew what they were looking for as they excavated the ruins below the modern street level—not because they had a map, but because the Aztecs had created a series of miniature versions of Tenochtitlan outside of Mexico City that they could compare their work to. These miniature "models" of Tenochtitlan also had at their center a holy shrine that paralleled the one in Tenochtitlan. They were ultimately memorial cities to the great mother city that existed no more. Some of these memorial cities were constructed in the time when Tenochtitlan still existed, but others were built afterward from the memory of the pilgrims who had seen it during its heyday. The people in the Aztec nation constructed these miniature versions in the areas around the ancient Aztec capital, in Otumba, Huexotla, Xaltocan, and Yautepec, for example, so they could vicariously live in a city that they might never be able to enter, since Tenochtitlan was restricted to a certain population of the Aztecs. These miniature Tenochtitlans were relatively easy to excavate and were not built up like Mexico City. We know who the Aztecs were by viewing these memorial cities.

When I was in Mexico City visiting with one of the archaeologists excavating the ancient city of Tenochtitlan, she related to me something that became very important in our search for Atlantis. After she and her colleagues started excavating Tenochtitlan, they realized they would not be able to excavate the entire ancient city because it was buried beneath many of the most important structures of modern Mexico City. She said this is the reason it is important to have these mini-Tenochtitlans to compare and contrast with what we are unable to excavate. In the museum they have a large model of Tenochtitlan, largely based upon a projection of the miniature versions around the countryside. At each of the memorial cities, there was a shrine, designs on the walls, artifacts, architectural features, and site planning that allowed these people, far from their mother city and long after it no longer existed, to remember their ancient heritage. It was extremely poignant for me. This is very similar to what the Jews did when their own central shrine in Jerusalem was destroyed. The Jews created a miniature version of the Temple in each and every synagogue of the Diaspora. Inside were versions of the holy altar, the ark, the menorah, the symbols of the pilgrimage on mosaic floors and carved into the rock decorations. No sacrifices were allowed, but new versions of the religion of the ancient Israelites were created in those synagogues. The Jews even called a synagogue a *mikdash me'at*, a "miniature Temple," in recognition of the Temple of Jerusalem that was no more. I didn't forget this piece of advice when we started our work in the southern swamp of Doña Ana in southern Spain. It would turn out to be the key to understanding what happened to Atlantis.

Learning to Be a Literary Archaeologist

In my 2009 book, *Digging through the Bible*, I demonstrate that one of the biggest problems in the study of the evidence of the Israelite exodus from Egypt was the obsession of some scholars who insisted upon reading an ancient text as if it were a modern newspaper. Instead of understanding how an ancient text works and critically analyzing it using modern (scientific) literary analysis, they sometimes ended up reading it in a literal fashion. One problem that they faced when they read the text literally was how many people left Egypt. If the Bible says that 603,550 men left, archaeologists took the number, calculated at least 2.5 children and one or two wives, and some came to the "scientific" conclusion that the exodus would have had at least five million potential participants—a nearly impossible number given the population of Egypt at the time. The sheer number is so improbable that it immediately led many archaeologists to throw up their hands and assert that the biblical exodus could not have happened, just because of the numbers! In *Digging through the Bible*, I reviewed the numbers and carefully examined the text of the Bible's use of numbers only to discover that the number who exited Egypt at any one of what I think were multiple exoduses was probably only about eight thousand or so. This was a very manageable and historically accurate migration pattern even in antiquity. The ancient writers of the Bible used numbers such as forty years in the desert, forty days and forty nights of the Flood and Moses' stay on top of Mount Sinai, and so on, not as exact numbers but rather as general markers of time. These numbers were intended to invoke a general time frame (forty days equals a long time; forty years equals a very long time and the four hundred years that the Israelites were in captivity equals a very, very long time).

We have a similar situation with archaeologists and geologists who are in search of Atlantis. They read the text of Plato like it was a newspaper and often read it literally without any scientific or critical apparatus. Like the exodus of the Israelites from Egypt, it is important to have a clear idea of when Atlantis really existed in order to search for it. In fact, the biggest problem in searching for Atlantis is related to the date of its disappearance. If you are not looking in the right time period, then anything you find will be problematic.

We have no idea when Atlantis was created. I think Plato saw its beginning as taking place in a very ancient time period (he makes no attempt at defining the time of its creation), and he saw the destruction taking place in a time period that, although far in the past, was at least in a definable period (much further in the past than most historians of his own period would even attempt to speculate). In the time of Plato, the Greeks did not yet have a fully developed chronological sense of time. Greek historians such as Herodotus started to develop a sense of chronological time (which went backward and forward into their own time) of the ancient past, but it was never beyond the scale of more than a few generations. Like the biblical authors who developed a sense of relative time associated with major events like kings, earthquakes, wars, and dedications of major institutions, Plato used a relative chronology for understanding when Atlantis existed. They rarely ventured to calculate time the way that moderns and even medieval groups did. The Jewish calendar, for example, in 2011, boasts a date of 5771. This is a medieval calculation that would have been unimaginable in the biblical period. The seventeenth-century archbishop John Ussher calculated the creation of the earth as having taken place at nightfall of October 22, 4004 BCE, by literally reading the Bible's listed generations (and providing missing pieces from many interpretations as well). This obsession with a running calendar, which began in antiquity and continued until our own time, is a phenomenon that seems to emerge only in the early Middle Ages. In fact, most writings of the ancient Greeks, Egyptians, Mesopotamians, Hindus, and the Bible seem to use numbers more as markers to distinguish a relative chronology. Unfortunately, far too many modern archaeologists employ these markers as if they are exact numbers, both in the Bible and in Plato. In the case of Atlantis, this is even more important.

To begin with, Plato himself admits that there is a complex transmission history associated with the story he is writing about. He admits that he did not hear the original account about Atlantis, but that it was first told some three hundred years before his own period to Solon, a well-known Greek legislator, poet, and literary figure. Solon heard it from Egyptian priests during his visit to Egypt. The priests apparently read it off of hieroglyphic "texts" that existed in their own time. Solon is related to Critias (for whom the book is named), who is himself telling the story to Plato (who wrote it down), and Plato tells us that the story had been passed through the family of Critias for three generations until it reached him. If Plato had not described all this himself, we would need to consider whether the ancient tradition that Plato had before him had gone through oral transmission problems, but because he tells us this, it helps us understand where the transmission problem begins. It is possible that any one of the different sources may have simply miscommunicated some elements of the story. But there are other literary and/or manuscript transmission issues that may be at work here as well. Plato had a style that was distinctive and followed literary conventions of the period. So first and foremost, we must consider how and why Plato writes the way he does to understand an account like this. But once Plato's work was set down, there was an additional layer of transmission problems that were introduced by scribal errors and accretions. Although scribes were excellent transmitters of the manuscripts they were copying, they inevitably added elements (sometimes inadvertently and sometimes purposely when they thought they knew better). Those who read Plato seriously must consider whether what you are reading may contain an accretion or two. I know that this happened to Plato's texts in particular. This, too, is part of the transmission history that we must examine while "excavating" this text.

We know that Plato's *Timaeus* and the *Critias* are probably some of the latest and most mythological of all of Plato's works. The traditional date mentioned by Plato ("that nine thousand was the sum of years which had elapsed" from the time of the origins of Atlantis) has, I think, misled most archaeologists in their search for Atlantis. This number, "nine thousand" years before Plato's own time period, just does not match any reasonable time period that Plato would have used and certainly does not correspond to a historical period. But yet, most of the archaeologists and geologists that I dealt with in Spain were always obsessing about reaching a layer or stratum that could be dated to nine thousand years before Plato, or somewhere deep into the Stone Age. The problem is that this is an enormous time frame for a philosopher such as Plato. In ancient Greek, nine is a very powerful and mythical number, often used to show that an entire sequence is completed. "Forty" is a similar number in the Hebrew Bible, symbolizing a long period of time. Greek readers would have read nine thousand and understood this to mean a very, very ancient time. It is a marker to indicate a relative time frame ("in the very ancient past") rather than a specific time frame. It is hard to know where this number nine thousand came from (Solon? the priests of Egypt? Critias's father? etc.), but it is possible that Plato used it to express a very ancient time period and not exactly nine thousand years before his own. Some scholars who read Plato as literalists and look at the number nine thousand and immediately dismiss the text and the entire site of Atlantis as a myth are not understanding the nature of ancient writing. For Plato, Atlantis was very ancient—the "grandmother of all civilizations"—and he placed it into an ancient literary context beyond the history of Athens or Egypt using a literary convention that the ancient reader would have understood. He was not writing for modern-day archaeologists or historians.

Searching for Atlantis and Tarshish in Harlem, New York

Every once in a while, in the search for an ancient site, one comes upon evidence in the most unlikely place. The trek of archaeology usually has two different routes, which are both simultaneously important and necessary. One is field excavations, and the other is in libraries and archives. We build our theories on the shoulders of giants who came before us, worked in far-flung places, and did research in a world that was far simpler and technologically less sophisticated than our own but which was filled with the awe of the unexplored. I like to say that my search for Atlantis began in Omaha, Nebraska, on 65th Street, and my search for biblical Tarshish began in an archive at the Hispanic Society of America in New York City on Broadway between 155th and 156th Streets on the edge of Harlem. The Hispanic Society was founded in 1904 by Archer Milton Huntington, and it is one of the gems of New York City that few people see. It is also a wellspring of information on archaeology in Spain. It has libraries, collections, and exhibitions, and it is housed in beautiful turn-of-the-twentieth-century architecture where the archives of modern Spanish life and culture are found in the United States. At the Hispanic Society, I was able to examine all of the original correspondence and writings of a twentieth-century giant of Spanish archaeology, George (Jorge) Bonsor, who was the first to do a systematic excavation in Doña Ana and declare it to be the ancient city of Tarshish. Elected to the Hispanic Society of America in 1905, Bonsor was seen in Spain and all of Europe and in the Americas as one of the great archaeological figures of the nineteenth and early twentieth centuries. His correspondence and his major writings were archived at the Hispanic Society following his death in 1930. I looked at more than a thousand of the massive pieces of documentation of his work in Spain. I also looked at the original twentieth-century attempt to establish both Tarshish and the lost city of Atlantis as being located in modern-day southern Spain. Bonsor had done an excavation of some of the most important sites in Spain and had a very special interest in a site in the Doña Ana Park in the early 1920s. (The name as it is found in nineteenth-century mapping and in Bonsor's correspondence is not consistent; it appears as Doña Ana, Doña Ana Park, Dona Ana, Dona Ana Park, Donana, and the Donana Park. The modern names of the location are Estación Biológica de Doñana and the Espacio Natural de Doñana. I will use Doña Ana Park or Doña Ana to refer to the large marsh under investigation where our work and the work of Bonsor took place.)

Bonsor became well known at the end of the nineteenth century for his systematic excavations of the north and the south of Spain, and he had much experience in working with pre-Roman and Roman materials. He also developed a curiosity about and a specialty in ancient burials. He visited and worked the burial chambers that were carved into soft rock, as well as the in-ground burials of both cremated remains and the bones of the ancient people who occupied Spain. He was able to distinguish throughout the country burials of the pre-Roman, Roman, Christian, and Islamic periods. He noted with interest the differences between burials in caves, the different periods of cremation, and the receptacles used to store the remains. He recognized the existence of multiple layers of burial places. His contributions were invaluable to the field of archaeology. During my study of Bonsor's work, I learned about some burials that were from what he called ancient Phoenicians, with Roman period burials on top of the same areas. The existence of Spanish Phoenicians was really one of the great discoveries that I made as I researched this topic. Unlike common wisdom, which placed the Phoenicians only in the Middle East and North Africa, the Phoenicians, their language, and their culture were seemingly everywhere in the Mediterranean, including Spain. Spanish Phoenicians appeared to be a manifestation of a culture that seems foreign to Spain. However, in reality, no one is sure whence the Phoenicians came or what happened to them. We know that the Greek and later Roman cultures subsumed what was left of Phoenician culture and language into the Greco-Roman civilization, but we have to ask: Where did the culture of the Phoenicians originate? This question interested almost every major writer of the twentieth century, and in the case of our research on Tarshish and Atlantis, it would ultimately have extraordinary answers. These answers were informed by the small details and clues in the excavations of these nineteenth- and twentieth-century archaeologists such as Bonsor.

Bonsor notes the existence of sarcophagi (a kind of coffin) that were made of stone, marble, and pottery. The use of the three materials seems to indicate some form of economic divide. As Bonsor saw it, Spain was a crossroads of ancient civilizations. According to him, the Celts invaded the Iberian Peninsula in the fourth century BCE and somehow displaced an already existing major group of Phoenicians and Carthaginians who lived in the south. The south of Spain remained a major port of call for all ancient peoples during the time of the Celts and the Greeks. Despite catastrophic environmental events that had closed more and more sections of the ancient bay (which went from present-day Cadiz and Huelva in the south all the way to Seville in the north), Bonsor notes that small river boats could still reach Seville in the north through the first century CE. The great swamps and marshes of the Doña Ana Park in southern Spain were a silent reminder of what had been an active marine economy and perhaps one of the largest protected port sites in the ancient world. Bonsor spent many years charting the ancient routes and rivers of Spain and was very impressed by the Guadalquivir River, which continued to change direction and shape with great frequency through the Middle Ages, and which created the great 250 square miles of the Doña Ana Park of Spain. The effects of the tectonic plates shifting and the massive tsunamis that accompanied the earthquakes in the region would only be fully understood years after Bonsor's work in the 1920s. But he already recognized the changing river routes and the changing settlement patterns of the region (from the ancient Mediterranean coast to the smaller Roman period rivers that ran through Doña Ana Park) changed history.

The Mystery of the Names *Atlantis* and *Tarshish*

Just as Atlantis disappeared mysteriously from the literary record, so too did Tarshish. As Tarshish was a port city at the end of the known world, so too was Atlantis. In much the same way that speculation ran about the lost port city of Atlantis, by the middle of the nineteenth century, ancient Tarshish had been placed by explorers and geographers in India, Spain, Crete, Cyprus, and off the coast of Lebanon and Turkey.

The search for Tarshish was often a surrogate topic for the search for Atlantis. As the greatest archaeologist of ancient Spain, Bonsor was not immune to the allure of the topic. Tarshish was important to Bonsor because he was classically trained, and he knew from the Bible and classical sources that it was a port city at the farthest end of the Mediterranean. He also knew that the area of southern Spain was known by two very distinctive designations, Tartessos and Al-Andalus. Classical sources such as Herodotus, Strabo, and Pliny's *Natural History*, as well as the late Roman source, Avienus's literary itinerary *Ora Maritima (Sea Coasts)*, all mentioned Tartessos in southern Spain.

Ora Maritima is an interesting and unusual source since it is a poetic work that connects many of the pieces that none of the other ancient literatures (besides Plato) do. Written by Avienus in Latin in the fourth century CE, the poem *Ora Maritima* purports to be conveying information that goes back a thousand years earlier (perhaps to the time of Plato), and traces the different parts of ancient coastlines and peoples that must have still been known in that time period. Avienus writes about the ancient coast of Spain, and he is especially conversant with the area at the Pillars of Hercules. He also is aware of the name of the island of Gadir (Cadiz), which he says was originally called Tartessos. Although it is hard to know if he is alluding to an earlier island in the area or not, he relates the area to the tenth labor of Hercules in Geryon and places it, as do other ancient sources, beyond the Pillars of Hercules. It is hard to know if Avienus was aware of these connections from sitting in a library or from actually visiting these places in antiquity. His knowledge of the specifics of the rivers that seem to approximate the rivers in the Doña Ana is one of the reasons why Adolf Schulten and George Bonsor took this literary source seriously in the 1920s.

By the fifth century BCE, Herodotus specifically placed Tartessos "beyond the Pillars of Hercules" (*Histories* 4.152)—the same place that Plato's source had placed Atlantis. The first-century CE Roman historian Velleius Paterculus dates the founding of Tartessos to the twelfth or eleventh centuries BCE. In my research, the first questions I asked were whether Tartessos was predated by an island beyond the Pillars of Hercules, and whether the ancient name Tartessos preserves the biblical name of Tarshish. There are just too many coincidences here that tie Tartessos to the location of Tarshish. Most scholars think that if there is a close linguistic link (which is their similar names) and some points of convergence of ancient sources, then the two places are connected. The second area I was most interested in during my research was exactly where the city and port of Tartessos/Tarshish was located in the large southern coastline of Spain. There are those who contend that Tartessos/Tarshish is the modern city of Huelva, which does indeed have Bronze/Iron Age contexts that could be consistent with a Phoenician port city. Some think Tartessos/Tarshish was located at ancient Cadiz (near Huelva). Bonsor's theory was that Cadiz and Huelva were ports in the period of Tarshish, but the original Tarshish (or Atlantis) was located inside the vast expanses of the ancient Doña Ana marsh.

Most people rarely consider the derivation of a name. When I study the story of New York—or its previous name "New Amsterdam" or the alternate name "Manhattan," which are all multiple names for the same place, New York City—I have to think about why the name changes took place and what the origin of the name is. The ancient name of the city of Jerusalem, for example, is often linked to Egyptian texts from the nineteenth and eighteenth centuries BCE that write about a "Rusalimum"—which sounds vaguely like "Jerusalem." Most scholars think that the name "Jerusalem" may come from two separate Semitic words: *yeru*, which means "to establish," and *Shalem*, which is the name of a well-known god of the region. The book of Genesis even mentions by name a person, Melchizedek, king of Shalem, which is another name that sounds similar to "Jerusalem." If so, the name "Jerusalem" developed and changed even as the city became a central place of pilgrimage for the ancient Israelites and Judeans. I am not sure of the etiology of the names "Atlantis" or "Tarshish," but I know that if the name was important, then history teaches us that either it would be updated or changed over time (like Manhattan/New Amsterdam/New York) or it would be developed to suit ancient sounds into something different.

Although Tarshish appears regularly in the Bible, there is clearly not a regular three- or four-letter Semitic variant root for it. The famed archaeologist William Foxwell Albright related "Tarshish" to the Akkadian word *tarsisu* (meaning a refinery for the transport of raw materials for smelting), but he also linked the word with the seventh-century BCE annals of the Assyrian king Esarhaddon to an area in the far western region of the Mediterranean: "All the kingdoms from [the islands] amidst the sea from the country of *Iadanan* and *Jaman* as far as [the country of] *Tarshishi* bowed to my feet and I received heavy tribute." Some scholars have linked Tarshish to ancient Greek designations for "oar" (*tarsos*) and "sea" (*thalassa*) and have even connected it with the city of Tarsus. Although Tarsus and Tarshish might have been a good match, Tarsus is relatively close to the coast of ancient Israel, and it would not have been a great journey to arrive there, even in the Iron Age.

Tarshish may indeed be named for one of the minerals found there, since seven of the Tarshish references in the Hebrew Bible are to stones called "tarshish." Ten references in the Hebrew Bible are to special types of Tarshish boats that were apparently of great size; they are found in an almost apocalyptic vision in Isaiah 2 and in the final return of the exiles in Isaiah 60. This reference to a type of ship may have a wonderful parallel in the writings of the fifth-century BCE Greek historian Herodotus, who wrote about the city of Tartessos in his histories. According to his account, the Tartessians were discovered by a fabulously wealthy Greek merchant named Kolaios. It is from the Greeks that we get the name Tartessos, from the root *trt/trd*, which is seen in a number of indigenous names used for the southern region of the Iberian Peninsula. The Tartessos name may not only preserve the ancient Tarshish name but also the name of the type of ship, with oars. These large ships with large numbers of oarsmen may have preserved the Tarshish brand of ship even after the city no longer existed as a port. Some of the most fantastic materials used in the building of the Temple of Solomon in Jerusalem came from Tarshish in the tenth century BCE. The number of biblical references to the Tarshish ships coming and going laden with materials for the building of the Temple of Jerusalem is impressive. This Temple was, even until the Roman period, one of the most important sanctuaries in the eastern provinces of the Roman Empire, but it was originally built by skilled Phoenicians with materials brought by Phoenician boats.

The Greek writers state that silver, iron, lead, and tin came in the ships of Tartessos to Mediterranean ports such as Tyre. In 2 Chronicles 9:21,

Tarshish has a similar cargo and ports on the Mediterranean, where it is stated that "every three years once came the ships of Tarshish bringing gold, and silver, ivory, small monkeys and large monkeys." The interesting part is the delivery of monkeys. The only European port where monkeys still live in the wild is at the tip of Spain at Gibraltar. If Atlantis was located near Gibraltar in southern Spain and if Tarshish boats were arriving at a port on the Mediterranean with monkeys at Gibraltar, it is possible that Tarshish and Atlantis may be two names for the same port.

Tarshish disappears from the biblical record between the fifth and fourth centuries BCE. The location of Tarshish was well known to writers from the tenth to the fifth centuries BCE, and then by the end of the Bible it was gone. The prophet Isaiah in the eighth century BCE mentions that some natural disaster may have affected the port of Tarshish in this period. Isaiah 23:1 states, "The burden of Tyre. Howl, the ships of Tarshish: for it is laid waste, so that there is no house, no entering in: from the land of Kittim it is revealed to them." Are Tartessos and Tarshish the same? By the first and second centuries CE, Greek geographers linked Tartessos and Tarshish. The second-century CE writer Pausanius states that

> Tartessos [the present day-Guadalquivir] is a river in the land of the Iberians, running down into the sea by two mouths, and that between these two mouths lies a city of the same name. The river, which is the largest in Iberia, and tidal, those of a later day called Baetis, and there are some who think that Tartessus was the ancient name of Carpia, a city of the Iberians.

The final step to the connection between the Hebrew Tarshish and the Greek Tartessos is preserved in the last occupation of southern Spain of the Arab Muslims. The Muslim conquest in southern Spain began in the eighth century. This southern stretch of land at the edge of Spain was called Al-Andalus. The Arab chronicles of their conquests often preserve the ancient dialect and names of places. In the nineteenth century, Edward Robinson, the explorer and grandfather of all Israelite archaeology, heard the local people call a site "El-Gib" in a local Arabic dialect and thought that the oral tradition of the bedouin may have preserved the ancient biblical name Gibeon. Over a hundred and fifty years later, a random discovery in a well at the site and systematic excavations confirmed the identification of the site as Gibeon. In the same way, it is possible that the Arabs still had an oral tradition in the eighth century CE that preserved in Arabic the name Al-Andalus, which is a version of the most ancient name for the region: Atlantis.

The Fifth Clue: Doing New Research at the Doña Ana Park—From Bonsor to Celestino

Ancient Tarshish's location was something that grabbed Bonsor's professional attention as early as 1918. He wrote a whole project for Tarshish in an outline I found in his correspondence at the Hispanic Society of America dated to 1918. This included one of the most beautiful and carefully mapped areas for the ancient island/port of Tarshish that I have ever seen. He mentions in the second paragraph of his proposal that in September 1910, German professor Adolf Schulten's research in the area had motivated his own interest. His 1918 treatment argues for the need for Spanish researchers to do the work on a Spanish expedition. Letters from Schulten to Bonsor are in the Hispanic Society files and include one dated April 22, 1910, that was about the significance of the undertaking. In this same file, there was one particular envelope that caught my attention. In a rather large white envelope marked "Very fragile" was a map that was from the original work of George Bonsor, dated August 25, 1921. On the map, he indicated where he thought the places to dig were for the ancient island/port of Tarshish.

I also found a single envelope that had ten of the most beautiful photographs of the ancient Roman buildings that Bonsor found in the area where he thought Tarshish was originally located. These photos were not of a small and humble fishing village put together from stones that had to be shipped in from far away, but rather of massive and ancient stonework that is some of the finest that I have ever seen in southern Spain.

Beyond the photographs and the maps that Bonsor included in his work, he wrote about the significance of the discovery of a place such as Tarshish for the people and the culture of Spain. Archaeology, as much as it is a scientific discipline and directed by dispassionate investigators about artifacts, is also about people. Scholars who choose to excavate one site over another are doing so as a conscious choice. As much as Bonsor was interested in the ancient Tartessan people and this site of Doña Ana, he was also interested in the national identity of the people of modern Spain as it relates to the discovery of Tarshish. As much as his investigations of ancient Spanish sites were about the ancient people of Spain, they were also about the dignity and identity of the modern nation. In writing *Digging through History*, I discovered that as much as ancient historians are writing about the past, they are also writing for the modern public. By the beginning of the twentieth century, Spain's time as a major superpower had passed. Bonsor's work reflects his interest in establishing Spain as the site where civilization began. He writes to Huntington, founder and president of the Hispanic Society, on February 21, 1920, about his recent (first) visit to "the supposed" site of Tarshish. He was taken to see a variety of items that were from the Roman period, but the abundance of building materials in the marsh indicated to him that the "island" area at the tip of Doña Ana had indeed been inhabited in a period before the Romans. As he himself notes, "When we begin digging there [at these Roman places] we may find underneath like in the site of Troy, the ruins of an older town, Phoenician or Iberian." His enthusiasm for this project was enormous. He wrote of his encounter with the local leadership: "When those quaint aristocratic people . . . heard that I was pretending to discover a mysterious place in their property, where many thousands of years ago King Solomon had sent expeditions for materials to build and adorn his magnificent temple . . . their surprise was extraordinary!" It is clear that Bonsor saw this project as the great pinnacle to his extraordinary career of archaeology for and about Spain.

In July of 1921, Bonsor authorized the publication of his work, titled *Tartesse*. This was the first of his own research on Doña Ana as the location of Tarshish. He knew that in 1902 a Roman period settlement had been discovered at the southern end of the Doña Ana area. As an archaeologist who had excavated many other areas of Spain in this period, he knew that it would be unusual for the Romans to build an isolated Roman period settlement in an area that had never been inhabited before. The Romans were keen observers of human development. They looked for roads (or ancient travel routes) that led in and out of a more ancient settlement, for settlement patterns that allowed commerce and agriculture or an economic base of some kind, and for water, city planning, and so on. They rarely just established a settlement that was unsustainable. So when Bonsor discovered that a complex Roman settlement with building materials and burials had been found in the remote southern marsh area of Doña Ana, he suspected that there was a more ancient settlement below it. In this area of Spain, that generally meant a Phoenician settlement nearby, but in the lonely swamp of Doña Ana in the dunes, it seemed unusual for the Phoenicians to have established a remote settlement of this kind that did not allow easy access to the Mediterranean. He suspected that this Roman settlement was a later version of a city on an ancient island at the mouth of the Gudalquivir River that disappeared in the very ancient period of the Bronze Age. The island of Cadiz had already become the further target of his study, and he saw that area as a twelfth-century BCE creation. As I read through his correspondence with Huntington at the Hispanic Society, it became clear that Bonsor saw the landlocked settlement in Doña Ana as a more ancient settlement that had become sedimented in, and that Cadiz might have been a later incarnation of the city. If so, the mysterious Doña Ana settlement might be older than the twelfth-century BCE Cadiz settlement—and effectively the most ancient settlement of Spain. This would make it the mother of all other settlements in Spain and indeed in all of Europe.

The manuscript of *Le Coto de Doña Ana: Une visite archaeologique a l' île du delta de l'ancien Tartesse* in the archives of the Hispanic Society of America is Bonsor's proposal for the research on Tarshish and Atlantis. The central pillar of the work is the idea that this is where civilization began. Spain, which had suffered humiliating defeats in the nineteenth and early twentieth centuries and had lost its status as one of the great powers of the world, was where all civilization began. It was no longer the place that had been colonized by the ancient Phoenicians, as was once thought, but it was the birthplace of a unique and ancient people that rivaled the Phoenicians. In reading the original manuscript of *Le Coto* that was received by President Huntington at the Hispanic Society of America on August 15, 1922, one sees that this work was Bonsor's attempt to claim Tarshish in the name of Spain, and therefore reclaim the power and the glory of Spain. As I read this work, I sensed that Bonsor was genuinely convinced of the possibility that this was the ancient port city of Tarshish.

In his opening assessment in *Le Coto*, Bonsor begins with the ancient Roman source *Ora Maritima*. His reading of *Ora Maritima* convinced him that the Romans knew that the site in Doña Ana was much older than the Roman period. I remember reading for the first time the words that Bonsor wrote in 1922: "On sembleait déjà voic reconnu que cette grand atendue de terrain formait jadis une île, l'île de l'antique Tarshish ou Tartesse" (page 14). He also notes that this ancient Tarshish may indeed be Atlantis (page 20). He was the first scientist in the modern period that I had ever noticed in all of my research who could make the jump between the ancient coast of Tyre and the ancient coast of Spain. In 1673, the Spanish author José Pellicer de Ossau suggested that Atlantis was buried between the islands Mayor and Menor, located near the Cerro del Trigo site. By the beginning of the twentieth century, de Ossau's hypothesis associating Atlantis with Doña Ana had made its way back into the popular Spanish consciousness in Juan Fernandez Amador de los Rios's book *Antiguedades Ibericas* (1911). Bonsor may or may not have been influenced by this, but it's clear that he saw southern Spain as an ancient port of call, and he seems to imply in *Le Coto* that if the island/port of Cadiz-Gadir was created in the period of the eleventh century BCE, then the area to the northwest of Cadiz, in the Doña Ana Park, must have hidden earlier remains. In his treatise, he places the final destruction of Tarshish in the sixth century BCE (page 23). Even earlier than Bonsor, in 1910 Professor Adolf Schulten had seen the same series of literary pieces and he too had concluded that Tarshish was located in the Doña Ana. Bonsor notes that in the latter part of the nineteenth century, other Spanish archaeologists had already concluded that this area in the farthest edges of Doña Ana's swamps (especially by the dunes) was worthy of investigation (page 26). He concludes his own research as I did after two years of working on the materials. He has a time line in which he establishes Tarshish in the south of Spain in the twelfth century BCE (he writes 1100 BC; see page 31). He sees the demise of the city happening by the eighth century BCE, and by the sixth century BCE, it does not exist anymore. As I sat in the archives in Harlem, I felt as if I was having a conversation across the generations with Bonsor, who was working on the same issues we were except we had the technology to solve more of the problems he faced.

In his correspondence with President Huntington, Bonsor writes on June 27, 1923, of the continued enthusiasm for the work that he—and now his German colleagues, including Professor Adolf Schulten of the University of Erlangen—had for the project. He realized that the project really belonged to the Germans (since Professor Schulten had begun work on it several years before), and it had been helped along by the permission of the Duke of Tarifa in Spain. However, his idea was that this was not Germany's Tarshish, but Spain's. He felt that one of the most ancient periods of the life of the people of Spain was going to be discovered there, and if he did not join Schulten, then Spain would not be represented. So he reluctantly decided to join the Germans' expeditions.

It is hard to understand some of the subtle issues that were at play. By the beginning of the twentieth century, forms of nationalism and national identities had developed, which played out in pages of archaeology and historical research. Although the Industrial Age had presented new opportunities for technology to resolve many of the scientific questions of the nineteenth century, some scholars expected more. I found this in the letters of Bonsor as well. In his letter to President Huntington from September 20, 1924, Bonsor writes of his frustration at the limitations of his technology and time. For example, he found the water table at two meters below the Roman site in Doña Ana, which was very high and needed a special pump to go deeper where he suspected the earlier, more ancient Tarshish was buried. He thought about doing the work himself, since the Germans and his geologist Otto Jessen all were leaving at the end of the month. But he realized that this would not be an acceptable proposal to the Germans and writes emphatically, "[I would not be able] to work alone after they left as it is understood that Tarshish must be discovered *in their presence.*"

This was really the end of the Doña Ana project for Bonsor. The limitations of the pumping technology, the Germans pressing for their own discovery of the site's most ancient remains (one senses competing nationalisms at work here), and Bonsor's age (he complains to Huntington of being sixty-eight years of age and notes that this was one of his last excavations) frustrated him. He would never complete what he started. He left the area, unsatisfied, without a final conclusion, and he passed away in 1930.

The Rediscovery of Atlantis in Omaha, Nebraska

It was filmmaker Simcha Jacobovici from Associated Producers who in 2008 at a conference in Omaha, Nebraska, introduced me to the idea of doing research on Atlantis and Tarshish. Simcha is more than just a filmmaker. He is, as many know, the *Naked Archaeologist* of TV fame and he often has amazing and insightful hunches about archaeology. The conference I was attending in Omaha introduced me to the idea of doing research on Atlantis being in Spain. I think that he thought I might be interested because I had spent the past twenty-five years in search of the ancient port of Bethsaida on the northeast shore of the Sea of Galilee and because we had pioneered the use of geophysics for finding ancient sites. After our initial meeting, he introduced me to a cast of characters that no one could ever have dreamed up in Hollywood, and I have come to have more and more respect for the hunches of Simcha. Later, as I worked in the archives of Harlem, I realized that Simcha was asking the same thing that Bonsor had asked a century before: What was hidden in this ecological park and swamp in southern Spain? Was it Atlantis and the ancient port city of Tarshish? Projects that have mythical status rarely provide the modern archaeologist the certitude that is demanded in the field. It is rare for an archaeologist to take a site that has achieved this status of "myth" and transform the site into reality without many critics. I know that the teams I was involved in Spain were risking ridicule and scholarly banishment by even suggesting that they were looking for Atlantis and/or Tarshish. But I also know that if one has the courage to follow a hypothesis, it may end up providing discoveries that might not otherwise have been found.

As I mentioned earlier, I was involved in twenty-five years of excavations at a mythical site called Bethsaida, one of the great missing port cities of the sacred geography of the New Testament. If I had not worked on this project, I too would have been skeptical of the possibilities of recovering Atlantis. Bethsaida was not found until 1987, despite the fact that thousands of pilgrims had searched for it on the shores of the Sea of Galilee. When I was a student in the 1970s, it was considered mythological, and some believed that the writers of the New Testament made up (from "whole cloth") the stories about it. Bethsaida (literally, "the house of the fisherman") was the place where some think Christianity began. It was home to many of the most important apostles, and the place where many of the major biblical miracles happened, and yet no one could find it in the rather small area of the Sea of Galilee. (The Sea of Galilee is really a lake, and not even a big lake at sixteen miles by six miles wide.) It has only been through the twenty-five years of excavations at Bethsaida that the mythical city has been proved to be a reality. It was a risk to the reputations of all of the archaeologists, historians, and professors who worked on the project to continue to work and uncover the data that made Bethsaida a physical location on the northeastern shore of the Sea of Galilee once again. If I had not been involved with Bethsaida, I probably would never have thought that Atlantis and Tarshish could be found. More important, I thought about the reasons why Bethsaida could not be found, and they seemed to parallel some of the reasons why Atlantis and Tarshish could not be found. People were just looking in the wrong places!

Three Hypotheses: Bonsor-Schulten/Wickboldt-Kühne/Lozano-Morales

In the case of Atlantis and Tarshish, we decided to test three very different hypotheses about related geographic locations that were being researched by three different (and unconnected) teams of researchers. I developed a shorthand for each of the three hypotheses as we worked through them. They all involved the search for Atlantis in the Doña Ana Park. The three were all looking in different parts of the Doña Ana: the southern, the central, and the southernmost areas. Bonsor and Schulten represent the southern Doña Ana project, Wickboldt and Kühne the central Doña Ana project, and Lozano and Morales the southernmost Doña Ana project.

As often happens in fields of study, different researchers can try to answer similar questions using different methods and, very often, not communicate directly with one another. In this case, I discovered that not only were the three groups not in direct communication with one another, but they were also separated by disciplines and even periods of research. My theory was that they were all solving parts of the same problem.

As I looked at all of the different theories, I began to suspect that they were all pieces of the same puzzle and could be linked together. In the beginning of my own study, I could not understand why the information gathered in the 1920s by Bonsor and Schulten was not being utilized by later researchers in the Doña Ana Park. I learned that, in fact, this happens quite a lot. A later researcher often will look at the data collected in an earlier generation of research and determine that the methods and conclusions were not as meaningful in the contemporary period as when they were first collected. In the case of Bonsor and Schulten, a follow-up of their Cerro del Trigo (southern part of the Doña Ana Park) research was in fact done by a leading archaeologist of Spain. After this scientist returned to the site, he determined that, although there was an enormous amount of building materials located in an unusually landlocked location in the Doña Ana Park (and that there was no source for the building materials readily available in this period nearby), the material culture they found at the site was from the Roman period—much later than the period that the Atlanteans would have been there.

In the 1923 excavations, however, Bonsor found one major "smoking gun." He saw that the Cerro del Trigo site was clearly used by the Romans. He was convinced, however, that the stones that were being used by the Romans in this now landlocked location in Cerro del Trigo were in fact in secondary use by the Romans. He could not look below the foundations of the Roman village because the water table was too close to the surface, but he did find one stone that showed him what he needed to know. This stone was found in a burial that was incised with an inscription in an ancient dialect of Phoenician that was located near the Roman installation. He probably concluded from that one stone that the stones in the site were from a location that predated the Romans by almost a thousand years. In the 1990s, the archaeologists' research in this area was meticulous in investigating only the surface finds of the Roman site, but it also overlooked one major issue that I have learned to consider from working at many different Roman sites. Generally, ancient peoples—and especially the Romans—would build in a place where there was access to abundant building materials. In this case, the Doña Ana Park had no indigenous building materials in close proximity. So where did the Romans get their materials to build at Cerro del Trigo? The idea of bringing in enormous amounts of material to build a non-monumental and non-strategic location such as this in the Roman period would not have made sense, and Bonsor states as much in his publication *Tartessos*. I concluded the same thing when I saw the site that the Romans had created, but I thought I knew where the stones came from—they came from the site we were working on to the north only a couple of miles away.

Bonsor concluded over eighty years ago that these building materials came from another location nearby, but he did not know exactly where. While working at the Doña Ana Park in 2009, a marine archaeologist, Claudio Lozano, told me that he thought he knew where similar building materials could be found. He had seen some of them just off the edge of the park in the coastal waters where he had been scuba diving. It was in that one moment that I realized I had the three different pieces of the puzzle: the visual identification of a satellite photograph of an ancient cityscape in the central part of the park below the ground; the building materials in the southern part of the park (Cerro del Trigo); and the building materials that the marine archaeologist had discovered in the coastal waters off the edge of the park. These were not three separate locations with random evidence at each place. They were all evidence of the same event dispersed from the middle of the Doña Ana Park to the present-day Cadiz Bay! The three research projects, spanning nearly one hundred years, are all pieces of the same ancient puzzle, and the destruction line that extended across miles of this barren landscape was in fact pieces of the same ancient city spread in varying layers below and above the surface. In a sense, all three of the hypotheses were correct.

This is the way good science is done, standing on the shoulders of people who came before us. You do not just go and propose to excavate; you must have a hypothesis that you are testing, and someone must have started the work. Lucky for us, there have been plenty of scientists in southern Spain who have proposed rival theories about Atlantis and Tarshish. I started with George Bonsor (perhaps the most famous of all Spain's archaeologists) and his search for Tarshish and Atlantis in the Doña Ana Park in the 1920s.

From George Bonsor to Claudio Lozano

George Edward Bonsor Saint Martin was in many ways one of the grandfathers of modern archaeology in Spain. It is fitting that I start with his hypothesis because he was so well known. He was a giant in his field and an innovator in archaeology. His work was some of the most important in Spanish archaeology in the early part of the twentieth century. Born in France, he came to live most of his professional life in Spain, including at a site in the Doña Ana Park. Adolf Schulten, as mentioned earlier, was a German historian, geologist, and archaeologist who came to work in Spain with Bonsor in the 1923–1925 excavations of Doña Ana that inspired him to write *Tartessos*. Schulten, like Bonsor, was one of the giants of the field. He is seen as one of the founding fathers of modern geology and archaeology. Bonsor and Schulten together on this excavation in Doña Ana would have been seen as the equivalent of the archaeological "dream team" of their time period, and they thought that the search was worthy of their reputations. They both held that ancient Tarshish was located in an area near Cerro del Trigo in the Doña Ana Park and thought that the accounts about Tarshish and Atlantis were somehow interwoven. Their work was based upon this hypothesis, and it is the first of the three hypotheses upon which we based our research.

The second hypothesis we were following was that of Werner Wickboldt and Rainer W. Kühne, who proposed in the early part of the twenty-first century that the central marsh of Doña Ana was the location of Atlantis, based upon a satellite image that shows a series of features that he interpreted as walls in circular arrangements and a single entrance in and out of the main circular feature. This location is to the north of where Bonsor and Schulten had excavated.

Finally, I call the third hypothesis we followed the Lozano-Morales hypothesis. It is centered in an area that is not inside the Doña Ana Park but just off the coast in front of the park's edges. In the Cadiz Bay, between Chipiona and Rota, Professors Claudio Lozano (the marine archaeologist) and Juan Antonio Morales (a marine geologist from the University of Huelva) found monumental pieces of architecture (ancient stone walls, columns, and pavement). Lozano and Morales proposed that these stone pieces were the last remnants of an ancient city that had been located nearby.

Following the Building Materials: Cerro del Trigo and Beyond

In many detective stories the seasoned detective says to the rookie that in order to find the criminal you must "follow the money." In archaeology, a similar rule of thumb exists. You need to always follow the stones: where they were quarried, how they arrived at the place where they are being used, who used them before, who used them after. Usually, if you can understand where the stones came from you can understand who brought them there and why. When we compared for the first time the stone wall configurations found off the coast of Doña Ana Park with the stone wall configurations at the Cerro del Trigo site within the park, I immediately realized that the building materials in the Cadiz Bay and the stone walls at Cerro del Trigo that Bonsor saw in his excavation were connected. Both the walls in the water and the stone walls at Cerro del Trigo were brought from another location, and their similarity suggests that they both had one source nearby. Bronze Age stone walls tend to have a special character; they were carefully crafted, with close-fitting joints that did not need cement. Stone walls constructed in later periods used cement and were not nearly as well-fitting. Stones from the Bronze Age that were crafted in the former way may be used again (as in the Roman period, for example). When viewing the ancient stones that have been used again, even if they are used with cement, it is easy to see that they are pieces cut in the Bronze Age that were used again in a later period. Tracing the pattern of stone distribution from the Bay to Cerro del Trigo is important. The distribution pattern indicates that the stones at Cerro del Trigo probably came from the bay. More important, the dispersement pattern of stones in the bay indicates enormous force had been exerted on the stones and had torn them off the shelf in the area in front of the Doña Ana Park.

Lozano and Morales used a sonar side-scan technique that was extremely effective in delineating the formation and the beds of "cut" debris stones that they found under the surface. The "splatter" pattern of the stones in the southernmost area of the Doña Ana Park and Cadiz Bay show us just how and where they came from. They originally came from the ancient floor shelf of the Cadiz Bay and then were deposited in the park, probably by a very ancient tsunami that started the building possibilities for Atlantis thousands of years before. The geologists identified a unique geological formation or shelf right off the Doña Ana Park that they (informally) called the Chipiona-Rota formation. It contained beautifully cut pieces of stones that probably provided the stone cut walls that we saw at Bonsor's excavation in the Doña Ana Park. They were indeed the same types of stones (large, nicely cut quartz blocks) from this unusual formation just off the coast that not only provided the stones for building in the park but also created a protected bay status for the original Tartessos Bay in antiquity.

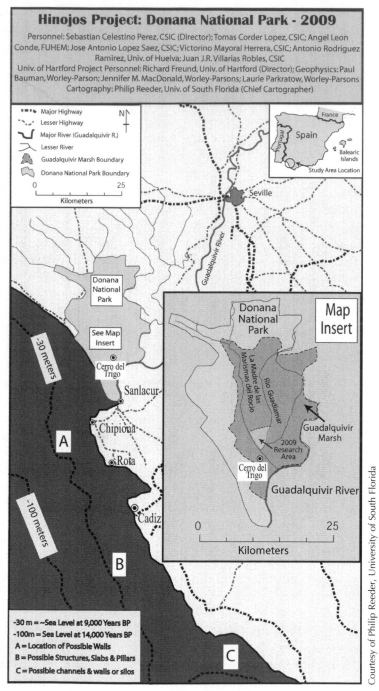

Hinojos Project: Donana National Park - 2009

Personnel: Sebastian Celestino Perez, CSIC (Director); Tomas Corder Lopez, CSIC; Angel Leon Conde, FUHEM; Jose Antonio Lopez Saez, CSIC; Victorino Mayoral Herrera, CSIC; Antonio Rodriguez Ramirez, Univ. of Huelva; Juan J.R. Villarias Robles, CSIC
Univ. of Hartford Project Personnel: Richard Freund, Univ. of Hartford (Director); Geophysics: Paul Bauman, Worley-Parson; Jennifer M. MacDonald, Worley-Parsons; Laurie Parkratow, Worley-Parsons
Cartography: Philip Reeder, Univ. of South Florida (Chief Cartographer)

Major Highway
Lesser Highway
Major River (Guadalquivir R.)
Lesser River
Guadalquivir Marsh Boundary
Donana National Park Boundary

0   25
Kilometers

N

France
Spain
Balearic Islands
Study Area Location

Seville

Guadalquivir River

Donana National Park

See Map Insert

Cerro del Trigo

Sanlacur

Chipiona

Rota

Cadiz

-30 meters

-100 meters

A

B

C

Map Insert

Donana National Park

La Madre de las Marismas del Rocio

Rio Guadiamar

Guadalquivir Marsh

2009 Research Area

Cerro del Trigo

Guadalquivir River

0   25
Kilometers

-30 m = ~Sea Level at 9,000 Years BP
-100m = Sea Level at 14,000 Years BP
A = Location of Possible Walls
B = Possible Structures, Slabs & Pillars
C = Possible channels & walls or silos

Courtesy of Philip Reeder, University of South Florida

Figure 2.2.   Map of the projects

Claudio Lozano Guerra-Librero is an unusual scholar in Spain. He is both a historian and a marine archaeologist who has spent his life working on the history of the southern coast of Spain—working in many different periods. The theory that Lozano and Morales advanced is based upon their observations of materials on the floor of the present-day Cadiz Bay and their expertise concerning the geological forces that brought them to this location. Both paving stones and pillars were located directly off of the ancient Tartessos Bay. These appeared to be from an ancient Bronze Age city that was located in the Doña Ana Park nearby. Lozano and Morales' theory is based upon their understanding of the specific geological forces of southern Spain, and on evidence of massive building materials that are unlike anything else they had seen off the coast of Spain.

Seeing these three theories from the three different teams, as well as looking at the evidence we have assembled, one gets the clear understanding of how one single, unifying theory can tie this all together. I call this type of theory a tsunami splatter, or dispersion theory.

A Tsunami Splatter or Dispersion Theory of Atlantis's Stones: Why the Three Hypotheses Are One

The area right in front of the southernmost edges of the Doña Ana Park on the southwest central coast of Spain has a long history of tsunamis and earthquakes with catastrophic results over the past three thousand years. Known and recorded accounts for the past two thousand years show at least sixteen major historical tsunamis between the third century BCE and the twentieth century. Most were generated by high-energy events associated with earthquakes and volcanic activity in the Mediterranean, and more specifically along the Azores-Gibraltar fracture zone, located between the European and African plates. In 1755, a well-documented earthquake affected Lisbon, Portugal, with sixty-foot waves, and hundreds of thousands of pounds of coastal sand and architecture were stirred and redistributed over areas scores of miles away from the Portuguese coastline. On the Portuguese coastline, two ancient tsunamis (five thousand to six thousand years ago) moved hundred-ton boulders over scores of miles. In the Doña Ana Park in southwest central Spain, two additional estuaries (the Boca do Rio and the Guadalete) show enormous deposits of ancient sand and materials that were brought there by what most geologists assume were tsunamis that closed the central portions of the ancient Tartessos Bay by the end of the Bronze Age.

If there had been an island/port in the central part of the ancient Tartessos Bay during the early Bronze Age (built on an earlier deposited sand bar, for example), the building materials would have been shipped in during that time. The remains from the ancient port city in the center of the marsh were dispersed southward, with some continuing to be available for building materials in the Roman period while others were brought out to sea. A series of catastrophic events filled in the entire ancient Tartessos Bay, leaving little in the marsh but the enigmatic telltale circles that could be viewed by satellite photo (see figure 2.3), with random finds at differing strata in the park. Any leftover remains were distributed in the Cadiz Bay itself.

The Sixth Clue: The 2009 and 2010 Hinojos Projects at the Doña Ana Park

Beyond our interest in ancient ports, it is really the technological advances that have been made using ground-penetrating radar, electrical resistivity tomography, magnetometry, and digital mapping that have made our projects so successful. All of these were used, but especially electrical resistivity tomography (ERT). ERT uses electrical impulses and collects the reflections down to thirty feet on a computer, and then interpretations by geophysicists are made of what is below the surface. Material culture, rock, sand, bone, plastic, and metal all have different reflective properties that are interpreted differently by the software and the geophysicist.

I have been lucky enough to work with some of the best and brightest geoscientists and archaeologists in the world. In the case of the search for Atlantis, this was the key to whether we would succeed or not. The Doña Ana marsh dries out for a very short period of time in the summer, and it was necessary to do our work during that brief window. The people I work with start with a plan that we work out during months of discussions, but they were always creatively problem solving as we worked in the field. This process is one that is extremely interesting to the public, and with the topic of Atlantis, the filmmaker Simcha Jacobovici decided to film our work for a documentary on *National Geographic*. Our method is to begin excavations only after there is evidence of some material culture spotted by the subsurface mapping. Even then, we generally know exactly where and what we are excavating. It is called pin-point archaeology, and after fifteen years of use of this technique at over two dozen sites, it is more than experimental. When we had decided that I had the right people in place to do the work in Spain, Simcha Jacobovici put me in contact with a group

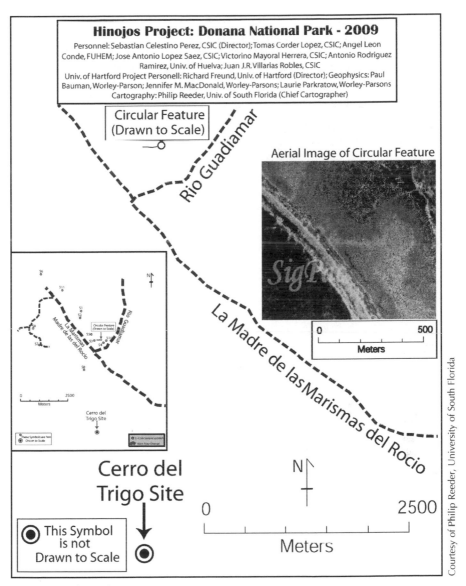

Courtesy of Philip Reeder, University of South Florida

Figure 2.3.   The project map

of archaeologists, historians, geologists, and archaeologists in southern Spain who had a theory to test. They had a theory in a place that would allow only limited access for research, and we had a method for testing the theory in a short period of time without years of excavations. It was a marriage made in heaven. The location we worked in in the marsh was the famous Marisma de Hinojos (thus the University of Hartford Hinojos Project), the marsh where the concentric circles were identified by satellite photography. The *marisma* (marsh) is hundreds of square miles in size and is only open for licensed professionals to conduct research and only for a short time every year when the topsoil dries out enough to drive cars on the marsh.

The hypothesis that the Spanish archaeologists were investigating was called the Wickboldt-Kühne hypothesis, based on the research of Werner Wickboldt and Rainer Kühne from the University of Wuppertal, Germany (discussed earlier in this chapter). Although neither of these researchers was an archaeologist, they identified the location of an anomaly in the Doña Ana Park through a careful assessment of a satellite photo. They also had historical reasons for suggesting that Atlantis was in this area.

The twentieth century produced a whole crop of archaeologists and historians who focused upon this mysterious swamp that is hundreds of square miles in southern Spain, to the south of Seville and extending all of the way to the present-day Mediterranean between Cadiz to the east and Huelva to the west. The problem is that the massive size of the swamp and the fact that it is flooded from October through June made any possibility of serious research difficult. When I arrived in southern Spain in March 2009, I was skeptical about the ideas in the Wickboldt-Kühne hypothesis, which I had read about in a journal. Atlantis is just one of those accounts that is almost too good to be true, a place from which all ancient civilization began. I went to the Doña Ana Park in March with a well-known Spanish archaeologist of southern Spain, a historian, and a geologist. We were part of an investigation to see if the claims had any possibility of being checked. (Many good hypotheses began as claims that simply could not be scientifically checked.) I wanted to see whether the hypothesis could be tested and whether the techniques that we had used so well in twenty other archaeological projects would work to resolve the claims of an Atlantis in southern Spain. It turns out that we were able to contribute to this issue in a way that no other group could. When I went to Doña Ana in March 2009, the site we needed to check was underwater. Everyone asked me what I could learn from a place that was basically inaccessible. What I went to see was the people we might be working with and what the conditions of the site were. When I went in March, it was to check the salinity of the water at Doña Ana and the conditions in the biological park. It turned out that the water was salty, which provided us with a clue for our research. It meant that any research using ground-penetrating radar would not be effective. So we were not surprised to discover that the Spanish team had not had any serious results using this technique. This also meant that we were limited to ERT for our work. Excavation was difficult even during the dry season, from July to September. The possibility of excavating was fraught with problems of how and where to dig, and the water table was near the surface in some places and deeper in others. We decided that the most effective and telling technique would be a combination of a surface survey, ERT in a very specific part of the park, coring, and radiocarbon dating, all of which is summarized in figure 2.4.

This was the first part of the scientific work in southern Spain. I spoke to my colleagues in the field regularly about their understanding of the ancient prehistory of the Iberian Peninsula. This is a topic that constantly fascinates the Spanish historians, since they have always wondered whether Spain was colonized or was itself a colonizer in antiquity. Many national myths are predicated on these discussions, and they affect the way people view their national history. If a people was colonized, they somehow have lost their original, indigenous ethnic identity and have accepted the identity of foreigners. If, however, the nation has been a colonizer, then the original ethnic identity of the Iberians is intact.

If the Phoenicians colonized Spain, then Spanish culture is a secondary creation of a colonized people, but if Atlantis was in Spain and preceded the Phoenicians, then the Spanish are the colonizers of all other Mediterranean cultures. I call this the Big Bang theory of civilization. The question is whether culture spread from east to west or from west to east. I have always wondered whether civilization was created from one single point and spread outward, or whether it was the result of a series of simultaneous, small steps throughout a very diverse world (like the theory of evolution and the Big Bang theory for the creation of the universe). The idea of Atlantis as the birthplace of all civilization is not just a modern speculation attempting to impose national identities upon ancient history. It seems that Plato himself delved into this issue in his own writings. In the same book in which he wrote about the creation of the physical universe, he also wrote about the creation of the cultural universe of Atlantis.

So we began where others have before us, in the Doña Ana Park. The massive swamp of Doña Ana today has no permanent settlements. Geologists have determined in conjunction with the archaeological settlement

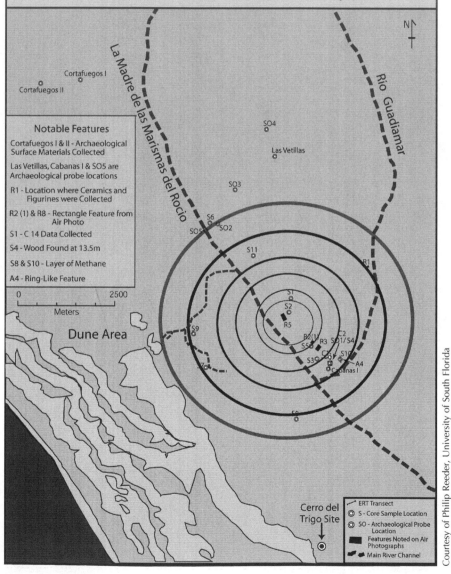

Hinojos Project: Donana National Park - 2009

Personnel: Sebastian Celestino Perez, CSIC (Director); Tomas Corder Lopez, CSIC; Angel Leon Conde, FUHEM; Jose Antonio Lopez Saez, CSIC; Victorino Mayoral Herrera, CSIC; Antonio Rodriguez Ramirez, Univ. of Huelva; Juan J.R. Villarias Robles, CSIC

Univ. of Hartford Project Personnel: Richard Freund, Univ. of Hartford (Director); Geophysics: Paul Bauman, Worley-Parson; Jennifer M. MacDonald, Worley-Parsons; Laurie Parkratow, Worley-Parsons Cartography: Philip Reeder, Univ. of South Florida (Chief Cartographer)

N

Cortafuegos I
Cortafuegos II

La Madre de las Marismas del Rocio

Rio Guadiamar

SO4

Las Vetillas

SO3

Notable Features

Cortafuegos I & II - Archaeological Surface Materials Collected

Las Vetillas, Cabanas I & SO5 are Archaeological probe locations

R1 - Location where Ceramics and Figurines were Collected

R2 (1) & R8 - Rectangle Feature from Air Photo

S1 - C 14 Data Collected

S4 - Wood Found at 13.5m

S8 & S10 - Layer of Methane

A4 - Ring-Like Feature

S6
SO5   SO2

S11

R1

0   2500
Meters

S1
S2
R5

Dune Area

S9

C2
R2(1)   R3 SO1/S4
S5G
C5   S10
S3G   A4
Cabanas I

C8

Cerro del Trigo Site

ERT Transect
S - Core Sample Location
SO - Archaeological Probe Location
Features Noted on Air Photographs
Main River Channel

Courtesy of Philip Reeder, University of South Florida

Figure 2.4.   Summary of data map

patterns that the city of Seville had a massive gulf that extended all the way up to Seville until the middle of the Bronze Age, and then slowly, something began to happen. The layers of sediments show that this ancient gulf was sedimented in specific events. It is not known when exactly the first event happened, but the geologists of Spain could easily see that the gulf of ancient Seville could not have suddenly been totally sedimented in one particular event—it must have been a series of events. The Vikings could still navigate through the Guadalquivir River at the edge of the marsh up until the seventh century CE. This fact indicates that the sedimentation was a slow but consequential process. The series of events would leave remains of the original location. The work that we did in 2009 really started over twenty years earlier with a satellite photograph and its subsequent interpretation.

Atlantis: The Anomaly in the Park—Kühne's Circle and the Line from a Satellite Photograph

Our group has one big advantage over most archaeological teams that gather to excavate sites around the world. We are an interdisciplinary group, made up of geographers, geophysicists, and historians, with whom I have now been working with for the better part of fifteen years. Paul Bauman, a geophysicist, is one of the team members. He is a cross between the TV character MacGyver and one of the main protagonists from a *Mission Impossible* movie. Usually, we present him with a problem, he evaluates first what kind of equipment he needs, and then he will assemble his team. We spent almost a year deciding what equipment needed to be brought from Canada to southern Spain. First, we were most worried about whether the Doña Ana swamp was fresh or salt water. We found it was very salty water—which turned into salty mud and dirt as it dried out in the summer. We had chosen a spot that was over ten miles from the coast, where the anomaly of the circle and the line was prominent.

We began our research looking for something that no one could see very clearly from the surface. The plant life that grew in the soil of the marsh provided clues as to what was below the surface. The patterns of vegetation dried in certain patterns every year because there were chemicals in the soil that leached up from below to inhibit the growth of certain plants in particular areas. This vegetation is what had created the circles. We expected that the reason the circles were visible from the air was not because the ancient walls and the architecture was still there, intact, after more than four thousand years. Instead, we were looking for clues as to whether the vegetation circle designs were the result of chemicals from below that had leached into the soil in patterns, and whether these chemical signatures would still be visible through ERT. If they were, we could interpret them as ancient holes where walls and architecture once stood. The walls and architecture had disintegrated over thousands of years, but much like the empty holes in the gums where extracted teeth once lived, the empty holes tell us the story of what once lived in them. Looking for the telltale signs of a long-distant past and missing architectural features, which are visible only from the vegetation designs on the surface, is much the same as all archaeological work. You are looking for signs on the surface of ancient activity below. Geophysicists can detect slight changes in the soil strata that would never be apparent even to the most skilled archaeologists. The geophysicists on my team, Paul Bauman, Laurie Pankratow, and Jennifer MacDonald, are all from WorleyParsons. This is one of the largest gas and oil exploration companies in the world and is headquartered in Calgary, Alberta, Canada. Paul listened carefully to what the Spanish archaeologists wanted him to do, and we began with the concentric circles and the circle and the line. If you can see the concentric circles from space, there must be a reason.

The geophysics team checked three different areas of the circle. Each one of the areas was one hundred meters (three hundred feet) long. Huerta Tejada, the hunting lodge on the edge of the Doña Ana Park, was where we all met up on September 5, 2009, in the evening after flights from Canada and the United States. The equipment, fifteen large crates of extremely sensitive geophysical apparatus, all came in through Madrid and had to be driven seven hours down to the site. We had a series of licenses from the federal and regional governments that allowed the five of us non-Spaniards to enter and leave the biological park each day during a negotiated time period.

ERT works well when you have a very resistant subsurface. Geophysicists place the lines in a specific grid with multiple electrodes that are connected together and then linked with cables to a battery. Electrical signals to the electrodes are first directed into the ground and then sent back by cables to a computer that immediately receives the signal "bounce" and interprets it. These lines of electrodes are placed at intervals and present themselves to the computer software as individual lines that are connected by the computer into a running interpretive signal. Interpreting the signal is the most important part of the work. Paul Bauman, after thousands of hours in the field and over twenty archaeological excavations, is perhaps one of the most skilled geophysicists in the interpretation of archaeological phenomena. I think what Paul does is more an art rather than pure science. He is able to do what other geophysicists cannot, after working on twenty different archaeological sites. He can interpret geophysical signals and see how they fit archaeological features. Other people and companies own the same equipment and are unable to successfully understand the data that they have collected in the field for archaeologists. Paul can because he has done it so many times.

On the first day of work, as the team set up their first one-hundred-meter circle, we went with the others to look at the edges of the swamp that were bordered by a fence. In the first area, some two miles from the site of the concentric circle and the fault line that we examined, we were able to survey an area that had apparently had had a building on it up until a few hundred years ago. The existence of an area such as this is important since it indicates that there might have been ancient foundations for the building that were reused in a later period. Indeed, as we got out of our Jeep for the first time and surveyed the area, the first things I noticed were pottery shards. Within a few minutes, our group, which was divided into three groups to survey an area that is about a square mile, started collecting shards. When we came upon one particular artifact in the dirt, I was shocked. We looked at each other and could not believe that we had found something such as this. It was a small female figurine—an Astarte (the Phoenician goddess of fertility)—which was so perfect that we passed her around and stood in awe of what clearly was one of the most ancient finds ever located in this swamp. We began calling her the Astarte of Atlantis. Because Astarte was indeed one of the most ancient female goddesses of the Phoenicians (and indeed all over the ancient Near East), finding something like this was a piece of a very complicated puzzle about where a proto-Phoenician Atlantis had been located.

The "Venus de Milo" of Spain—The Astarte of Atlantis?

Even with its arms and head missing, the Astarte resembled the type of Astarte I had seen in ancient Near Eastern collections. Also, the type of rock it had been shaped from was common—but not in this region! It appeared to have been brought from another area, and the rock and the colored white limestone top had been shaped by an expert. We all speculated on the history of the Astarte and how the Atlantis story might indeed be connected to the ancient Phoenicians.

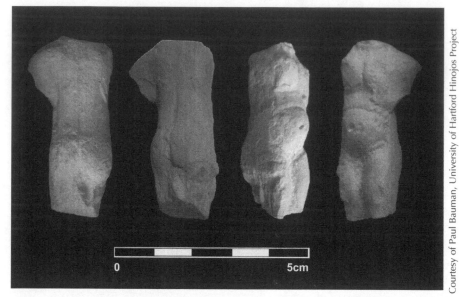

Courtesy of Paul Bauman, University of Hartford Hinojos Project

Figure 2.5.   The Astarte of the Doña Ana Park

We studied the figurine's distinguishing features. We did not have to look very far. At the University of Hartford we have a small collection of antiquities that were donated by Joel and SusAnna Grae, which includes a series of classic three-thousand-year old Astartes from Mesopotamia and the Mediterranean. Astarte figurines are well represented in this extraordinary collection because Astarte was venerated as a fertility symbol and is emblematic of the Phoenicians because she appears in all of the places where they had ports. Characteristics of Astarte figurines include a prominent stomach and navel, a headdress, breasts, and bulging thighs. Most of the figurines seem to be either free standing or in relief. Ishtar may be crafted with one or both hands on the stomach or breasts, seated, beak-faced, or with hands upraised. In excavations in ancient Israel, Astarte with upraised arms is found many times in excavations. In all likelihood, the figurine we found in the Doña Ana Park had had upraised arms, but the fragile arms had been broken off.

The fact that Astarte was found in the Doña Ana Park was not so unusual for southern Spain. In Granada there is the alabaster seated Astarte from a seventh-century BCE necropolis of Galera (near Granada) with winged sphinx figures nearby. In the outskirts of Seville an Astarte from the Iron Age had been discovered, and the variety of Astartes even in this region suggested that a sitting or standing Astarte was a well-known an-

Figure 2.6.   A traditional Near Eastern Astarte drawing and pose

Courtesy of DreAnna Hadash, University of Hartford Hinojos Project cient figurine. But to find an Astarte in a surface survey on our first day was outstanding.

The Astarte or Ishtar is either free-standing or on a background. One of the oldest and most important goddesses of antiquity from Mesopotamia is Inanna, who is later identified both as Ishtar and by the Bible as Anat, Ashera or Ashtoret, and Astarte. The Canaanite goddess Anat, whose fundamental affinity with Inanna and Ishtar is well known, was likewise deemed the Queen of Heaven in Egyptian sources. And she has also been identified with the planet Venus. The celestial goddess figures prominently among the pagan gods mentioned in the many sections of the Hebrew Bible, and apparently ancient Israelites burned incense to honor the Queen of Heaven, which vexed the prophets of ancient Israel. A figurine of an Astarte in ivory was found in excavations in Israel as well. It had the same type of hair as the figurine we found in Doña Ana, and it also had the pregnant stomach feature.

The worship of Astarte spread far and wide, and in time, she was glorified by the Philistines, the Greeks, the Romans, the Sicilians, and in many parts of Europe and Africa for almost four thousand years. Examples from the Middle East are very well known. So I convinced my colleague Sebastian at the ERT work site that we needed to do more of a systematic surface survey while Paul and the geophysicists completed their work. On the next day, September 7, Sebastian and I with the entire film crew went to the area where we had found the Astarte. As we stepped out of the van, we immediately saw a tableau of legs of another Astarte at our feet and began an intense two-hour search of the area. Sebastian discovered another unusual form of a goddess statuette that was clearly not Christian, Roman, or Greek. It seemed to have the same headdress of an Astarte with a place for a diadem on the forehead.

Finding a Phoenician goddess figurine in the middle mudflat made me think about the connection between the Middle Eastern Phoenicians and the Spanish Phoenicians. As we began to date the organic matter in the Hinojos mudflats (through carbon-14 testing) to near 4000 BCE, it made me rethink the idea of direction of cultural influence. Although we could not date the stone figurine, if she were a part of the most ancient parts of the mudflats, she would predate the Phoenicians of the Middle East by nearly a thousand years. What if this was indeed a Phoenician settlement from the Bronze Age but was established before all of the most typical Phoenician groups were even settled in the western Mediterranean? What if, instead of coming from the Middle East to Spain, the Phoenician culture was actually spread first from the west and then transplanted to the Middle East? What if the first seafarers and Phoenicians originated in Spain and went from the west to the Middle East (and then later returned as Phoenicians)? That would make Atlantis the prototype for all other Phoenician outposts. I remember telling Sebastian all about this as he stood holding the two statuettes, and I speculated on what else might be found in this marsh in the area of the mysterious circle that had been identified by satellites and now investigated by ERT technology.

The Second Day of the Expedition

On the first day of the expedition, our geophysicists tried a one-hundred-meter section that was not in the middle of the circle where the most prominent feature was viewed in our aerial shot. On the second day, September 7, 2009, the actual center of the circle was the target. It was not altogether clear that there would be anything at the actual center of the circle. Nothing could be seen on the top of the dry marsh fields in which we had worked, and very little was visible even from the vantage point of our helium balloons that hovered above the sites in which the geophysicists were working. When the next one-hundred-meter section was placed over the area in the center of the large circle that is seen from space, it was clear that this was a crucial detail in the work. There was a distinctive marking in the ground in the places where the concentric circles of the inner city of Atlantis would have been located. Since the day before had yielded no clear indication of any activity below the surface with the ERT, it was a good test for the second day. When intermittent undetected inner breaks were found in the ERT, it took all of us by surprise. The intermittent breaks in the ERT layer were the remnants of the ancient walls of a Bronze Age city that had been there thousands of years before. The chemical signature of the different walls was probably plastered with an ancient limestone plaster over a rock cut wall that was no longer there. The intermittent breaks in the ERT layer in the center of the circle were just the chemical footprint of that which was gone but not forgotten in the layers of sediment that exist there now. This was the clue to why the vegetation had grown in the way it had and why it could be viewed from above. Once a layer disappears, it leaves behind only a "shadow" or chemical signature of the original feature. Often when we find ancient bodies that have been incinerated in a cataclysmic fire, for example, all that is left is a chemical signature and a shadow in the place where the body had been. In the case of the walls of Atlantis, the ERT showed the circle shadows in the places that, if traced, would indicate circles in the sandy marsh, with breaks on both sides of a large area.

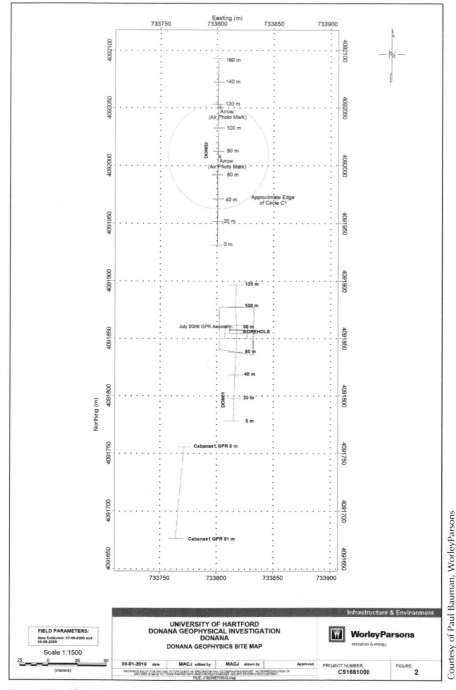

Figure 2.7.   The ERT survey of the circle

Courtesy of Paul Bauman, WorleyParsons

The Seventh Clue: How Carbon-14 Tests Help Pinpoint Atlantis

The seventh clue in determining whether we were working in an ancient Bronze Age site that might be Atlantis is real dating processes. Today, it is not enough just to say that something compares favorably to another Bronze Age site; it must be accurately dated to an ancient time period by multiple radiocarbon dating. My colleagues in Spain took a very thorough radiocarbon dating sampling from the area we were investigating. They checked and rechecked at two labs before providing the dates. It was very important to the entire project and was the seventh clue that this would be a suitable place for the ancient city.

A word about the process of establishing scientific chronology, or a time line, and its terminology is necessary. Archaeologists and geologists use different sorts of chronological terminology to sort out ancient periods of time. Archaeologists prefer to use a combination of historical and cultural designations together with technological advances. For example, in this book I use the designations that are used by Middle Eastern archaeologists—Chalcolithic Period (4500–3200 BCE), Bronze Age (3200–1200 BCE), and Iron Age (1200–586 BCE)—but these divisions are sometimes based upon technological advancements (and other times upon conventions) in the use of new materials, combined with major historical events in the region. These periods are followed by the Persian period (536–332 BCE), the Greek period (333–63 BCE), the Roman period (63 BCE–325 CE), the Byzantine period (325–638 CE), the first Muslim period (638–1096), the Crusades (1096–1200 CE), and so on. Geologists use a much more general term for the most recent period of human history (the last five thousand years) and have developed terminology for the hundreds of thousands of years that came before our human history. In addition, in our Atlantis project, the use of Before Present (BP) in our carbon-14 (C14) measurements of time corresponds to a convention among geologists that is used to date the decomposition of carbon, from a date in our own period (1950 CE) to the ancient period. (See the simple chronology just after the table of contents if this all becomes too complicated.)

My point is that the time periods we reference in our project are based upon the combination of historical guide points and technological advancements. Much of the history in this book relates to the Middle East and Europe (although these designations are slightly different in Europe). Radiocarbon dating uses an absolute (and not culturally based) measure. It is usually used together with other dating practices such as geological layering and architectural styles, as well as with, in later periods, pottery styles. The advent of coins offered another chance for evidence that can be used alongside the carbon-14 dating to give greater specificity to the dates. The basic principle of carbon-14 dating is based upon the presence of the carbon-14 isotope in all organic matter, such as bones, parchment, and textiles made from animal and vegetable matter. Even though the isotope decays at a precisely measurable rate, the micro-conditions of any setting can affect the scientific analysis of the data. Carbon-14 is a reliable way to analyze organic matter for dating purposes, especially when you have something such as architectural types or artifacts to compare to the dating. Since carbon is one of the elements that have a well-known and trackable decomposition rate, a test was developed about sixty years ago for analyzing the carbon in organic remains found at a specific archaeological stratum. It is not a perfect test, since it generally has a broad plus-or-minus factor, but the more you know about a site and the specific elements of a layer, the use of all dating techniques together makes the C14 test more accurate.

At the Doña Ana Park site, we had multiple samples of C14 that were analyzed. The samples taken at the S1 site are in the middle of the famous circular site that I opened the chapter with. They are samples that are all very close to the surface (about 200 cm–1200 cm), and all are from the Bronze Age. Then the S4 sample, taken at a depth of 13.5 meters (over 40 feet below the top layer), is also very ancient. The wood sample is local and is located below all of the other layers of sediment that had accumulated on top of it. It is from 4400 ± 40 years BP. The genus of the wood found deep below the sediments is local oak, suggesting that the boat made with this wood was made in Spain and not in the Middle East. This means that the site was in use somewhere around 2500 BCE. It does not tell us when the site was destroyed, but we know that by the eleventh century BCE, there was already another site that had developed on an island/port farther to the east of Doña Ana at today's Cadiz. The depth that the wood sample was found at (13.5 meters) suggests that some catastrophic event or events buried the wood under massive sediments. But finding the wood below so many different layers and located in the middle of the circular feature in the ancient Tartessos Bay suggests that in the early Bronze Age, there was an ancient island/port active in the now sedimented Doña Ana Park.

The wood sample led us to ask when did the island became sedimented in. The general parameters of when the change occurred are between 2500 BCE and 1100 BCE, but I think I can narrow it down even further. In order for an entire bay the size of Tartessos to be sedimented, it would require an enormous force. Some of the few forces on earth that can cause this type of cataclysmic change are earthquakes and volcanoes (and sometimes both—one causing the other). The volcano of Santorini (on the Greek island of Thera, now called Santorini), eight hundred miles from Spain in the Mediterranean, is known to have caused damage as far away as the coast of Israel, some seven hundred miles away (depositing ash and pumice). The timing of the eruption is generally understood to be in the middle of the seventeenth century BCE, and the explosion is now blamed for the decline of Minoan civilization. The possibility that Santorini initiated the earthquake that caused the tsunami in Tartessos Bay is one element that has to be considered.

Plato writes a description of this event that is very specific in its details. In antiquity one might expect that mud brick might be the major type of construction. In *Critias* 116, Plato specifically states that the buildings were "surrounded by a stone wall on every side," with different-colored stones (white, black, and red) used in the construction. The different-colored stones are indicators of geological formations, but the fact that these walls are constructed in a period before cement means that stone workers would have to cut the stones so they fit in very neat arrangements. While many of the other elements such as mud brick, gold, and silver would have disappeared over time, the type of stone that Plato is describing is exactly what archaeologists look for in ancient architecture. The fact that Plato's descriptions single out the stone walls as unusual leads us to think that the regular walls of construction for the palace and all of the other buildings were mud brick, which would have been covered in a plaster and made aesthetically more beautiful by a covering of mud brick or tile work that was painted or covered in gold and silver. This is the reason that the ERT revealed only the chemical signature in the strata directly below the surface. But stonework from antiquity is still evident thousands of years later and is the best indicator of an ancient city. None of the ERT work (that can be viewed down some sixty feet) found any stone evident at the site. If the areas were hit by a tsunami, it is possible that the stone walls—probably blocks cut and placed together one on top of another without cement—would have been taken out to the sea. Finding the stone walls was therefore the most important part of the search for Atlantis. If Doña Ana Park held only the last chemical signature of the impressive walls and the contours of the concentric circles of Atlantis, it would be difficult to say that we had found evidence of the ancient city. But with the evidence at Cerro del Trigo and in the Cadiz Bay (the stone building materials found by Bonsor and mentioned earlier in this chapter), there were pieces that could be connected back to the Hinojos marsh site that we were studying.

The Lozano–Morales Hypothesis: How a Tsunami Can Change an Ancient Bay

In 2009, when we were working in the Doña Ana Park, we were joined by a number of geologists, geographers, archaeologists, and especially marine archaeologists from the area. Claudio Lozano was one of those marine archaeologists who were fascinated by our work. As discussed earlier in this chapter, Claudio said that he had encountered a site in the Cadiz Bay off Doña Ana where there were indeed unknown massive stone walls lying on the floor of the bay. As mentioned, he theorized that a tsunami moved the stone walls away from the Doña Ana Park location, and I found this intriguing. His work involved a side-scan sonar, a boat, and divers, and was captured on film by a film crew as most of this work was filmed. In August 2010, he found the stone walls, without the cement, intact, and in a random "splatter" pattern off the Doña Ana Park location. This was the best evidence of a tsunami dropping the stone walls in that location. He and his colleagues brought up photographs. These stone walls are just some of the artifacts that together explain why we think there was a buried city here in antiquity.

The work of the marine archaeologists in the present Bay of Cadiz is very significant. The stones that they found randomly arranged on the floor of the Cadiz Bay tell a story of the destruction and environmental cataclysm that sealed the Tartessos Bay forever. The pattern of the stones indicates that they were originally sheared loose from the geological formation in front of the ancient Tartessos Bay and mined for building and then ultimately hurled back into their present location. These are enormous forces of nature and tell us how the fate of the ancient Tartessos Bay was sealed sometime in the Bronze Age. The stones in the present-day Cadiz Bay would turn out to be the most direct connection to the ancient tsunami(s) that we assume destroyed both Atlantis and what would later be the follow-up port of Tarshish in the area. After I was shown the evidence of the destruction on the floor of the bay, I was asked whether I thought these were the stones of Tarshish or the stones of Atlantis. I imagine that the same stones that were used to build Atlantis were used by those who rebuilt the later island/port of Tarshish. This was a cycle that was repeated by the Romans at Cerro del Trigo.

So What Happened to the Altanteans/Tarshishites?

When I looked at all of the evidence we had gathered, it told me about the destruction of the city. Now we wanted to know what happened to the Atlanteans/Tarshishites. Even if we could track the destruction pattern of the tsunami into the Cadiz Bay, we needed to find out what happened to the refugees who survived this destruction. Did they rebuild their city/port again? Did they get on boats and find another location on the Mediterranean where they could ply their trades and skills? Did they go to live in another new settlement farther to the east and south on the island/port of Gadir/Cadiz or did they move to another location farther west on the Iberian Peninsula? I have made a career out of searching out where refugees escape to following national and regional disasters. In our work on the Dead Sea, at the Qumran site, at the Cave of Horror (in Israel), and at the Cave of Letters, we tracked the refugees from the first and second century CE rebellions of the Jews against the Romans to caves and settlements in the Judean desert. At Yavne, we tracked the refugees of Jerusalem and Judea's destructions from the first century CE to a village some twenty miles to the west of the Mediterranean Sea. One of the most poignant series of settlements that I have found were villages in the north of Israel in the Galilee and Golan that were built up after the city of Jerusalem and the area of Judea was devastated by war. In the north of Israel we found that the refugees built villages and constructed synagogues that were miniature versions of the Temple in Jerusalem that they could no longer visit. I wondered if the Atlanteans and Tarshishites did the same thing in Spain. They did.

The Miniature "Atlantis" Ritual Cities: Tartessos of the North

I think that the descendants of the same people who built Atlantis may also have built Tarshish nearby. But it appears that by the eighth century BCE Tarshish was no more, and the Tartessos Bay where they were located was seen as a hostile environment. In one of the most unique tests of a hypothesis, I asked Sebastian Celestino, one of the leading archaeologists of Spain, if there were other known Tartessan settlements in Spain or Portugal. His reaction was one of joy. "Yes," he said. "There was a Tartessan culture that developed farther to the west, and there are Tartessan settlements some 150 miles to the north of the coast." In fact, this was an understatement. Professor Celestino spent the better part of two decades excavating one of the most important Tartessan cities ever discovered in Spain. So on a September day after we completed the work in the Doña Ana Park, Professor Celestino took me to Cancho Roano for the biggest discovery of the Atlantis project. As I looked at it for the first time, I knew

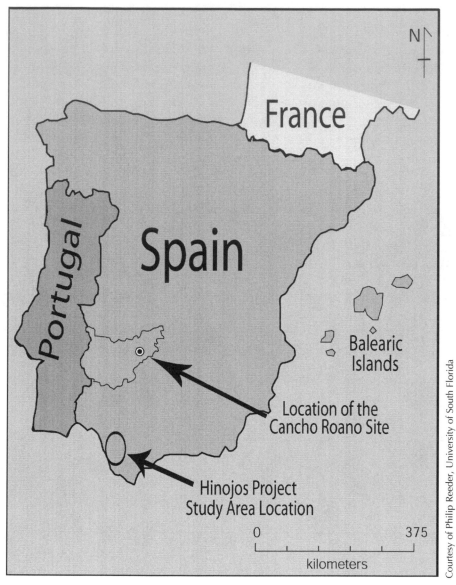

France

Spain

Portugal

Balearic
Islands

Location of the
Cancho Roano Site

Hinojos Project
Study Area Location

0   375
kilometers

Courtesy of Philip Reeder, University of South Florida

Figure 2.8.   The research areas

in that moment that I was looking at the most compelling evidence for the existence of Atlantis. It was a miniature city built in the image of the Atlantis described by Plato.

We first drove to Almendorjalegos, which is not the geographic center of Spain but it could be. It is in the region called Extramadura and sits in the middle of an area with wine and olive trees that reminded me of areas in the Middle East. On September 9, 2009, we took our ERT to help Sebastian with an excavation of a group of cities he called Tartessan cities of the north. We worked at the site at Cerro Bartolo for a morning, and we could just barely see the central shrine with rooms around the outside as the stones poked through the ground. He explained to us that we were looking for features that he had identified at the site of Cancho Roano in nearby Zalamea de la Serena. We arrived at Cancho Roano in the early evening. It was at Cancho Roano that we all realized what had happened to the Tartessans and the Atlanteans. As we walked toward the site from the parking lot, it was clear to all of us who saw it bathed in the light of the late afternoon. Cancho Roano was one of many monumental cities in the region that were created (as I later learned from Sebastian) by a mysterious group of refugees from the south, the Tartessans, who came there probably in the ninth or eighth century BCE from the south and stayed. When we arrived to see Cancho Roano, we saw that we were looking at a site with one solitary entrance into the city that was completely surrounded by a large, artificial canal that had been dug with great difficulty around the outside of a series of concentric circle rooms around a central shrine. We were looking at a miniature version of what we had been looking for in Doña Ana Park.

When I asked Sebastian who had lived in the city, he told me that it did not appear that anyone had actually lived in the building. It was a ritual Tartessan city/building built for pilgrims to visit and then return to their homes. As I looked at the building it struck me that there were too many anomalies in construction to explain away. For example, the canal that surrounded the city, which during the rainy season would fill with water, was not natural but rather was cut (at great expense and effort) into the bedrock. It surrounded the entire building (except one entrance that jutted out in the center over the top of the canal), giving the city the appearance of an island when the canal was filled with water. If Cancho Roano had been the only city in the region like this I would have thought it was just a coincidence that it resembled an island, until I discovered that other monumental cities in the region also had this canal surrounding the building with one entrance/exit. There were a number of these ritual cities that had been created with the same elements: a central shrine, a canal, areas for sacrifice, and a single entrance in and out through the canal into the city. It was evident walking through the rooms that they had different purposes. Some were for storage of items brought by the pilgrims, and then we saw a decorated ivory piece on a sign that immediately caught my attention. The ivory piece resembled the winged cherubim (the image of an animal with decorated palmettes and columns around the outside of the piece clearly were not like anything I had seen before). This image is often associated with the Phoenicians throughout the Middle East, and here we were in the inner sanctum of a building on an artificial island in the middle of Spain.

As we entered the holy of holies shrine, it was clear that the symbol on the floor was an indicator of the most cherished part of the Tartessan culture. It was a symbol that I recognized from ancient Middle Eastern sources, which is found atop a famous stele built by the Pharaoh Ahmose I in the sixteenth century BCE in Egypt. This honored group within Egyptian society practiced an artistry and science that was not well known to all peoples. It was metallurgy, and the symbol of the metallurgists sat in the middle of the holy of holies of Cancho Roano. One of the most prized secrets of the ancient world—the origins of how metal ore was smelted into a workable form—was shrouded in mystery. The ability to create and forge the ancient mineral resources of antiquity was part science and part religion. Shaping gold, silver, tin, bronze, and iron was the difference between low tech and high tech in antiquity. The jewelry, weapons, ritual objects, and one of the technological advances that made Atlantis famous were here preserved in a single symbol on the floor of the holy of holies shrine in the center of the artificial island/city. Here it was at the center of this miniature version of Atlantis, 150 miles from the coast. If I had not seen it with my own eyes I would not have believed it. This miniature version of Atlantis preserved the memory of the high technology, the architecture, the decorations, and the ancient seafaring past—not hidden in a marsh but hidden in plain sight.

Cancho Roano had one more element that was shared by all of the other Tartessan cities of the north: a signpost that indicated who had built the cities, as well as what they were memorializing. My guide, Professor Celestino, took me to the museum where the remnants of the Tartessan civilization are housed in the city of Badajoz, and it was there that the final clues to the mystery all came together.

Symbols of Memory: The Eighth Clue to the Identity of the Northern Tartessans

I immediately was aware of the many symbols of memory that I started to see around me in the museum of Badajoz. There were stones, symbols, decorations, and inscriptions that connected these people with an ancient past that went beyond their own period. When you begin to add up the number of elements in each of these cities you realize that you are looking at the largest assembly of evidence for the ancient, proto-Phoenician Atlantean culture. One of the mysteries of the building of Cancho Roano, for example, was a single room located on the left as we entered the site through its only entrance and exit. This small room, which had what looks like the remains of a window structure looking out or ventilating the room, also had a pavement of an extraordinary nature. All of the other rooms were clay or dirt and not particularly interesting. This room was paved with slate and also filled with artifacts. This single, slate pavement room in Cancho Roano was identified as perhaps the only place that indicated that someone lived at Cancho Roano. The archaeologists identified it as a single room on the left side as you entered the first ring of the inner city after stepping over the threshold. The archaeologists had labeled this room as the place where the priest or officiant from the site stayed. It was this officiant who would perform sacrifices for the citizens who would visit on pilgrimage. Unlike the other rooms that were packed with local dirt, this room was paved with a slate floor.

Slate is an abundant stone that was a well-known paving stone in the coastal region of Spain but was unusual in the middle of the country. In fact, during my visit to Bonsor's excavations in the south, one of the few stones still *in situ* (meaning in its original location) that had not been buried by the "preservation" teams in the 1990s—was slate. Looking around the Badajoz Museum, I saw how valued slate was, and those decorated slates in the collection were there because they were seen as special items that were venerated by the locals in the earliest periods of their history. One of the things that we do in archaeology is to follow the building materials in order to evaluate the influences upon a site. By following the stones, you can track the cultural influences. Paving with slate in ancient sites is rare in the middle of the country (it is found mainly in the north and the south), but it appears that it served another purpose at the holy site of Cancho Roano. The room thought to be the officiant's is the only one paved with slate. I think it provided the officiant with a memory of a place, probably from the south, where slate was abundant, and that was no more: Atlantis.

The Final Clue: The "Message in a Bottle" of the Atlanteans and a Map of the Lost City

I have had only a few "aha!" moments in my life. It was in the Badajoz Museum that I had one such moment. Hanging on the walls of the Bada-joz Museum (near the site of Cancho Roano) were other reminders of the life that was no more. On the second floor of the museum were the steles that stood at the entrance to each of the northern Tartessan cities. Most had the same symbol etched into the stone—a symbol like no other symbol that I have ever seen on any ancient stele. These steles are called by the museum the "Warrior Stelae," because many have a standing warrior on the front with weapons scattered on the ground next to (or in front of) a warrior; sometimes he is carrying a spear or a sword, but for the most part the weapons are scattered near his feet. Some of the steles have ancient chariots alongside the warrior, and others have a variety of other elements of life. But all have in the center, on the top, to the side and always near the warrior, three concentric circles with a small line leading from an edge into the center of the circles. The image on nearly every one of the steles

Figure 2.9.   A Tartessan stele on display at the Badajoz Museum

Courtesy of Associated Producers

almost leaped off the wall. The concentric circles were a perfect match to the description of Atlantis in *Critias*.

I asked Professor Sebastian Celestino, my colleague from the work in the Doña Ana Park who had earlier brought me to Cancho Roano to see the excavations there, whether he thought it was odd that almost every recovered stele (including one from Cancho Roano) had this image. To his thinking there really was no other grouping like these steles. The stele of Cancho Roano had been found at the one entrance to the city. It had a standing warrior with his weapons at his right foot, and then isolated off to the left of the warrior was the mysterious concentric circles image. I asked him what the concentric circles image on the steles was thought to be by Spanish archaeologists. He told me that they were interpreted as shields. When I asked why the shields were often so much bigger than the warrior (and in some cases there are no warriors, just the symbol of the concentric circles), disconnected from the other weapons, and always drawn with this symbol on them, he said that it was just a design. In fact, even if some of the images are shields, the symbol on the shield is more than just a design. It was a decoration of something that was powerfully important to the Tartessans, and it is often alone on a stele without warriors or any other materials. In my experience, perspective, proximity, and designs of symbols are always important and often follow something that is meaningful to the people who used it.

After seeing Cancho Roano the day before and now seeing all of these steles at once, it appeared that the concentric circles image was more important than I first imagined. Cancho Roano and another Tartessan site, La Mata, have been reconstructed to allow visitors to see what the original planners did. Each city had a dug canal or band of water around the outside of the city, and inside the main structure one could see the additional concentric circles of rooms with a central shrine (the holy of holies) in the middle. This was just too similar to the description of Atlantis to be ignored. And now this. It turns out there are scores of these steles with the same image of the concentric circles situated throughout the countryside in the area where the Tartessan culture flourished. Some have a sentinel guarding what I interpret to be the symbol of the concentric circle city. In the museum we could see that in city after city in the northern Tartessan settlements, there were these steles with the same symbol placed at the entrance to the city. The symbol and the city were re-creating an artificial island.

Writing, of course, was very important to most ancient cultures and especially the ancient Phoenicians, and I assume also to Atlantean refugees' culture. It is one of the ties that binds a people far from their original land to their ancient culture. I think the refugees used a language written in Phoenician script and inscribed upon stones at their new home, far from the coastal Phoenician culture and trade. Here in the middle of Spain we have inscribed stones with the Phoenician alphabet with cryptic messages written on some of the steles. Fixed to the wall in the museum of Badajoz were powerful reminders of how a people remembers who they are and were. Unfortunately for us, the meanings of the inscriptions remain a mystery that linguists have not been able to solve. The inscribed letters are a testament to the past and a mystery for the future.

So What Happened to Atlantis (and Tarshish)?

The tracking of the Atlantean refugees to the central part of Spain is perhaps the most exciting part of our work. What happened to the Atlanteans is as important as what happened to Atlantis. The study of these Tartessan villages (like Cancho Roano) will continue to enlighten us about how ancient peoples like the Atlanteans reinvigorated themselves after natural and man-made disasters forced them from their original

Figure 2.10.   The Tartessan inscribed stone

Courtesy of Associated Producers

homes. How they translated the rites and the rituals of an ancient Atlantean life and coastal religion into a new and very different locale is the story of all religions from antiquity. This is the story of how archaeology can help us understand the history of the world. Each discovery is a microcosm of the history of many of the world's religions that had to face (and continue to face in the modern world) new and untold challenges, as the foundational ideas and theologies continued to influence new generations of followers in different locations.

Our most important insight on Atlantis is that the same geological forces that brought it into existence probably destroyed it. The sediments that filled the original, ancient, open Cadiz Bay with enough material to allow the Atlanteans to create a canal-like port island/city like Atlantis after a very ancient catastrophic environmental event (earthquake and tsunami) are the same forces that later destroyed it. This later catastrophic environmental event (an earthquake and tsunami) sealed the remains of the city under thousands of pounds of mud and sand, but also disgorged many of the materials into the depths of Cadiz Bay in front of the Doña Ana Park. The remnants of this ancient city are buried in the midst of the park and in the Mediterranean Sea just beyond the Pillars of Hercules (Straits of Gibraltar), just as Plato indicated 2,500 years ago.

The Dead Sea Scrolls   **3**

One Archaeological Discovery That Changed How We Understand the History of the Ancient and Modern Worlds

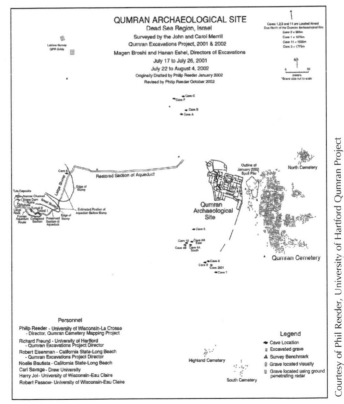

Figure 3.1   Mapping of the Qumran Excavations Project

Courtesy of Phil Reeder, University of Hartford Qumran Project

Could it be that the Dead Sea Scrolls, so amazingly exhumed from their long forgotten cave-burials and suddenly transported over the space of some twenty centuries to the attention of the world, were hailed unconsciously by myriads as a symbol of luminescent hope in an age of otherwise unrelieved darkness?

—RABBI DR. NELSON GLUECK, PRESIDENT, HEBREW UNION COLLEGE
(*NEW YORK TIMES*, NOVEMBER 1958)

Not the End, but the Beginning

AN ONE ARCHAEOLOGICAL discovery really change history? I could name six or seven different archaeological discoveries that have changed history, but I chose to focus on the Dead Sea Scrolls because, unlike other discoveries that changed the way we view the ancient world, the discovery of the Dead Sea Scrolls changed our understanding of ancient *and* modern religious history. More than any other archaeological discovery of the past century or more, the Dead Sea Scrolls stand as an example of how a discovery has caused historians to go back to the proverbial drawing board and reconsider the ideas or preconceptions that they had about Judaism, the origins of Christianity, and the Bible.

Many of my students think that all of the mysteries of the Dead Sea Scrolls have been solved since they are now available to scholars all over the world online. In fact, the importance of the Dead Sea Scrolls will continue for the future as scholars puzzle over the meaning and the influence of the ideas in the scrolls. Like Plato's writings on Atlantis, the Dead Sea Scrolls are connected with many different places. One place, Qumran, and the caves nearby on the Dead Sea, is considered the location where the scrolls were written. But it is not altogether clear that Qumran was the only place from which these scrolls came. In addition, the Dead Sea Scrolls and other manuscript discoveries from around the Dead Sea and the Judean desert are themselves a part of a larger mystery of why this desert region seems to have served as a repository of so many almost unparalleled ancient religious ideas. In our own work at the University of Hartford's projects in the Judean desert from 1998 to 2002 at caves along the Dead Sea and at the site of Qumran, a village near the eleven caves where the scrolls were discovered, I have become aware of how significant these discoveries have become not only for ancient history but also for modern religion. The original mystery of the content of the Dead Sea Scrolls has, for the most part, given way to a second mystery: What do the scrolls mean and how have they influenced modern religion? Part of our research included a search for other caves and to see if there is much more to the story. This is a thoroughly modern search using the high-tech equipment that we used in our search for Atlantis. Many of the maps we developed have utilized a global positioning system (GPS) location for future study, and I am certain that as the political situation on the West Bank improves, many new archaeological expeditions will follow. This is why archaeological research is a thoroughly modern part of historical research, at the same time that researchers try to unravel the original ancient context of the written material.

I was suddenly struck during our work at Qumran and the caves by just how the methodology of archaeology of the scrolls has changed over the years. Everyone admits that the scrolls were largely not discovered as a part of organized and scientific excavations. In fact, the provenance of the scrolls will always be a question because they were largely found and brought to scholars by local bedouins, who rarely shared the exact location of their discoveries. We puzzled for almost a decade over the scrolls that were eventually assigned to the Cave of Letters from other caves nearby. Once the large number of unique Psalms scrolls and fragments of the Pentateuch were reassigned to the Cave of Letters, the cave suddenly had a totally different "religious" meaning that it lacked when Yigael Yadin excavated it in 1960–1961. Today we still marvel over the discovery of the letters of Bar Kokhba in the Cave of Letters, but we also puzzle over the religious authorities who produced the scores of Psalms manuscripts that were taken from the cave in the 1950s (and assigned to a nearby non-Israeli cave) only to be reconstituted and reassigned to the Cave of Letters thanks to excellent scholarship. The context of the discovery counts, and at Qumran it is not only the context but also assumptions about the Dead Sea Scrolls in the eleven caves that continue to influence our understanding of the scrolls.

Sometimes a technique helps redefine the archaeology. Our method of using ERT and another technique, ground-penetrating radar (GPR), at Qumran and in the caves has redefined the way that ancient caves can be investigated. Since almost all of the discoveries in the caves were discovered on the top layer of all of the roof debris in the entrances to the caves, our work suggests that this may just be the beginning. Otherwise, it would be tantamount to an archaeologist just excavating the top layer of an archaeological mound and never attempting to see if there are other layers. Our work has confirmed that we need to have a new generation of research on the caves. The thousand or more caves along the Dead Sea that were quickly investigated by many different projects need to use the GPR/ERT approach to see if the caves contain buried materials as we found in the Cave of Letters. This may usher in a new era of Dead Sea research.

Sometimes method and the public telling of the story of the scrolls do help define and sharpen what we know about the scrolls. An example is the new Shrine of the Book at the Israel Museum in Jerusalem, which displays some of the scrolls. The Israeli curator, Dr. Adolfo Roitman, has redefined the way the scrolls are displayed, and by doing this he has also redefined the way that the scrolls are understood by the museum public.

We started our work at Qumran in the mid-1990s when the "old" Shrine of the Book was still telling a story that had been defined from the 1950s and the early 1960s. It was an interesting tale of a little-known sect of Jews living on the Dead Sea primarily before the rise of early Christianity. The archaeology of Qumran revealed that there was indeed a massive defensive feature; they had multiple water installations, a sophisticated system of capturing the water, a large area to eat, a pottery shop, no apparent living quarters, a cemetery containing men and women in more than twelve hundred in-ground burials, a strange structure in the midst of the cemetery with a single burial within, and an unknown relationship with the scrolls in the nearby caves. There is still no absolute consensus about who the Qumranites were or if the scrolls were even written there. If we judge the water installations by later rabbinic interpretation, they are not easily categorized as rabbinically Jewish. The burials tell us little about the ethnicity of the individuals interred there, and comparisons with the mysterious sect of the Essenes continue to vex scholars. Yet, beyond doubt, the discovery of the scrolls and the village of Qumran captured the imagination of the world in the 1950s and 1960s in a way that no other archaeological discovery has done. But the meaning of the scrolls became after 1965 a part of the national narrative of the modern State of Israel, and they were enshrined in their own iconic Shrine of the Book as a part of the new pantheon of the Jewish state. Even with no Temple and no priesthood, the Dead Sea Scrolls and their home at the Israel Museum in Jerusalem became the new Temple of the modern religion of Israel, and the curator became the equivalent of the modern high priest of this secularized society.

We began working with the new curator of the scrolls in 1996 when the scrolls were being displayed in the "old" Shrine of the Book in the mid-1990s, and we continued to work with him as our own work at Qumran progressed. We made a short documentary of the young curator, Dr. Roitman, in 1997 (titled *The Shrine and the Scrolls*), which featured him scrambling around Qumran trying to tell the story that he had been taught by his predecessor about the relationship between the scrolls and the caves that were located in close proximity to the village of Qumran. Over a decade later, Dr. Roitman has built a new conception of the scrolls and has chosen to display them at the shrine in a different context—and to tell another story. Today it is a story of the ancient manuscripts of the Bible and the group (or groups) that preserved these traditions, and it is about the modern State of Israel. Our short documentary was the first video that involved the new curator and the legacy of the scrolls and the shrine that housed them. The Shrine of the Book had become famous in Israel and the world as the modern-day "holy of holies" of Israel. I use the video today in class to show how change in archaeological work alters the message of the same buildings, artifacts, and texts in the blink of an eye. I realize how different the new story of the scrolls is from the old story of the scrolls, and it tells us a lot about how history works.

Our work at Qumran paralleled the new shrine's progress. Just as the shrine was embracing its role as more than simply a "mausoleum" to house the ancient scrolls, it became a way to help the Israeli and non-Israeli public understand the ancient story and the modern import of the scrolls. It was the parallel series of changes in the archaeology, the display, and the understanding of the scrolls that prompted me to see the importance of the scrolls today. Most people think that because biblical archaeology deals primarily with the ancient period our understanding of the history is static. In fact, it is in flux. Every single discovery can change the way we understand an ancient site or discovery, and in the case of the scrolls our work has changed the way cave work can be done. It became clear just how fluid this changing history can be when I saw one of our famous discoveries cited in a book in 2006. In the last figure and the last words of the book *Handbook of Geophysics and Archaeology*, titled "From Dinosaurs to Dead Sea Scrolls," Alan J. Witten writes about how new technology has revolutionized the study of archaeology, using our work at Qumran as an example. He ends his book with these words: "While this feature is likely a cave, it remains to be determined if this cave contains any information dating to the period of the Dead Sea Scrolls" (page 317).

The figure is used there to demonstrate how new technology is revolutionizing the study of archaeology and how just when we think the history of a place and time has been written, we have to go back sometimes and reinvestigate the same site for more information. In this book, part of why the Dead Sea Scrolls is an excellent example for understanding the influence of religion and archaeology in the writing of history is because while new methods and techniques in excavation may actually force us to rewrite the history of a location, that history is influenced by a whole series of layers of history writing as well.

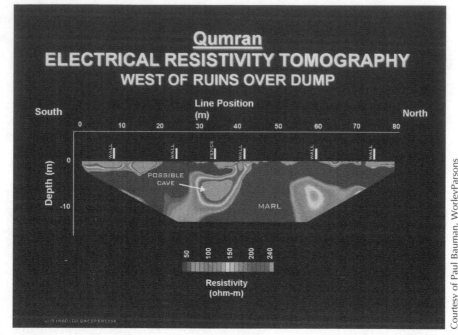

Figure 3.2.   Electrical resistivity tomography of Qumran

How Pottery, Fruit Pits, and Nails Changed Our Understanding of the Dead Sea Scrolls

I thought I would give one small example of how an archaeological discovery has changed our understanding of the scrolls. In our 2001–2002 excavations at Qumran, we discovered some collapsed caves. They were located in some of the most inaccessible cliffs of the village, but in close proximity to the other caves that also ringed the Qumran cliff-face. Using ERT and GPR scans, we discovered the cave and went in, and instead of scrolls we found some mats, ancient pottery, and ancient fruit and olive pits. While we were excited to find the collapsed cave, we were at first puzzled by the signs of human activity inside a cave. One of the great mysteries of Qumran and the Dead Sea Scrolls has always been the question of where the people who wrote the scrolls lived. There are no living quarters inside the ruins, and this fueled speculation that the scrolls were placed there by Jerusalemites and not by the Essenes. The Essenes are a mysterious and ascetic group mentioned in the writings of the first-century

CE historian Josephus Flavius (and others). They were one of a number of sects of the Greco-Roman period (the Pharisees, Sadducees, and Zealots are others, for example). The Essenes resided on the shores of the Dead Sea and were supposed (by most scholars) to have been the authors/scribes who wrote and deposited most, if not all, of the scrolls in the caves around this village.

Despite these ancient accounts about the Essenes, the odd, missing pieces of the archaeological record at Qumran allowed people to say that it was not inhabited by a large group like the Essenes, but rather that it was a winter palace (the Dead Sea is warm even when it could be snowing up the road in Jerusalem) for some official, and the settlement has nothing at all to do with the writing of the scrolls. It has always been speculated that like other desert dwellers the group lived in makeshift tents that would not have survived, and so there is simply no evidence of their domiciles. But it does unsettle archaeologists to base an argument on the lack of evidence, so the debate continued. Therefore, the discovery in a cave of human activity may signal something of great importance that does affect our understanding of the scrolls. The human activity in a cave indicated to us that some caves may have been for living and some for storing scrolls. In fact, about six years earlier, Hanan Eshel and Magen Broshi, the archaeologists we worked with during our 2001–2002 project, had discovered (using a metal detector) a mysterious trail of tiny, ancient nails that led toward the caves. These nails, which may have held together sandals that were worn by some of the inhabitants in the Roman period, show that the residents trekked out to the caves regularly. The debate over how many people lived at Qumran and whether these are the people who wrote the scrolls is still open. A new form of pottery analysis has aided this debate. Today, thanks to two new technologies, we know that the chemical signature of some of the pottery jars in which the scrolls were found is in fact the same pottery that came from the Qumran site. So it appears that at least some of the scrolls and some of the people of Qumran lived, worked, and were involved in the placement of these scrolls in the caves where at least some of them lived (either for short periods, during the hot days, or permanently). Although the arguments about the archaeological finds that surround the scrolls continue (the original excavations from the 1950s were never completely published), the scrolls themselves have changed the way we look at ancient history and modern religious history.

Why Ancient Writing Continues to Inspire Us in the Modern Period

Our knowledge of the ancient world is so limited and fragile. We have ancient texts from excavations in India and China that no one can read or understand. Because of a series of fortunate events, we have been able to unravel the library of discoveries from ancient Egypt and Mesopotamia, and so we have something to compare to the Bible. The Bible is a very limited knowledge base. It is made up of just a fraction of the stories and accounts that were circulating in antiquity. Perhaps one of the most controversial issues of archaeology and literary studies today concerns when Hebrew began to be written as a distinct language. It is controversial because many of the traditions of the Hebrew Bible point to very ancient events—for example, the creation of the world, the ancient Flood, the patriarchs and the matriarchs, the sojourn in Egypt—that all occurred long before the ancient Israelites had their own written language. In what language were these original stories communicated? When did the ancient Bible scribes write down these traditions for the first time? Who were the sources of this information? How much leeway did a scribe have as he wrote down the word of God?

Although people realize that oral traditions have been maintained by many religious groups for thousands of years, the process is very mysteri-

Courtesy of the Joel and SusAnna Grae Collection

Figure 3.3.   The 1536 Psalms book from the Joel and SusAnna Grae Collection

ous. Who were these faithful people who served as "human books" of memorized information? In Islam and Judaism to this day, memorized and recited materials are maintained together with printed and read materials. People who can memorize large portions of holy texts are venerated in Buddhism, Hinduism, Islam, and Judaism, and Jews still refer to the Talmud by the ancient designation of "Oral Law," despite the fact that it has been written down for fifteen hundred years. The earliest Hebrew writing (which may have been a creative adaptation of the Egyptian hieroglyphs or pictographs) did not emerge as a full-fledged and distinctive language until the ancient Israelites were already settled in the land of Israel and coalesced as a people sometime in the tenth century. The discoveries in archaeology over the past 150 years taught us this.

The past one hundred years of systematic archaeological excavations have turned up only a handful of written pieces from the historical land of Israel that allow us to date the development of Hebrew in the eleventh or into the tenth century BCE. This seems to coincide with what we know from the history of the Bible and the development of the ancient Israelites. In the period of the United Monarchy of ancient Israel (which was the period of King David, in the tenth century BCE), Hebrew emerged as one of the examples of this unique, united people to whom we refer as the Israelites. Even though the first seven books of the Bible refer to events that took place before the tenth century BCE, the archaeological evidence points to the fact that these traditions only began to be written down in the unique Semitic dialect of Hebrew in the eleventh and into the tenth century BCE.

Like a child maturing to the point that he or she can ask, "Where did I come from?," so too the unique written accounts preserved in the scrolls provide Jews, Christians, and even Muslims with a way to understand how their foundational doctrines are all rooted in these same texts. These are the oldest Middle Eastern manuscript versions of the biblical-esque apocalyptic scenarios shared by these religions. These are the some of the oldest manuscripts that trace some of the basic ideas shared by these religions of initiation, anointing, covenant, belonging to and rules of the order, cosmic war, sexual conduct, leadership, succession, and a host of other themes that became standard parts of later rabbinic Judaism, Christianity, and Islam. Because these documents can be dated before the rise of rabbinic Judaism, Christianity, and Islam, in a sense we can say that these scrolls are the tangible launching pad for these faiths in a way that is different from just the Hebrew Bible.

Writing was an amazing, unusual activity in the ancient Near East, so the discovery of something as large and diverse as the almost a thousand scrolls is really unparalleled. Most writings that have been discovered through systematic archaeology from the ancient past usually consisted of tomb and symbolic artistic presentations, record keeping, receipts, religious registers for internal purposes, correspondence between high officials or religious figures, or purely theological documents to ensure that the leaders of the cult knew what they needed to know. The great accounts of Mesopotamia and Egypt that were preserved are so fragmentary that even when they are pieced together, they do not give us a coherent system of religious ideas. The notion of having ancient narratives put together in a running national epic was revolutionary in antiquity. We appreciate Homer's labor in the *Iliad* and the *Odyssey* precisely because it was a unique endeavor. The Egyptian *Book of the Dead*, which continued to develop for over a thousand years, is an example of how ancient writing was not a single author's work, but the labor of many hands.

By the tenth century BCE, some of the earliest parts of the narrative were being written down even as a new historical period had begun. By the ninth and eighth centuries BCE, Hebrew writing had developed in earnest. Unfortunately, there are no manuscripts of any sustained size from this period, just short graffiti, a few inscribed pieces of Hebrew writing on stones, steles, clay tablets, bones, amulets, signets, shards, and bullae. Even though the material culture does not tell a coherent narrative, it shows us that writing was important. From the ancient Bronze and Iron Ages, few papyri and parchments survive. The only place where manuscripts might be preserved would be in a hot, dry, constant climate with perhaps a salt deposit or two to preserve the materials' organic matter. The Dead Sea was that place. Israel has a few different and unique microclimate zones that have preserved its history in ways that simply are unique.

The fact that Jerusalem, the capital of the ancient kingdom of the Israelites and later the Judeans, was located close to this depository of the caves of the Dead Sea is also important. Located on one of the great land bridges of antiquity from Africa to Asia, the Dead Sea was the Fort Knox for ancient travelers from the Rift Valley of Africa to the depths of Asia. Travelers moving north and south and then east and west for tens of thousands of years followed the Syrian-African rift, a tectonic plate on the earth's surface that passes by the caves along the sea. The caves provided a convenient hiding place for the material culture of different peoples. On the Dead Sea, there are nearly fifty miles of limestone caves that are situated adjacent to the lowest point on earth. These natural limestone caves were created tens of thousands of years ago as the ancient Lake Lisan receded and left

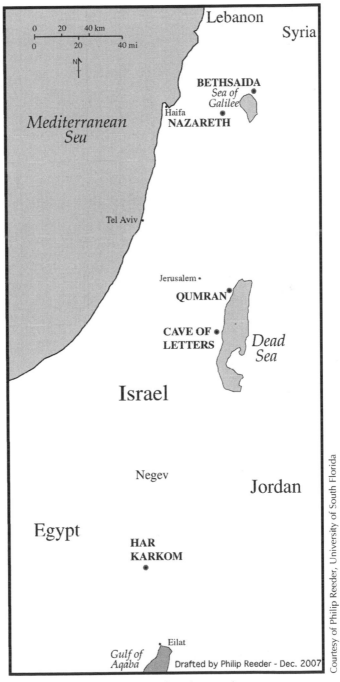

Figure 3.4.   Mapping ancient and modern Israel

Courtesy of Philip Reeder, University of South Florida

the Dead Sea and the Sea of Galilee dislocated from one another with the Jordan River connecting them.

A divine footprint left its mark on the Dead Sea. The Dead Sea has a unique environmental mark on the earth's surface; it is only there that these caves could exist, and it is only in these caves that manuscripts such as the Dead Sea Scrolls could have been preserved for thousands of years. What strikes people first and foremost about the story of the scrolls is that in precisely the place where we would need to have ancient documents preserved (ancient Israel), there is a natural environment (the Dead Sea caves) for the protection of ancient documents. After many years of speaking to people who have followed the story of the Dead Sea Scrolls more than any other archaeological story (save Atlantis), I have found that they see in the story of the discovery of the scrolls more than just a discovery of a cache of ancient documents—they see them as a type of "message in a bottle."

Yigael Yadin: The Scrolls, the State, and the Hand of God

The timing of the discovery of the scrolls and the creation of the modern State of Israel is perceived by many as more than just a coincidence. Many religious people refer to it using religious terminology such as "miraculous" or even "the Hand of God." Many secular archaeologists are uncomfortable with this type of terminology, but they realize that it is one of the reasons why Qumran and the Dead Sea Scrolls at the Shrine of the Book at Jerusalem's Israel Museum are two of the most visited sites for religious pilgrims. Yigael Yadin, in his book *The Message of the Scrolls* (1957), relates a version of the "unseen Hand of God" argument, not only because of the fortuitous timing of the discovery, but also because of the implications for the nascent State of Israel: "I cannot avoid the feeling that there is something symbolic in the discovery of the scrolls and their acquisition at the moment of the creation of the State of Israel. It is as if the manuscripts had been waiting in caves for the two thousand years, ever since the destruction of Israel's independence, until the people of Israel had returned to their home and regained their freedom."

The "Hand of God" argument works in many unseen and unfathomable ways. The discovery of the Dead Sea Scrolls in the caves along the Dead Sea could have taken place in the Middle Ages, or during the eighteenth and nineteenth centuries when French and British archaeologists and Bible scholars scoured the landscape of Israel for new discoveries. The bedouin, a nomadic Arab group who roamed this part of the Near

East in the 1920s or 1930s, could have discovered the manuscripts that sat silently in these caves. But it was only in 1946, a year after the end of the Holocaust in Europe, when a single bedouin boy, Muhammad ed-Dhib, entered what later became known as Cave 1 and discovered the first of more than nine hundred different manuscripts that would emerge out of eleven caves near the northern edge of the Dead Sea in close proximity to Qumran. This was also a crucial year for the British Mandate in Palestine. With the end of World War II and the liberation of prisoners from the concentration and extermination camps in Europe, streams of displaced persons from Europe and the former Ottoman Empire converged upon Palestine as a refuge. In 1945 and 1946, illegal and legal Jewish immigration took place to different areas of the British Mandate in Palestine, resulting in enormous tension between Jews and Arabs. The pressure to create a modern State of Israel for displaced persons grew as some Jews attempted to return to their homes in Europe only to discover that their neighbors did not want them. The cause was taken up by the United Nations, and the UN sought to create two distinct entities in the area that had been a part of the British Mandate. When I have heard religious people (Christians and Jews) refer to the coincidence of the discoveries and identification of the scrolls, they do so with the knowledge of the timing of the creation of the State of Israel. In many ways the scrolls helped give birth to a new national identity, and the new national identity became embodied in the Dead Sea Scrolls.

Why There Are No Coincidences in History

Albert Einstein once said, "A coincidence is God's way of remaining anonymous." Jewish history is replete with these types of coincidences, and this fits well with many different Jewish theological views of the work of the divine in this world. What I think Einstein meant by this is that when we see events in retrospect, they seem to fit together neatly in an organic fashion and may indeed be seen as a part of a larger divine plan. In the ancient period, one would have called these "miracles." Miracles are sometimes defined as the events that suspend the rules of nature. While this is certainly one definition, there are many other ways that the ancients saw the unfolding of events. It is clear that some of the ancient writers of the Bible and later rabbinic Jews were not completely comfortable with this definition. The idea of talking animals such as snakes and donkeys (which clearly suspends the rules of nature) was not altogether appreciated by all ancient Israelites. In the rabbinic Roman period document the Mishnah, for example, the rabbis have a tradition that God basically built into the rules of nature all of the elements that were in the text of the Bible and seemed to suspend these rules. If God had built them into the system from before the beginning of time, then they were not really miracles but rather preordained events and elements waiting to be discovered.

Another Jewish view is that coincidences of history are viewed as a stylistic ancient form of writing about extraordinary events whose timing suggests that there is a transcendental force at work. Many of these elegantly timed events would be "collapsed" into a single mega-event. A literary example that was nearly contemporaneous with the writing of the Dead Sea Scrolls is from the books of Maccabees. There are two books of Maccabees (actually there are four books designated as "Maccabees" in many collections of the Apocrypha, but I will compare only the first two). The first two books are really telling the same basic story but were apparently authored by different Jewish writers with varying ideas about miracles. The story of the Maccabees is associated with the desecration of the Temple of Jerusalem in the second century BCE, its ultimate liberation by the Maccabees, and the inauguration of a holiday celebrating the victory—Hanukkah (dedication or rededication of the Temple). According to 1 Maccabees, in approximately 169 BCE, Antiochus IV marched on Jerusalem and sacked the Temple, and two years later the city was burned, the Jews expelled, and the fortifications of the city destroyed. The 1 Maccabees author (who does not favor the suspension of the rules of nature even for the victory against the Greeks) writes that the ultimate coincidence occurred during the final battle: "On the very day that it [the Temple] had been profaned it was restored." The author of 2 Maccabees favors all types of miracles, including the suspension of the rules of nature to ensure victory. There is the miraculous death of Antiochus IV, and the Maccabean commander, Judas, is helped by supernatural beings; he leads his men to victory and purification of the facilities on the *exact same calendar day* as when it had been profaned two years before. What the two authors share is the idea that a coincidence was a form of divine intervention. For these ancient writers, this was how the divine worked. Events that were coincidences were seen as a result of some hidden divine plan. To this day Jews recite on Hanukkah a special prayer for the many "miracles" that were wrought on their behalf at this particular time of the year. Although the Jewish sources are not in total agreement as to which miracles they are referring to, it is clear that those who redacted the prayer are collapsing a number of different sources and coincidences into one single prayer of thanksgiving.

So-called coincidences that occur in the process of uncovering archaeology are also well known. Few archaeologists like to write about them. Many point to coincidences that sent explorers in the direction to discover (or better, rediscover) ancient temples and tombs. The diaries and writings of explorers such as Hiram Bingham at the site of the ancient Inca site of Machu Picchu, Howard Carter at the tomb of Tutankhamen in Egypt, and even Heinrich Schliemann at Troy are filled with what they considered to be a series of fortunate events that led to their discoveries. The tales of the rediscovery of Mayan and Aztec temples and cities are replete with coincidences that happened to the archaeologists who found these cities in far-flung jungles and rough terrain after many others had trod the same locations and found nothing. We constantly hear—in reports on the rediscovery of European cave dwellings, buried treasures in fields, and the recovery of ancient and premodern artifacts—how the people involved had been drawn to the spot by more than just informed intuition. There is, however, a dark side to this line of thought. The discovery of the tomb of Tutankhamen in the 1920s, for example, was followed by a series of unfortunate events. These catastrophic coincidences gave rise to the notion of a "mummy's curse." The idea that there was a supernatural power at work can also unleash a Pandora's box of energy. It may indeed just be a random series of unfortunate events. The explanations never quite satisfied the skeptics, who viewed a direct cause and effect in events. History, however, is full of incidents that look like a direct cause and effect but can also be reasonably viewed as not direct cause and effect. This is one of the reasons why some people view spontaneous healings as divine miracles and some physicians just see them as a fortuitous series of natural processes. The events of history rarely speak for themselves, and events, after the fact, can be organized in a variety of ways to show very different things.

The "Miraculous" Discovery of the Dead Sea Scrolls

The events associated with the discovery and early recognition of the value of the Dead Sea Scrolls involve a series of coincidences that could not have been scripted even in Hollywood. The coincidences are worthy of study themselves and are well known to the excavators as well as to the many thousands of commentators on the scrolls. The timing of the discovery was seen by some as the unseen "divine hand" (the *deus ex machina*) reaching into history to allow a window to open on a past that was both fortuitous and significant for humanity. In many of the books, articles, and pronouncements that were published in the 1950s, it is clear that numerous Christians saw the discovery as more than just accidental. Theodore Heiline's 1957 book, *The Dead Sea Scrolls*, has an entire section titled "Timed Events," and he writes:

> Important events of this kind do not fall out haphazardly. They come to pass when the time is ripe for their emergence. They are called forth by man's thoughts, by the inner activity of his spirit, by his soul's needs. The discovery of the *Dead Sea Scrolls* is clearly such a timed event. The present religious revival and spiritual renewal that is everywhere manifest has created such a state of mind that earnest seekers after deeper truths can profit in a tremendously important way from what the scrolls reveal. It is safe to say that never in the course of the two thousand years during which they have remained hidden could their uncovering have had the significance that it has at this particular time. The questions they answer have not yet been asked so generally nor with such insistence. Today the contents of the scrolls, together with their many implications, are of first importance. Such is the tension, the inner and outer stress and strain of these terribly confused, chaotic and tragic times, that any evidence touching upon the validity of the spiritual basis whereon the Christian faith rests, is eagerly grasped by the many striving to pass from skepticism to faith. The strengthening foundations of faith were never so urgent. So the scrolls have come to light at just the right psychological time (pages 29–30). . . . All of which points to the fact that now is the "appointed time" for the discovery of ancient scrolls containing a message as important to the present generation as it was to the generation to which it was addressed two thousand years ago. (page 75)

Many Christians saw the discovery of the scrolls as initiating some new countdown for the Second Coming, or as a message in a bottle precisely addressed to modern skeptics and people disheartened by the inhumanity of World War II and the Cold War. Scholars and locals had had other historical opportunities to discover these scrolls in the caves along the Dead Sea, but only in 1947 were they suddenly discovered and authenticated. The first major written accounts about the scrolls that were presented to the general public connected the "sudden" discovery of the scrolls and Christianity's apocalyptic "end of days" scenario. The scrolls were a type of mild corrective to the forms of the original religion of Jesus, which had somehow, through the course of time, become something other than what it originally was intended. The scrolls were a revelation and reformation event for modern Christians.

In the United States in the post–World War II era, American Christianity saw the need to flex its muscles as a legitimate and indeed authentic form of Christianity. Sermons and writings of prominent Christians show just how much the footprint of the scrolls could demonstrate the authenticity of American Christianity. For example, Dr. Charles Frances Potter, pastor of the All Souls Church (a Unitarian church) in Washington, D.C., used the scrolls as a way to teach how American Christianity in the 1950s was the natural continuation of the ancient Essenes (a Dead Sea Jewish sect) in his 1959 book *The Lost Years of Jesus Revealed*. Potter saw American Christianity through the lens of the scrolls. American Christianity was something different than what Christianity had been in earlier places and times. Potter preached and wrote that Jesus was no longer the original and miraculous incarnation of the son of God, preexistent in heaven and sent to earth as the long-awaited Messiah. He was seen as a product of his times. Jesus was the natural outgrowth of Jewish messianic views espoused by the Essenes, and after the discovery of the Dead Sea Scrolls he is seen as a latter-day "Teacher of Righteousness," the leader of a group mentioned in the apocalyptic texts of the scrolls. In 1958, Dr. O. Preston Robinson wrote *The Dead Sea Scrolls and Original Christianity* and found in the scrolls many of the ideas of some of the foundational texts of the Church of Jesus Christ of Latter-Day Saints.

The Unseen Hand of God in the Discovery of the Scrolls

It was a different path to the scrolls' acceptance within Judaism. For the most part, many Jewish scholars were skeptical of the sudden "discovery" of the scrolls by bedouins. There had been scandals in the nineteenth and early twentieth centuries with new discoveries of ancient Jewish manuscripts that were actually frauds or not as ancient as their discoverers made them out to be. But the connection between the discovery of the scrolls and the events unfolding in Israel in 1947 and 1948 made many Jewish scholars take a second look at the Dead Sea Scroll discoveries. The "Hand of God" argument (or, as some would call it, mythologizing) manifested itself in different ways to Jewish scholars. One of the famous coincidences (which has come to be seen as more than just a coincidence) has to do with the date of the identification of the scrolls: November 29, 1947. Eleazar Sukenik, a well-known Jewish archaeologist and paleographer, was an expert on the handwriting of ancient Hebrew scripts, through his work on ancient stone ossuaries (stone bone burial boxes). He (along with many others) had developed a system for dating Hebrew writing based upon a series of developments in the lettering systems. In the closing days of 1947, the Jewish immigrations to British Mandate Palestine had created enormous tension between the Jews and the Arab populations of Palestine. (This turned into Israel's War of Independence, which lasted until 1949.)

When the Dead Sea Scrolls were discovered, some scholars thought that they were medieval manuscripts of little value. Some thought they were fraudulent manuscripts created for profit, and others just did not know what they were. It was important to have a legitimate independent source evaluate what the manuscripts were to determine if they were of any importance, and indeed to figure out what they said. But as the UN vote on the creation of an independent Jewish state in Palestine was about to take place, the violence throughout the area made it dangerous to travel between the Jewish areas of the country and the region where the recovered manuscripts were housed (in Bethlehem). On November 29, 1947, on the very day that the modern State of Israel was sanctioned by a vote in the United Nations, Sukenik journeyed at great personal risk to Bethlehem to see the mysterious scrolls. According to the story told by Sukenik and his son, Yigael Yadin, at the hour when the historic vote of the United Nations was announced on the radio, Sukenik was sitting in his home in Jerusalem and identified the significance of the scroll that he was looking at as the oldest manuscript copy of the Hebrew Bible on the planet. He identified it as almost a thousand years older than the oldest then-existing manuscript. At the time when the United Nations was voting on the fate of the new State of Israel, he had identified the most ancient example of the antiquity of the new state. Yadin wrote in *The Message of the Scrolls*, "It was a tremendously exciting experience, difficult to convey in words . . . knowing that some of the biblical manuscripts were copied only a few hundred years after their composition and that these very scrolls were read and studied by our forefathers in the period of the Second Temple" (page 14).

Sukenik (and later his son, Yigael) realized that on that fateful day, November 29, after the darkest moment in human history and especially Jewish history (after the Holocaust and in the midst of the violence against the displaced Europeans waiting in camps to get into Palestine), Sukenik's identification gave new meaning to their struggles. Yadin's explanations are by far the most extensive Jewish expression of the semi-divine force at work in the discovery of the scrolls. In *The Message of the Scrolls* he wrote:

I cannot avoid the feeling that there is something symbolic in the discovery of the scrolls and their acquisition at the moment of the creation of the State of Israel. It is as if the manuscripts had been waiting in caves for two thousand years, ever since the destruction of Israel's independence, until the people of Israel returned to their home and regained their freedom. (page 14)

Yigael Yadin knew better than most just how he and his father were a part of both the rise of the modern State of Israel and the identification of the scrolls. Yadin served as a well-known military figure, and he enhanced his research skills by writing his doctoral dissertation in ancient warfare. Both Sukenik and Yadin saw the fateful backdrop of the Holocaust and the rise of the modern State of Israel as inextricably connected. In his book *The Message of the Scrolls* (published in 1957—a decade after the discoveries), Yadin quotes his father as saying, "This great event in Jewish history was thus combined in my home in Jerusalem with another event, no less historic, the one political, the other cultural" (page 24). There are few examples when archaeologists actually sense they are in the midst of a special event that transcends the excavation of just any material culture. So November 29, 1947, was not simply the announcement of the UN partition plan, which brought into existence the modern State of Israel. It was not just the date of the identification of just any ancient manuscript. These events were seen by Sukenik and Yadin as the examples of a mysterious process of history in which they were participants.

The battle to get the Dead Sea Scrolls for the State of Israel was complicated by all of the religious and political events of Israel's War of Independence in 1948 and through the early 1950s. Other coincidences would follow. Attempts to sell the scrolls by the church in Jerusalem that had them in their possession is a famous story that is still being told. Attempts were made (and even some money paid to purchase some of the scrolls), prompting the church to put a now famous advertisement in the *Wall Street Journal* classified section in 1954. This advertisement leads us to one more coincidence in the discovery and the recovery of the scrolls.

June 1954

One last coincidence associated with the discovery of the scrolls happened about seven years after the first event and again involved Yigael Yadin. On June 1, 1954, a rather small, unassuming advertisement appeared among the other classified ads in the *Wall Street Journal*, declaring that four "Biblical manuscripts dating back to at least 200 B.C. are for sale. This would be an ideal gift to an educational or religious institution by an individual or group." It just so happened that Yigael Yadin was in the United States that day on a lecture tour and was alerted to the ad. (This was in a time before e-mail and electronic media.) Yadin was by then a well-known archaeologist and fully capable of understanding the significance of the scrolls both for the State of Israel and the archaeology of the new state. The timing was so fateful that many people have written about just how opportune it was. During World War II, art and artifacts from many museums throughout the world had changed hands and were often advertised in a very unassuming way so that a collector might find another private collector to sell a questionable item to. Many of these treasures were purchased and consigned to private collections, and little was known about these holdings after the purchase. If not for this coincidence, the scrolls might have been purchased by a private collector—or worse, languished in the safety deposit box that the church in Jerusalem maintained in New York City for the scrolls, until they were only dust. What is the likelihood that someone from Israel who knew intimately about the significance (and the location) of some of the scrolls would have seen that classified advertisement for "Biblical manuscripts that date back to 200 B.C." on that June 1 day and understood that these were the Dead Sea Scrolls that his own father had identified almost seven years earlier? Below the advertisement for the biblical manuscripts, the *Wall Street Journal* had an ad for 10,000- to 18,000-gallon steel tanks and two electric welders, and below that an ad for a rental space in Knoxville, Tennessee. Reading it today, I cannot imagine that most readers would have picked up that this advertisement was for the Dead Sea Scrolls. But Yigael Yadin was alerted to the advertisement, and history was subsequently made.

Yadin realized that these were probably the same scrolls that his father had identified almost seven years earlier. More importantly, because Yadin was a famed military commander, he also possessed the organizational skills to construct an elaborate plan to purchase the scrolls through an informed intermediary and ensure that they could be easily sent out of the country and back to Israel without the seller knowing that the buyer was the State of Israel. The use of an informed intermediary was a very important part of the plan, since the scrolls needed to be authenticated by someone who could immediately tell the difference between a fraud and the real thing, and the person needed to keep the selling price from escalating by not letting on that it would be for the State of Israel. The price would have become astronomical (or impossible to pay) had the seller known that it was the State of Israel that was purchasing the scrolls. Few Israelis had as many connections in the government of Israel, among world Jewry, the financial world, the scholarly world, and strategic planning to plan the purchase and movement of the scrolls in a short turnaround time. We can all now sit back almost sixty years later and say that it was a well-oiled plan that was carefully carried out, but in reality each part of the story required so many preexisting conditions to be in place as to suggest an enormous accident of history. The right person had to be at the right place at the right time and have all of the surrounding conditions in place for the plan to be successful. I still marvel at the way that the scrolls purchase was planned and executed. Yadin was perfectly placed to carry out the plan and knew the man who would become the intermediary as a trusted scholar and colleague in the New York area. Few Jewish scholars had dealt with the scrolls in the way that this mysterious fellow (code-named simply "Mr. Green") had. The scholar had to be unassuming, trustworthy, and able to recognize a fraudulent manuscript in a "blink" moment. Any hesitation and the plan could have fallen through. The mission was executed and the scrolls were on a plane back to Israel the next day; they are displayed to this day in the Shrine of the Book at the Israel Museum in Jerusalem. Yadin and others involved in this plan saw that the entire series of events was more than the sum of the parts. It was the ultimate unseen "Hand of God" in play in the rather mundane setting of a bank vault in New York City.

The "what-ifs" of history are one of the reasons why the Dead Sea Scrolls are included as a chapter in this book. Another reason is because my own discoveries at the ancient site of Qumran were themselves replete with coincidences, which led us from our original excavations at Bethsaida to the Dead Sea "Cave of Letters" excavations and then to Qumran during a period from the 1990s to 2002 (chronicled in my books *Secrets of the Cave of Letters* and *Digging through the Bible*). Over the past decade of studying our research, I discovered how much the scrolls affected Western civilization and how different they were from any other archaeological discovery.

Why Are the Scrolls Important?

I think that the scrolls are a microcosm for the reason why archaeology can change our understanding of history in a short period of time. The Dead Sea Scrolls are arguably the most famous and significant archaeological discovery of the twentieth century for many reasons. The more than nine hundred different manuscripts discovered are significant because they pushed back the date of the earliest (Hebrew) biblical manuscripts by almost a thousand years. Suddenly, the text that was used by Jews as their primary religious document went from being suspected as a late antique text created to justify rabbinic Judaism to a truly ancient Near Eastern text. Before the discovery (especially at the end of the nineteenth century and the beginning of the twentieth century), academic biblical studies had come to extremely disparaging conclusions about the text of the Hebrew Bible, and indirectly about Judaism. The lack of a complete, ancient manuscript of the Hebrew Bible had led some radical critics in the twentieth century to view the book as a late "pious fraud" that was used to bolster the faith of rabbinic Jews, and to claim that the "true" biblical faith was that which emerged from the New Testament. The Dead Sea Scrolls gave Christians a new respect for the antiquity of Judaism and the Hebrew Bible and simultaneously made them see how Christianity had indeed emerged from Judaic roots.

The Dead Sea Scrolls contain the oldest manuscripts of a type of commentary on the Bible that is central to Judaism, Christianity, and even Islam. Without the scrolls, the fluid notion of religious ideas that were in transition could never totally be tracked. Not only do the scrolls comprise the oldest manuscripts of the first five books of the Hebrew Bible, the Torah (or Pentateuch) that the Jews use in their worship service, but they also include works that were written by ancient Jews who were commenting on the meaning of the Torah traditions in the ancient period. Many of the Dead Sea Scrolls' biblical commentaries—such as the Genesis Apocryphon, for example—tell an entirely new story about the patriarchs and matriarchs that is not found anywhere else. What these scrolls give us is a way of seeing how ancient and fluid the traditions of the Bible were in antiquity. When I read the Quran's story of Joseph and his brothers (which is a much more amplified story about what happened to Joseph than the Pentateuch gives us), I no longer wonder if amplified versions of ancient characters and events existed in antiquity. The scrolls tell us that they were present and that we have only a fraction of the total of the ancient traditions that were circulating in antiquity. Ancient commentaries on the Bible are very important for delineating ancient religious ideas as well.

Commentaries on the Bible are really attempts at clarifying what is written in another text. Many modern and medieval Jews understand the story line of the Bible through the lens of a twelfth-century Jewish Bible commentator (Rashi, for example) and rarely consider if this is the original meaning of the biblical text or just a medieval attempt at harmonizing the text for later readers. Although these medieval commentators are important for pointing out religious ideas that are not always clear in the rabbinic or church traditions, they might be telling us more about medieval practices than about the early traditions of the Israelites and Jews. The scrolls' commentaries give us a window to the past that allows us to compare and contrast what Jews in a much more ancient context believed. We have the first-century CE historian and commentator on the Bible, Josephus Flavius, whose attempt to create a more flowing understanding of the Bible is preserved in his multivolume *Antiquities of the Jews*. His effort can be called one of the earliest complete commentaries on the entire Bible and the postbiblical tradition to his own times. Although Josephus is a commentator of the biblical text, manuscripts of his work were carefully monitored and "updated" by the early Church, and it is difficult to know exactly whether they are all his original thoughts or whether they have been manipulated by later Byzantine or medieval hands.

The Dead Sea Scrolls are something totally different. They provide the earliest *manuscript* discoveries of how the Bible was read by Jews, and no one has had access to them to change or manipulate them. The other ancient Jewish commentators, Philo Judaeus, Josephus Flavius, the Aramaic language translation/commentary called Targum Jonathan, and so on are all slightly later than the scrolls, and their commentaries have been carefully scrutinized by the many hands of later medieval scribes and censors. The scrolls are the original manuscripts without later interventions.

The book of Jubilees, for example, is seen as the oldest commentary on Genesis and is found in the Dead Sea Scrolls. The book is attributed to Moses and is said to have been dictated by the "Angel of the Presence." It is designated by modern scholars as pseudepigraphic ("falsely" attributed to an ancient author—like Moses—and even though it is ancient, it is not part of the canon of the Hebrew Bible) and was probably written in the Hellenistic period. It shows us what Jews over two thousand years ago were thinking about what the book of Genesis meant in their own day. The word "Satan," for example, appears in Jubilees (despite the fact that it is not in Genesis), and in it Satan is a very specific being. Satan in Jubilees is a totally independent agent from God, despite the fact that this is not in the Hebrew Bible. In many ways, one of the most important parts of the Dead Sea Scrolls is that they give us a critical part of the lost history of the development of the Jewish, Christian, and later Islamic ideas of good and evil. We now know that some of the Talmudic and Midrashic descriptions of *gehennom* (hell), the Garden of Eden, and even the messianic aspirations of the rabbis are rooted in the earlier views of the Dead Sea Scrolls. The history of ideas is an important part of history. Scholars of religion ask how we get from the Hebrew Bible's rather limited "end of days" scenario to the Christian New Testament book of Revelation. Without the scrolls we would never know how it developed. Even scholars of Islam ask themselves where the highly evolved Quranic and Hadithic concepts of punishment in heaven and hell and the idea of a spiritual "holy war" came from—and the scrolls lead us back to an antecedent.

Can Archaeology Really Change Modern Religion?

Many archaeological discoveries, even those of textual information, do not seem to have had a direct effect upon modern religion, but they often have had an indirect effect. Archaeological discoveries both inside and outside Israel have affected the study of the Bible, Judaism, and Christianity. The discoveries of Israelite cult sites throughout the land of Israel in the Iron Age (both in the north and the south of the country) changed the way that people understood the biblical Temple of Solomon in Jerusalem. Up until the discovery of many different altars, shrines, and sites that were clearly Israelite in different parts of the country, the history of ancient Israel was guided largely by what was written in the biblical text. The biblical text spoke about the one Temple of Solomon, and it was assumed that any of the other "high places" mentioned in the Bible were simply decommissioned with the establishment of the Temple in Jerusalem. Archaeology has revealed that the picture was far more complex, with competing Israelite altars, shrines, and temples throughout the entire classical biblical period (twelfth to sixth centuries BCE).

Many of the most profound influences upon modern Judaism and Christianity come from archaeological discoveries that included textual materials. The discoveries of texts related to the New Testament and early Christianity found in excavations at Oxyrhyncus, Egypt, in the 1890s and Nag Hammadi in the 1940s, for example, told a different version of the life and beliefs of Jesus and the early Christians and inevitably affected the way that modern Christians viewed their own faith. In 1896, excavations at Oxyrhyncus discovered mounds of texts. These were found to be fragments of noncanonical and canonical gospels as well as Christian hymns, prayers, and letters. In 1945, a large number of versions of the gospels were found in pottery jars buried in a field at Nag Hammadi in Egypt. The fifty-two texts were in Coptic, translated from Greek, and they record parallel versions of the gospels that were written down in the early centuries of the Common Era for an audience who became known as Gnostics. Although their theological ideas were different from those of Christians, they provide a glimpse into the traditions of Jesus and the Holy Family. These texts found in systematic excavations are nearly contemporaneous with the manuscripts of the canonical gospel accounts, and they led some Christians in the modern period to decide that religious and theological diversity in the modern period was authentic and valid. Before these discoveries, religious diversity among Christians was thought to be the result of modern forces associated with the Renaissance and the Enlightenment. With the discovery of these ancient variants, some modern Christian groups reevaluated their own ideas with a new sense of empowerment. The Gnostic Gospels and the Oxyrhyncus texts are not usually consulted by modern Christian groups in their church settings, but when they are cited by one Christian group or another, it is usually to demonstrate how diverse Christianity was in its origin and to justify the proliferation of sectarianism and denominationalism as a normative part of the Christian religious identity. The texts are cited regularly in comparisons between the canonical gospels and standard manuscript readings of the New Testament and materials from the Church Fathers in some Bibles that are used for church study. The early liturgical formulations are sometimes quoted to clarify one religious view or another in different denominations. This methodology that archaeological discoveries can not only illuminate the understanding of the past but also influence modern religious practice has developed in the present period with postmodern archaeological interpretation.

The Nineteenth-Century Cairo Geniza and Its Influence on the Acceptance of the Twentieth-Century Dead Sea Scrolls

Few archaeological discoveries have had a direct effect upon modern Jewish practice and doctrine like the discovery of the Cairo Geniza in a medieval synagogue in old Cairo. A *geniza* (a Hebrew word meaning "hidden") is a well-known repository for old prayer and holy books that are no longer usable in many synagogues. Often these texts are buried in a formal ceremony in a Jewish cemetery after first being collected in the *geniza*. The Cairo Geniza, in the Ben Ezra Synagogue of Fostat, Old Cairo, is unique because Egypt was a crossroads of Babylonian, North African, and European Judaisms from the Islamic period (eighth century onward) and a center of medieval Jewish life. The hot, dry conditions of Cairo facilitated the preservation of many of these texts, and the Cairo Geniza has been visited and commented on since the eighteenth century. With the development of Wissenschaft des Judentums (the scientific study of Judaism that started after the Enlightenment, in the nineteenth century), Jewish scholars endeavored to write, and often rewrite, the history of Judaism in light of systematic research of all of the documents of Jewish life. This development marked a change in the understanding of Judaism, which up until the Enlightenment was based upon doctrinal and ideological guidelines that were strictly interpreted by rabbinic leaders. The discovery of the *geniza* in Cairo also coincided with the development of new forms of rabbinic Judaism that are generally called Reform, Conservative, and Orthodox Judaisms.

The Wissenschaft (scientific scholarship) and the discovery of new texts that were not part of the rabbinic canon created a remarkable synthesis for modern Judaism. The Cairo Geniza became especially important in end-of-the-nineteenth-century discussions of modern Judaism after some of the manuscripts were brought to Solomon Schechter (then a professor of rabbinics at Cambridge University) for evaluation. The Cairo Geniza contained almost two hundred thousand fragmentary texts; with a significant percentage at nearly one thousand years old, these texts changed the way that Jewish scholars understood religious diversity in Judaism, both in ancient and modern times. In the beginning of the twentieth century, when the Cairo Geniza was not well known, two leading Jewish institutions of higher learning in the United States, Hebrew Union College in Cincinnati and the Jewish Theological Seminary in New York, developed two different attitudes toward the fragments, which rapidly changed over the course of the century. Schechter came to regard the fragments as originating with an ancient sect of the Sadducees and not the Pharisees. Others came to see the Geniza as representing a protorabbinic group that provided a more flexible Jewish law than had earlier been recognized. These ancient texts were used by the modern movement called Reform Judaism, as a vindication of some of the positions that they staked out for themselves that were different from traditional orthodox Judaism.

In 1903, after Schechter had settled in the United States, he had a discussion about the fragments with Kaufmann Kohler, the distinguished scholar and leader of Reform Judaism and the head of the Cincinnati-based Hebrew Union College. Here was the head of the historical positive school (later to be known as the Conservative Movement of modern Judaism) and the head of the Reform Movement discussing a single document. They were, on the surface, only discussing the text of an ancient religious idea in a single manuscript. In reality, their discussions were about the state of twentieth-century Judaism and the way that a single manuscript can impact modern religion. For Kohler, the fragments were a remnant of the religious system of the Zadokites, Sadducees, Samaritans, and Karaites, which preserved ancient and elitist traditions and practices in contrast to the progressive and populist notions of the Pharisees. As much as the Geniza fragments influenced the understanding of ancient Judaism, early on, they were seen as a vehicle for interpreting modern Judaism. Conversely the understanding of the Geniza was influenced by the discussions going on in modern Judaism. It was a two-way street. The Reform and Conservative Jewish scholars influenced our understanding of the Geniza through the lens of their movements' ideological stances as much as the Geniza influenced Reform and Conservative Judaism.

Geniza materials are not just cited in scholarly works. Thanks to the widespread use of the Geonic and *piyut* (liturgical) materials found in the Geniza, they were used to determine Jewish law and practice in the twentieth century in Conservative and Reform *responsa* (replies to questions sent to rabbis, made in written form) and even affected the prayer books. The Geniza discovery paved the way for the significance of the Dead Sea Scrolls for modern Jewish movements precisely because so many scholars from the lead institutions, Hebrew Union College (HUC) and the Jewish Theological Seminary (JTS), were involved in the deciphering of the Geniza. It contained many rabbinic citations that were unknown from other sources. This suggested that there were textual materials that showed a richer and more complex history than is suggested by canonized rabbinic texts. When Solomon Schechter identified Geniza fragments as Zadokite fragments of an unknown ancient sect (albeit in a medieval copy), he provided the future framework for the acceptance of the Dead Sea Scrolls. The Damascus Document (or "Zadokite fragments") was an antecedent of the Dead Sea Scrolls. The Dead Sea Scrolls' manuscripts corroborated Schechter's identification but his identification also allowed the Dead Sea Scrolls to have an immediate pedigree (of sorts) of authenticity as a Jewish text.

The discovery of the Dead Sea Scrolls, despite the controversies surrounding their meaning and the actual translation of the texts, did affect (like the Geniza discoveries) modern Christians and Jews in synagogues in a variety of ways. It is perhaps possible to say that without the discovery of the Cairo Geniza in the nineteenth century and its use by scholars and rabbis as an authentic expression of the varieties of Jewish practice, the Dead Sea Scrolls would never have claimed the position that they did in modern Jewish life. Beyond the sensationalism of early claims that either Jesus or

John the Baptist was the Teacher of Righteousness, basic ideas of Judaism and Christianity were affected by the scrolls. Suddenly the ancient ideas of the importance of baptism, resurrection of the dead, the observance of the Sabbath, eschatology, monasticism, rituals of daily and holiday observance, and so on demonstrated authentic religious doctrines that in some form had been accepted by Jews and then later by early Christians.

In Christianity, some groups used the scrolls as an authentic and influential voice of "pre-Christian Christianity." Dr. Will Varner, professor of Old Testament at the Master's College in Israel and the college's director of the Israel Bible Exchange program, wrote:

> Is it not striking that soon after this manuscript [of the Dead Sea Scrolls] was composed, a child was born who fulfilled the hopes of Israel and inaugurated a new age? Although the men of Qumran were mistaken in the details of their messiah, they did expect one whose general characteristics were strikingly illustrated by Jesus of Nazareth, the Son of God and Messiah. It is not known if some early Christian brought the message of Jesus to this wilderness community. We are left only to speculate on how they would have responded to the Wonderful Child born in Bethlehem who was the Prophet, Priest and King of Israel.

Christian eschatology, which during the past eighteen hundred years has developed around a set group of texts and writers (the New Testament, writings of the Church Fathers, and others), suddenly included writings of the Dead Sea Scrolls in their canon to develop new and different Christian eschatological views (for example, millenarianists, preterists, futurists, manifestations of Protestant reform groups).

For modern Judaism, the question is this: What is the impact of the scrolls beyond the obvious contributions to our understanding of ancient manuscript readings of the Hebrew Bible, and verification of certain historical beliefs about the Jews in the first centuries before and after the Common Era? Do the Dead Sea Scrolls actually affect modern Jewish synagogue theology, life, and customs? Are they used to establish (or reestablish) ancient customs and beliefs in modern Jewish life? Do they translate into changes in modern Jewish life in any substantive way? This chapter will go on to investigate how the discovery of the Dead Sea Scrolls and their translation and interpretation by the scholars involved in their dissemination trickled down into the pulpits of American life from the 1950s onward.

Reform Judaism, Hebrew Union College, and the Dead Sea Scrolls

Reform Judaism has a very close connection with the history of the Dead Sea Scrolls, because of the involvement of Rabbi Dr. Nelson Glueck (president of Hebrew Union College from 1947 to 1971) with Israeli archaeology—especially in the southern region of Israel and Jordan where the scrolls were discovered—and also because of his connections with the American Schools of Oriental Research (ASOR) in Jerusalem, where he served as director in the period right before the discovery. As a prominent student of William Foxwell Albright (a renowned biblical archaeologist), Glueck had worked as director of ASOR before returning to the United States in 1947 to take up his duties as president of HUC. It was at ASOR that the scrolls were photographed for the first time in 1947. It was Albright himself who had declared in early 1948 that the scrolls were the "greatest archaeological discovery of the century." Glueck's close relationship with Albright ensured that he was involved in the study of the scrolls from the earliest part of the discovery. The close connections between Glueck, Albright, and ASOR assured that the scrolls would be a part of HUC's legacy. In 1949–1950, Hebrew Union College, celebrating its impending seventy-fifth anniversary with the new President Glueck at the helm, positioned itself as the most prominent American institution involved with the scrolls by scheduling a series of distinguished learned society meetings at the college, among them the Society of Biblical Literature (SBL) and the American Schools of Oriental Research in late December 1949, and the American Oriental Society (AOS) in April 1950. Dr. Harry Orlinksy led the SBL and AOS conferences, at which there were almost a dozen presentations on the scrolls in those years. The events received national attention. Dr. Robert Gordis, the lone scholar who participated on behalf of the JTS, spoke on the correlation between the ancient Masoretic tradition and the Qumran Isaiah scroll. This is important since many Jewish scholars did not immediately accept the authenticity of the scrolls. Most Jewish scholars only slowly warmed to the idea that these scrolls were authentic and meaningful for the study of ancient and modern Judaism. Many Christian scholars were very accepting of the significance for early Christianity and modern Christianity and were enamored by the rather spectacular fashion in which the scrolls were presented.

The discovery of the Dead Sea Scrolls is not the main subject of this chapter, but it deserves some mention. The 1946 discovery of the scrolls by local bedouins in the area of Qumran is only the first stage. Qumran had been a well-known location from the nineteenth century onward, but the caves and the scrolls added immeasurably to its importance. The cemetery and the ruins of Qumran were associated with the Essenes and other Dead Sea groups mentioned in the first-century writings of Josephus, Philo, and Pliny. Reports of ancient scrolls in the Dead Sea region had been related in the nineteenth century but had never been proven. The passing of the scrolls from an antiquities dealer in Bethlehem to Mar Samuel, the metropolitan of the Syrian Orthodox Church in Jerusalem, occurred over the course of one year. By 1947, Mar Samuel's manuscripts were known and had been authenticated. By 1949, the scrolls were in the United States, and Samuel was in search of a buyer.

Some within the Reform movement had an ambivalent stance on the significance of the modern State of Israel in the 1940s, so the appointment of a scholar with close links to the State of Israel was important. Nelson Glueck's appointment as president of HUC and his connection to archaeology in Israel does have a connection to their early acceptance both by the Reform movement and among many scholars at HUC. Rabbi Glueck, as president of a major seminary for the training of rabbis, rarely spoke about why he thought the scrolls were so important to modern Jews, but it is clear that, unlike other Jewish scholars who dismissed the manuscripts, Glueck saw them as more than just museum and archaeological artifacts. In one of the few insights into why he saw the scrolls as so important, Glueck wrote in "Out of Yesterday, A Symbol for Today" (*New York Times*, May 11, 1958), "Could it be that the Dead Sea Scrolls, so amazingly exhumed from their long forgotten cave-burials and suddenly transported over the space of some twenty centuries to the attention of the world, were hailed unconsciously by myriads as a symbol of luminescent hope in an age of otherwise unrelieved darkness?"

In this pronouncement, he seems to be alluding to the dark days of the Holocaust, the wars of Israel, and American post–World War II conflicts and nuclear frenzy (the Cold War and Korean conflict), and he saw the scrolls as a form of a "message in a bottle" from a divine hand. "Message in a bottle" is not just an idle metaphor—the fact that these manuscripts had been placed in special ceramic holders was part of the mystery. These ceramic jars, so unusual in shape and size, were specially made to hold and preserve the manuscripts. The scrolls in the caves may have been a library not only for the ancient group who lived on the Dead Sea and who wrote the materials, but also for future generations of survivors of the "war between the sons of darkness and sons of light." The apocalyptic group that lived on the Dead Sea (whose beliefs are chronicled in the scrolls) feared that their holy texts—and they themselves—might not survive the "end of days" scenario predicted in those texts. In this way, the Dead Sea Scrolls are the ultimate "message in a bottle" to an unknown population. If they had been discovered (which some may have been earlier—it is hard to know), the message would not have been easily discernible nor would the message seem so dramatically translatable to people living in the pre-nuclear age. To those who look at the discovery today in the post–World War II and post–Holocaust era, it appears more likely that they may have made a conscious decision to preserve them for some distant future time and not simply put them in a storage area.

Dr. Nelson Glueck and Dr. Harry Orlinsky both knew the importance of the archaeology and manuscripts of the Jews and also understood the state of biblical studies, which up until the discovery of the scrolls was dominated by the nineteenth- and early twentieth-century "documentary hypothesis." For many, "the documentary hypothesis" (described in the following paragraph) minimized the historical value of the ancient Hebrew Bible, and placed it as a relatively late invention of what could be described as self-serving Jewish writers in the Greco-Roman period.

The circumstances that unfolded in New York City in the late 1940s and early 1950s are, as already noted, unusual, especially because an HUC professor played a central role in the purchase of four of the original scrolls (plus fragments). Rabbi Stephen S. Wise, the founder of the Jewish Institute of Religion in New York City, brought Dr. Harry Orlinsky from the Baltimore Hebrew College to teach at HUC in 1943. Orlinsky was well known in the 1940s and early 1950s because of his work on manuscripts of the Hebrew text (the Masoretic text), and he was favorably disposed to Israel in general. He was also in a perfect position to be the famous intermediary in the plan to return the scrolls to Israel. Yadin's plan to purchase the scrolls needed a person who intimately knew what the scrolls looked like and could authenticate them when they were purchased. The possibility of another less ancient manuscript being substituted at the last minute was a real possibility. The arrangements for the purchase were put into the hands of a very unlikely "secret agent," a grandfather-like, raincoat-wearing Dr. Harry Orlinsky. The diminutive, rather unassuming Dr. Orlinsky (known to the sellers only as "Mr. Green") was nonthreatening and believable in his role as a simple businessman who was purchasing the items for a collection. But the amazing benefit of Orlinsky's presence there that day in the bowels of a New York bank was his ability to immediately recognize and authenticate whether these were indeed the original Dead Sea Scrolls that Sukenik had identified, or just forgeries and/or other substitutions. As the esteemed Hebrew Union College professor of biblical literature, Dr. Orlinsky came to the Waldorf Astoria branch of Chemical Bank and Trust, examined the scrolls, and bought them on the spot. Dr. Orlinsky related the story in a number of different publications (this is taken from *Reform Judaism* 20, no. 3 (Spring 1992), pages 47–48): "I was to assume the name of Mr. Green, an expert on behalf of the client. . . . I was to say as little as possible and to admit to no identification beyond being Mr. Green. . . . After leaving the vault, I phoned an unlisted number and spoke the word *lechayim*, meaning the Scrolls were genuine."

D. Samuel Gottesman, a noted Jewish benefactor, financed the scrolls' purchase as a gift for the State of Israel to preserve the anonymity of the exchange and ensured that they would be sent back to Israel. The year 1954 (when the scrolls were sold and spirited back to Israel) was a particularly difficult time for relations between Syria, Jordan, and Israel, and without a donor like Gottesman the transaction would have been much more difficult and expensive. The looming threat from Egypt and the nationalization of the Suez Canal were still two years off, but the Israelis were taking no chances in losing this cultural symbol of the presence of the Jews in what amounted to Jordanian territory. The plan was flawlessly executed and was seen by many as a minor "miracle," given all of the possible pitfalls.

The scroll acquisition was finally announced only on February 13, 1955, some seven months after the famous clandestine purchase in New York. During this time period, however, HUC and the Reform movement in general continued to discuss the importance of the scrolls. The connection between the scrolls and Reform Judaism has continued publicly through the present day, both in the Dead Sea Scrolls course work taught for the rabbinical school and in graduate student work at HUC. What is interesting is how in this same time period the scrolls helped change the relationship between Reform Judaism and the modern State of Israel and Zionism. It would have been unusual in the 1930s, for example, for HUC and Reform Judaism in general to be as active in Israeli affairs as they became in the post–scrolls discovery era. Years later, in the 1960s, when President Glueck was establishing the HUC campus in Jerusalem and some of the leading orthodox Israeli rabbis were opposed to this, the role of the HUC in the Dead Sea Scrolls story suddenly took on added importance. The scrolls had an unanticipated and unusual ideological legacy. Beyond the technical details of the scrolls readings of the biblical and nonbiblical texts, and beyond the theology that was present in the writing of the Qumranites (which was different from Jerusalem), suddenly there were many new versions of ancient customs that did not correspond exactly to the medieval rabbinic codes (a book form, rather than a scroll). In a strange, ironic twist, the ancient texts indirectly provided the modern Reform movement with sources that validated their own differences with the modern orthodox Jewish movement. The scrolls also allowed Reform Jews to have some of the most intense and meaningful encounters with Christian churches and seminaries on a subject that they both could claim as their own. As Reform Judaism had already engaged in ecumenical dialogue from the early part of the twentieth century in the United States, the scrolls were just another new aspect to this fundamental tenet of American Reform Judaism. The scrolls were featured as a part of almost every major Christian seminary as well. The fact that the scrolls were important for theologians and the faithful I understand. They were mostly biblical texts and they did have additional theological messages that were not explicitly in the New Testament or the Hebrew Bible. What is interesting for this book is how ancient history (especially one that is rewritten because of an archaeological discovery) influences the modern history and how modern history and the writing of modern historians about the ancient period tend to be influenced by the modern period.

The Dead Sea Scrolls, Christianity, and Judaism: How the Modern Period Influences the Ancient Period

The sermon is a well-known and ancient Jewish art form that became a part of the Church in the Byzantine period. It was transferred from Christianity to Islam as a form of combining elements from the life of the people into religious textual reading for the week. Many thousands of sermons became famous throughout the generations as a way of informing and inspiring people through topics that were well known and contemporary. I begin by exploring Christian sermons about the Dead Sea Scrolls because there were just so many of them and they all seem to follow patterns. Jewish sermons about the scrolls were more difficult to find for a variety of reasons (some of which have to do with the immediate interest of Christian scholars and ministers in the obvious parallels to Christianity). The Christians sermonized about the scrolls at different periods of time than the Jews did. The early pronouncements that made the scrolls a "proto-Christianity" or a precursor to Christianity were perceived by Christendom as good; then there was a wave of reaction to these claims that was seen as bad. One of the major differences was the sensation caused by the pronouncements of a scrolls team member, John Allegro (the scrolls team was made up of only Christian scholars for most of the first forty years of Dead Sea Scrolls research). Allegro questioned the originality of Christianity in light of the small amount of information that was available in the 1950s, while Andre Dupont-Sommer, in his 1952 book, *The Dead Sea Scrolls: A Preliminary Survey*, presented the scrolls and the Essenes as the "original" Christianity and Jesus as the reincarnated Teacher of Righteousness of the scrolls. These kinds of contradictory presentations caused many Christian pastors to reinvestigate what the scrolls actually said, and it wasn't until the late 1960s that there was a change in attitude among Christian preachers.

The most impressive changes were attitudinal. American (mainly Protestant) Christians and Jews viewed each other's practices in different ways. While some Christians before the discovery of the Dead Sea Scrolls suspected that Jewish practices were inauthentic expressions of the life and times of Jesus, now manuscripts from before the time of Jesus delineated practices that were similar to and yet different from rabbinic Jewish practices that they wanted to know more about. The ideas of celibacy, vestments, liturgy, ritual meals and purity, relations between the genders, and organizational and leadership models that were found in the scrolls suddenly gave American Jews and Christians freedom to innovate and change their own traditions in the face of evidence in the scrolls. The "Jewish" identity of Jesus and Paul was not a homogeneous block but rather a series of different groups all attempting to understand how to carry out God's will in the new and very different religious reality of Judea in the Greco-Roman period. Even the literary form of exegesis, the explaining of a traditional biblical text in a totally new and distinctive (and contemporary) way, a hallmark not only of written interpretations that emerged in Judaism and Christianity but also of Jewish and Christian sermonizing, was suddenly laid out in texts that were over two thousand years old.

The majority of Jewish sermonizing probably took place throughout the Middle Ages and into the modern period at synagogue services. In fact, sermons in most churches around the United States in the 1950s and 1960s used the scrolls as a wonderful vehicle for teaching about how Judaism and Christianity were interrelated, as interest in ecumenism rose after the Holocaust and World War II. It was during World War II that Jews and Christians came to live in close quarters with one another in the armed forces. In the post–World War II era, the sermon in the synagogue and the church became a vehicle for expressing how Jews and Christians were a part of the American fabric. In Will Herberg's 1955 book, *Protestant, Catholic, Jew*, he shows just how this connection had developed. Jews in the United States found themselves working together in a multireligious society that, in the main, was populated by Catholics and Protestants that shared common interests in their churches with Jews in their synagogues.

In many Protestant denominations, the sermon came to replace the Catholic Eucharist. Its placement became the central piece in Sunday worship, exhorting the faithful to seek a deeper faith rather than fulfill rituals. In the 1950s, there were a prodigious number of sermons delivered by Christian pastors that included the Dead Sea Scrolls as a theme. Many of the sermons showed just how similar the formulas of Jesus's Sermon on the Mount are to many of the pronouncements in the Dead Sea Scrolls. Even without a proto-gospel text, the idea that New Testament language is so similar to Jesus's teachings made Protestant preachers use the scrolls as if they were church teachings rather than pre-Christianity teachings. Most of the sermons I examined began with a New Testament proof text (or a holiday theme) and used the scrolls as a means to interpret the New Testament or Christian message. Typical of this is the 2002 sermon titled "Following a Different Drummer," by Reverend Charles Rush at Christ Church, affiliated with the United Church of Christ and the American Baptist churches, in Summit, New Jersey. He began his homily on Matthew 4:12–23, where he developed the theme of Jesus and the apostles as unique individuals who followed their own way, just as the Essenes did (www.christchurchsummit. org/Sermons-2002/020127-DifferentDrummer.html):

> There were lots of these groups around too. One of the most famous, the *Essenes*, we know a fair amount about, because they gave us the Dead Sea Scrolls. They were a group of Jewish ascetics who thought the world was coming to an end soon and if you were living as an oppressed person in Palestine under Roman occupation, that would not be an unreasonable speculation. Evil was so evil that the caricature of Apocalyptic thought made sense.

The Dead Sea Scrolls are also used to discuss Jesus's resurrection. The Easter holiday theme may not seem a likely Dead Sea Scrolls comparison, but it is clear that the idea of the resurrection of the dead was one that rang true for Christians because even before Christianity we know that Jews took the concept seriously. Now it is true that there are particularly normative rabbinic texts that demonstrate the same thing, but the scrolls have the advantage of not being rabbinic. They are Jewish, ancient, and pre-date the New Testament, and yet they are not rabbinically Jewish. I find that many Christian pastors use the scrolls in the same way that Reverend Johnold J. Strey, pastor and acting principal of Gloria Dei Evangelical Lutheran Church and School in Belmont, California, did in his "Sermon for the Festival of the Resurrection of Our Lord" (2010). The sermon, a conclusion of his Lent season and his lead up to Holy Week and Easter, shows that the entire concept of Jesus's message would have been understood by the people listening. His church, affiliated with the Wisconsin Evangelical Lutheran Synod, echoes the sentiments of many other Protestants in his use of the scrolls (see http://pastorstrey.wordpress.com/2010/04/06/sermon-for-the-festival-of-the-resurrection-of-our-lord-2010/):

> I tend to follow news and happenings in the Milwaukee area, because that's where I'm originally from. The Milwaukee Public Museum is currently offering an exhibit of the Dead Sea Scrolls. Perhaps you have heard or read something about the Dead Sea Scrolls. These scrolls are a collection of manuscripts discovered in the Holy Land in the middle of the last century. Among these scrolls are the earliest known copies of the Old Testament. These Old Testament manuscripts can be positively dated to the B.C. era. That's extremely important, because prior to this, the oldest copies of the Old Testament that historians knew about were more recent documents, well into the A.D. era. Now, for the honest inquirer, we have solid evidence of a pre-B.C. era Old Testament.
>
> Why is that so important? Remember that the Old Testament contains predictions of the Messiah's resurrection from the dead—for example, Psalm 16:10 and Isaiah 53:11. Before the Dead Sea Scrolls were discovered, many critics of Christianity assumed that these Old Testament predictions were written long after Jesus' ministry and were made to look like they were predictions of his resurrection. With the discovery of the Dead Sea Scrolls, an honest person has to come to grips with the reality that these are truly prophecies and not carefully concocted statements after the fact. In other words, Jesus wasn't the first to predict his resurrection. God the Holy Spirit had made multiple predictions of Jesus' resurrection long before God the Son entered into our world.

Of course, part of the use of the Dead Sea Scrolls in Christian sermonizing is to create another mode for ecumenical common themes arguing for how theologically close Judaism and Christianity are by showing that the Jews can accept *multiple messiahs*. The scrolls' use of the two messiahs seems to have two purposes. One is clearly to present that Judaism has an active messianic tradition for ecumenical discussion purposes. Again, the rabbinic tradition is replete with active messianic references, but they are rarely cited. Another tack seems to use the scrolls' references to multiple messiahs in order to demonstrate that Jews accepted (and can therefore still accept) different messiahs. In Reverend David B. Smith's sermon, for example, on Acts 11 ("I Had a Dream"), Father Dave (as he calls himself) uses the scrolls to demonstrate this characteristic (see http://ezinearticles. com/?I-Had-A-Dream---A-Sermon-On-Acts-11&id=533143):

> There might well have been room within Jewish society to accept different beliefs about different Messiahs. Look at the literature of 1st century Israel and you will see that different groups had different Messianic expectations. Most people were waiting for a warrior leader. Some were waiting for a priest. If you look at the Dead Sea Scrolls, it seems that the Qumran community, who were a group of Jewish monks, were expecting both!

The Reverend Carl McIntire, president of the International Council of Christian Churches (a Christian fundamentalist denomination), with the type of zeal and interest in the scrolls that characterized the many different sermons that co-opted the scrolls for Christianity, wrote in the *Christian News* (October 28, 1991), just as the scrolls were being released to the general public (see www.carlmcintire.org/newspapers.php):

> When the International Council of Christian Churches was formed in Amsterdam in 1948, in its detailed enumeration of the common evangelical doctrines and the Apostles' Creed, it listed first their belief in the inerrancy and infallibility of the Scripture. These churches around the world can now rejoice and thank God that out of a cave alongside the Dead Sea, where all these years of church history rested, these Dead Sea scrolls were waiting for this hour when God would bring them out, and the correctness and accuracy of what He gave to Isaiah could be used in the salvation of many souls, both Jews and Gentiles. He has presented this to the church just before He comes back, as He promised, to gather His own to Himself in a new and glorified body like the one He had on His resurrection day. The Dead Sea Scrolls are the greatest archaeological discovery for the Church of Jesus Christ and the people of God in 2000 years.

The Dead Sea Scrolls and the Jews

For the Jews in the United States in the twentieth century, the sermon was a modern innovation to attract families and workers to synagogues on a Friday night (and not necessarily on Saturday morning) to talk about the events of the day in a time before everyone had radios and television

sets. Sermons that were preached in churches would not generally be repeated in a synagogue, but for the first time in the 1950s, rabbis saw the
same materials that were relevant to the Jewish community in the same
way that they were relevant in the Christian community. The sermon was
the place for ministers and rabbis to enlighten their congregations to the
week's news, wrapped into a biblical message. The Friday night service and
sermon was one of the central pillars of Jewish life, and a major difference
between Reform Jews and traditional Orthodox Jews, since it assumed that
Jews in America would only be able to accommodate the later service and
use it for their Sabbath experience, given that some of these same Jews
might be called upon to work on Saturdays to feed their families. I remember as a student in graduate school in the 1970s reading the monumental
study of Marshall Sklare in his 1955 book, *Conservative Judaism*, about the
importance of the sermon and the Friday night service.

In looking through hundreds of sermons from rabbis across America
at the American Jewish Archives in Cincinnati in this time period, one
notes sermons on the major events of the day from the post–World War
II era. There was discussion of the Cold War, the threat of a nuclear war,
the beginnings of the new State of Israel, the sexual revolution, the status
of women, the plight of children, wars across the world, books, movies,
music, performers, politicians, innovations in the law, civil rights, Communism, and major American holidays, among many other issues, but
there was very little about the major discoveries from the world of archaeology. The sermon was the vehicle for discussing basic ideas and religious
customs. Among the Jews, questions about intermarriage, women as rabbis
and equal participants in the service, theological problems related to the
Holocaust, gay and lesbian relations, Jewish-Christian relations, divorce,
and the pressing need for social justice were presented often for the first
time in Friday night sermons by far-thinking rabbis ordained at modern
rabbinical institutions. In fact, I encountered very little of the archaeological world in nearly sixty years of sermons that I investigated from the 1940s
to 2000. What I did find shows us how Jews and Christians were introduced to the world of archaeology and the Dead Sea Scrolls in a religious
setting and not in a university setting.

Jews Writing Their Own History in
the Scrolls' History: 1955, 1957, and 1968

There were a few very courageous and scholarly rabbis who saw the scrolls
as the "missing link" between how Judaism and Christianity converged.

The American "melting pot" allowed Jews and Christians to interact in society, but churches and synagogues were still very different and foreign settings with rare moments of common dialogue. The scrolls provided a few rabbis with the tools to narrow the intellectual and religious gap between the Jews and the Christians in America. To discuss how rabbis understood the scrolls in relation to the Jews, I will offer examples through the sermons of a select group of rabbis that characterized many of the different sermons of the time. Rabbi Harold Saperstein, who for almost fifty years was rabbi of Temple Emanuel in Lynbrook, New York, was trained at the Jewish Institute of Religion and ordained in 1935.

Saperstein was a prolific writer and activist of the period and saw the discovery of the Dead Sea Scrolls as significant for modern Judaism. On Friday night, December 16, 1955, he preached a sermon titled simply "The Dead Sea Scrolls." His motivation for this sermon may have been a series of different publications in 1955 that had mentioned the scrolls. For example, the writer Edmund Wilson wrote a popular article in the *New Yorker* magazine on May 14, 1955, called "The Scrolls from the Dead Sea." In this article, Wilson stated that the Dead Sea Scrolls and the Essenes "played no significant role in the development of Judaism." Saperstein does not seem to have accepted this idea, and his sermon explained his belief in the scrolls' importance to modern Judaism.

Saperstein's remarks included the elements from the scrolls that demonstrate the close relationship between Judaism and Christianity; this was a constant motif in the scrolls sermons that I saw. Most of the sermons that dealt with the Dead Sea Scrolls were usually placed in anticipation of Jewish-Christian ecumenical events and holidays when rabbis attempted to demonstrate the similarity between Jews and Christians (Saperstein planned his sermon for just before the Christmas holiday; the other popular period for Dead Sea Scrolls sermons was before Easter).

Rabbi Edward Klein (also ordained at the Jewish Institute of Religion) of the Stephen Wise Free Synagogue in New York City, in his Friday night, December 6, 1957, sermon titled "More on the Dead Sea Scrolls," notes:

> The authors of the Dead Sea Scrolls speak to us across two millennia of the amazing vitality and creativity of an ancient people, the rag-tag and bob-tail of the ancient world, a tiny people over-run by Greeks and Romans, able nonetheless to give humanity its God idea, its Bible, its prophets, its commandments to give more than half the world its faith. They bid Christianity to recognize a new and even greater debt to Judaism, than had before been known. On the eve of Chanukah and Christmas, the Qumran

covenanters urge that Christianity and Judaism, unique in their separate beliefs, yet even closer than before in the things they share, fulfill their mission as Children of Light, doing battle against the forces of darkness.

In fact, many different sermons were delivered on this particular Shabbat in December 1957 because it marked the tenth anniversary of the discovery.

The year 1957 was an important year for sermonizing, both among the Jews and Christians. For example, Rabbi Richard C. Hertz, the rabbi of Temple Beth El in Detroit, Michigan, delivered a sermon on December 6, 1957, wherein he specifically mentioned how the scrolls were a counterbalance to the scary nature of the 1950s arms race:

> In the 20th century of sputniks and rocket ballistics, it is good to gain a little perspective on the values of life and realize that there is still fascination in an ancient Jewish time, that new discoveries are constantly being unearthed. And it is also a little humbling to realize that modern man, for all his vaunted scientific and technical wizardry, still does not know everything about the long ago and far away.

The Dead Sea Scrolls did provide this opportunity for many preachers. Nelson Glueck (president of Hebrew Union College in Cincinnati, mentioned earlier in this chapter) observed in 1955 that the discovery was not reserved for just professional archaeologists and Bible scholars, for it had a potential influence upon Judaism in his own times. In his 1955 *New York Times* review of two books on the scrolls (Millar Burrows's *The Scrolls from the Dead Sea* and Eleazar Sukenik's *The Dead Sea Scrolls of the Hebrew University*), which Glueck titled "New Light on the Dim Past," he wrote, "Their very names [the Dead Sea Scrolls] excite the interest of all who are alert to the ideas and tendencies related to some of the main theological tenets of our own times."

Saperstein, like other rabbis of his period, assiduously followed the *New York Times* and its book reviews, and he had read Glueck's piece. On that Friday night in December 1955, he exposed the Reform Jews of Long Island to an idea that they might otherwise not have seen as subject matter that pertained to them: the significance of the Dead Sea Scrolls for modern Jews. Saperstein wrote:

> Now what do these discoveries have to tell us about religious history—first for Jews and then for Christians? As Jews as Professor Burroughs [*sic*] of Yale Divinity School has said, there was more variety and flexibility in Judaism than we have ever before supposed. It helps us to realize that there

was in ancient times in Judaism room for minority groups and freedom for minority people. But more important it helps us to know more about our own religious literature.

Rabbi Saperstein mentioned the scrolls only once in a sermon in 1955, but some thirteen years later, he mentioned them again. On Friday evening, January 5, 1968, he preached a second sermon on the Dead Sea Scrolls. I was there on that Friday night, and while one can never say what event helps a person make a decision about one's own future career, I remember being moved by his sermon. When I read the manuscript of the sermon for the first time in the American Jewish Archives in Cincinnati, I felt a shiver run down my back, as if Rabbi Saperstein had spoken the words yesterday. I recognized the note cards that were meticulously typed. In this period rabbis would write their sermons down word for word and usually read them exactly as they had written them. I read it and saw that Saperstein had put his finger on what I had discovered while researching the archives of rabbis and Christian preachers of the period. The scrolls were not just a simple ancient artifact; they spoke to ancients and continue to have importance for modern Judaism.

From June of 1967 onward, Rabbi Saperstein reported on the major events in Israel with particular vigor. In the years from 1967 to 1969, I remember being particularly inspired by his presentations of the modern life of Israel and especially the archaeology. Rabbi Saperstein held that Reform Jews were a modern continuation of the life and times of the historical Jews that extended back to the biblical world. He wrote:

> Now what is the importance for the understanding of Judaism of these greatly publicized ancient scrolls? Outside of the fascination of dealing with something which goes back 2000 years—do they throw light on our heritage? I think they do.
>
> First, they add great support on the accuracy of our current Bible texts. . . .
>
> Secondly, these discoveries make us realize that we are not the people of the book but the people of the books. We had come to feel that the only book that has come down from ancient times was the Bible. We suspected that there were many other books which had somehow got lost—there are hints of some in the Bible itself. But we had never seen any. Now suddenly we have come across a group of these books—each with a character of its own—and can better appreciate how rich the total literary heritage of our people must have been.
>
> Thirdly, we are reminded of the great variety of Jewish religious thought and practice during the time that the Jews were in an independent

nation. Judaism was never a monolithic faith. There was a great deal of
free religious searching. There were many differing, sometimes conflicting
groups. The break away from tradition by Reform Judaism in our day is
not an innovation in Jewish history at all.

Saperstein is one of many rabbis who made the leap that the Dead Sea
Scrolls, which had been purchased through the intervention of the Reform
movement, really did reflect as much about Reform Judaism's emergence
in the nineteenth century as it did about the Qumranites' emergence in the
second century BCE. Reform rabbis saw themselves in the twentieth century in much the same way as the Qumranites must have seen themselves
in the first century. Rabbi Saperstein finished:

> The ancient scrolls that come from the area of the Dead Sea still have the
> potential of life and light and inspiration for the people of Israel. Amen.

Saperstein and many other Reform rabbis preached about the scrolls as
a reaction to the press and the local interest in the content of the scrolls.
Rabbi Ferdinand M. Isserman, of Temple Israel in St. Louis, Missouri,
delivered a sermon on the Dead Sea Scrolls on March 29, 1957. It was, in
part, in commemoration of the tenth anniversary of the discovery of the
scrolls. On that Friday night, he conveyed what must have been the senti-
ment of many Reform rabbis and most Christian preachers:

> It is the literary record of this community that has been found. Among
> them is a book of hymns. These hymn books draw on biblical sources, but
> they reveal the originality of the community. They did exactly what we
> have done. We have a Union Prayer Book. In it there is a song centered
> around the 23rd Psalm. It is, however, not the 23rd Psalm, but it centers
> about it. That is what they did too. They were inspired by biblical litera-
> ture and the biblical point of view, but they composed their own songs.

The recognition that there was a possibility of composing new liturgy
was not a new idea. It had been written about especially by scholars of
liturgy at the Jewish Theological Seminary and Hebrew Union College.
Isserman was pointing to the ability of the inspired ancient author to
compose a hymn based upon the Bible, therefore having the same type of
inspiration that the ancient biblical author had had. The scrolls provided
Reform Jews (especially the rabbis) a validation of their "new" Union
Prayer Book and all of the corrective liturgical changes that had been going
on for nearly a century before the discovery of the scrolls.

Modern Religious Movements and the Dead Sea Scrolls

Preterism is a movement within Christianity that is based upon a specific interpretation of the "end of days" scenario of traditional Christianity. Preterism ("praeter" means "past" in Latin) holds that the biblical prophecy of the "end" was fulfilled by the destruction of the Temple of Herod in 70 CE. Preterists believe this is the original view of the early Church. Differing ideas from historical Christian thinkers added to the struggle, as Roman Catholics and Protestants struggled to find the "true" message of Jesus's teachings after the Renaissance and in the period of the Reformation and into the period of the Enlightenment. Among Protestants, the Dutch Hugo Grotius and later the seventeenth-century English theologians Thomas Hayne and Joseph Hall found preterism a way of understanding their own religious identity. By the twentieth century, many Preterists had only theological and philosophical arguments to stand on. The discovery of the Dead Sea Scrolls gave the Preterists a new way of arguing the same issues. The loose organization of preterist churches (which are subdivided into full, middle-of-the-road, and partial Preterists) is not one single movement, but the Dead Sea Scrolls show that there was a Jewish lead up to the types of final "end of days" scenarios that are in the New Testament and indirectly validated the preterist contentions.

Recently, in a similar way, the scrolls allowed a new group of Jews and rabbis to express an interest in very different ideological and theological stances than traditional rabbinic groups. Starting in the 1960s, precisely in the period when the scrolls were becoming known in American society, the group known as the Jewish Renewal began to grow. The name "Jewish Renewal" is a general term for a loose form (not necessarily a movement) of Jews who attempt to weave different historical ideas—mystical, Hasidic, musical, and meditative (drawn from a variety of sources that are traditional and nontraditional, Jewish and non-Jewish)—into a fixed set of Jewish spiritual practices that would be meaningful to the modern Jew. The movement began in the 1960s and 1970s in North America at precisely the same time that the scrolls had become known to a wider Jewish public in the United States, and most of the terminology was adapted from the scrolls. The Jewish Renewal movement includes prominent leaders such as Rabbi Zalman Schachter-Shalomi, teachers, and authors including Dr. Arthur Green and Rabbis Shohama Weiner and Arthur Waskow.

The original organization of the Jewish Renewal movement, "The B'nai Or Religious Fellowship," which Zalman Schachter-Shalomi described in an article titled "Toward an Order of B'nai Or," was derived from the terms in the scrolls. Schachter-Shalomi wrote, "The name 'B'nai Or' means 'sons' or 'children' of light, and was taken from the Dead Sea Scrolls material, where the 'sons of light' go to war against the 'sons of darkness.'" Schachter-Shalomi saw B'nai Or as a semi-monastic, ashram-like community, based upon the various communal models prevalent in the 1960s and 1970s. By 1969, taking some elements from the developing Havura movement, the Christian Trappist tradition, and the Dead Sea Scrolls, Schachter-Shalomi founded the B'nai Or Religious Fellowship (now called ALEPH: Alliance for Jewish Renewal) with a small circle of students. In 1974, he ordained the movement's first rabbi. Although his community has changed over the past forty years, B'nai Or did produce a number of important leaders in the Renewal movement and in Judaism in general. I often compare it to the influence that Martin Luther King Jr. had upon other Christian preachers and Christianity in general. The Renewal movement produced the *B'nai Or Newsletter*, a quarterly publication that presented articles on a variety of Jewish topics and Schachter-Shalomi's philosophy. The Dead Sea War Scroll may have provided the movement with an idea, but the modern battle for spiritual meaning of the Renewal movement is as fresh today as it was over two thousand years ago. Most of the associated congregations acknowledge that their followers wanted to use the meditative techniques that they saw present in the scrolls in their own modern religious development. Not only is the movement similar to the Qumran sect, but the followers also readily acknowledge that their original intent was to move to a desert setting to continue their group's spiritual practices. The idea that the archaeology of Qumran and the understanding of the ancient scrolls had given these two modern movements (Preterists and B'nai Or) a way to understand new spiritual practices is unique in the annals of archaeology, and I think it sums up how ancient history can influence modern history.

Modern History, Postmodernism, and the Dead Sea Scrolls: Why Archaeologists and Textual Scholars Are Only Human Beings

No book on history and the interpretation of history would be complete without a chapter that included one of the most significant intellectual movements in the academy in the past fifty years. The movement has changed the way that all scholars read and write history from the ancient to the modern period. The movement is called "postmodernism" because, unlike the nineteenth- and early twentieth-century attempts to present information in a purely scientific ("objective") way, scholars have begun to see how historical information can be influenced by the forces of the historical period in which the scholar writes. It is not so much that scholars are biased and trying to rewrite history in their own image; it is that they cannot help themselves. It is a by-product of being human to have your own independent thoughts that are inevitably influenced by your psychological, intellectual, and social circumstances. No scholar can ultimately be an island unto himself or herself.

Postmodernism, a loosely defined movement in a variety of very different disciplines in the humanities and social sciences (but especially in science, history, and literature), has at its root the attempt to deconstruct the motives of modern (and even ancient) writers and to see how the writers' own education, ideas, tendencies, and biases ("cultural, religious, etc., baggage") are reflected in what they are writing. In general, it tries to qualify the thing (events in history) about which the writer is writing from the thing (event) itself. It is an extremely important movement in most historical writing, but it is rarely applied to those who wrote the scrolls and those who write about the scrolls for the public. An ideological bent can be seen in the translations and interpretations of the scrolls from the beginning of the research, since almost all of the original researchers were Christians. In the 1950s, Christian writers used the scrolls all too often as an opportunity to present (in a not very veiled way) their own theological biases under the cover of writing about ancient texts. For Christianity, the Qumranites were the precursors of Christianity. The leader of the sect, the Teacher of Righteousness, prefigured either John the Baptist or Jesus and gave their roles greater antiquity. It is well documented that Father Roland de Vaux (the head of the Catholic group that first researched the Dead Sea Scrolls) interpreted the site of Qumran to be a monastery-like settlement, which paralleled the later Roman Catholic monasteries that he knew so well. Many other Christians found the parallelisms between the multiple stepped pools at Qumran and the gatherings of the ritual meals mentioned in the scrolls as direct parallels to the rites of baptism and communion, and they interpreted what they knew about the scrolls in light of modern rituals. In a sense their modern Christian identity informed their scholarly assessment of the scrolls, just as the scrolls informed the meaning of their own modern Christian identity.

The terminology of de Vaux's descriptions of Qumran followed the medieval monastery model with a refectory (dining hall), scriptorium (library), and so on. No one doubts that de Vaux's background influenced his own interpretation of the Qumranites as either prefiguring Christianity or as proto-Christian, but the recognition that one's background influences how one interprets the data (even within "objective" scholarship) is a tenet of postmodern interpretations. Father Geza Vermes, a Catholic priest, offers a classic example of how postmodernist interpretation can be seen. In his 1956 *Discovery in the Judean Desert*, he eliminates from the text of the scrolls any allusion to divorce to seemingly set up the Qumranites as proto-Catholics, and he ultimately demonstrates his own agenda through the scrolls: "And we know that their (i.e. the Qumranites') expectation of the imminent coming of the Lord, whether they knew it or not, was soon to be truly fulfilled."

In the 1950s, Orthodox, Conservative, Reform, and Reconstructionist Judaisms all commented on the scrolls in their official literatures and found ways of incorporating the insights into the type of Judaism that they practiced. As an example, we can look to the assessment of the Dead Sea Scrolls by Cyrus Gordon, a well-known eclectic scholar of antiquity during the period following the discovery of the scrolls. He developed his own understanding of them—which seems to fit in with the view of Reconstructionism. Reconstructionism, which originated in the United States from the writings and thoughts of Rabbi Mordecai Kaplan, teaches that democratic society and its diversity should be embraced. The American ideal of equality for all is consistent with Jewish historical civilization, and Jews should help in reconstructing Judaism in the modern period through these ideals. Gordon wrote about the scrolls in his article titled "The Dead Sea Scrolls" in the publication *Reconstructionist* on May 4, 1956:

> The Qumranites had a democratic, parliamentary government. Under priestly guidance, the majority ruled in accordance with deliberations in the community assembly. Any member who desired to address the assembly could do so after requesting and getting permission to speak. Once a member had the floor, no other member could interrupt him. Orderly parliamentary procedure, with each speaker taking his turn, is delineated in the Manual of Discipline. (page 14)

One of the most recent examples of this phenomenon and why it matters in our understanding of history comes from a controversy that erupted in 1990 in the scrolls story. In the late 1980s, the slow pace of releasing the translations of the scrolls by the small scrolls team became a major problem both for scholars and the public. The dismissal of the Dead Sea Scrolls chief editor (1984–1990), Professor John Strugnell, shows us just how background matters. Strugnell, a scholar who had worked on the scrolls from almost the beginning of the effort, was dismissed not for poor scholarship, but rather for something that he said which revealed how his views might taint his scholarship. The controversy erupted after Strugnell gave an interview to an Israeli reporter that was published in November 1990 in the Israeli newspaper *Haaretz*. In the midst of the transition to an enlarged scrolls translation team that included both Israelis and Jews (who had been excluded from the original scrolls teams), Strugnell's interview gave both scholars and the public an insight into how important it is to know who a scholar is. In the interview Strugnell was quoted as saying, "It [Judaism] is a horrible religion. It is a Christian heresy, and we deal with our heretics in different ways. You are a phenomenon that we haven't managed to convert—and we should have managed." One might ask why Strugnell's personal views were at all important. In modern scholarship we realize that scholars are human beings and their scholarship is a construct that contains their own modern views, which inevitably creep into their research—even if the thing they are researching is the ancient world. This is one of the great mysteries of religion and archaeology in the modern period. Archaeology is subject to interpretation by people who come to the scholarly table not as "empty slates" but full of their own views of the world. We cannot avoid this eventuality; we can only account for it as we as readers of scholarly materials evaluate scholarly arguments and balance their scholarly arguments against one another. Scholars and even archaeologists who excavate new materials are, at the end of the day, only human beings.

The Dead Sea Scrolls, perhaps because so little was revealed over a forty-year period, became a vehicle for understanding modern American religion in general and post–World War II America in particular. Strangely enough, modern religious, post–World War II (Jewish and Christian) identity seems also to have influenced the understanding of the way we understand the scrolls. Professor Tzvi Zahavy (in a 1992 paper at the Society of Biblical Literature conference and in his blog, http://tzvee.blogspot.com/2006/aa/my-postmodern-review-of-three-Jewish.html) assessed the work of three well-known Jewish scholars who wrote about the scrolls in the 1980s and showed that the scholarship of the three may indeed reflect their own religious backgrounds. According to Zahavy, the scholars and their books (which include extensive interpretations of the scrolls)—Shaye J. D. Cohen (*From the Maccabees to the Mishna*), Lawrence H. Schiffman

(From Text to Tradition: A History of Second Temple and Rabbinic Judaism), and Alan F. Segal *(Rebecca's Children)*—each reflected something about the religious background of the writers. Professor Zahavy demonstrates that as much as modern religion was influenced by the scrolls, the interpretation of the scrolls is influenced by modern religion. He attempts to show that the Jewish interpreters (like the Christian interpreters) of the Dead Sea Scrolls were guided by their own modern religious backgrounds. He writes:

> An Orthodox Jewish analysis will search for "Torah-true" ideals, emphasize ritual [e.g., prayer], focus on a textual canon, on elite rabbinic leadership, highlight internal sectarian debate and differentiation, downplay interfaith relations, ignore populist involvements in religious decision, deny the prominence of changes and adaptations based on social and historical circumstance, consider acculturation an evil, and emphasize particularism.
>
> A Conservative Jewish investigation will emphasize the analysis of family structures, democratic ideals, evolutionary change, institutional development [e.g., synagogues], communal leadership patterns, the interface of scholarship and rabbinic learning, rites of passage as opposed to other rituals, and treat acculturation as a struggle fraught with contradiction and ambivalence.
>
> A Reform Jewish approach will seek to differentiate Jews from Christians and highlight the opportunities for interfaith understanding and cooperation. It will emphasize theology in a Protestant model, acculturation as a positive force and universalism. Just how much do these three introductory surveys of the Second Temple and Early Rabbinic Judaism by three well-known Jewish scholars reflect their respective religious affiliations? Let us stipulate that all to some degree do come not only out of the minds, but also from the souls of their authors. There is no such animal as a "neutral academic account."

If Zahavy is right, we must be very careful to look out for the influence of the modern religious backgrounds of the scholars who interpret ancient religious documents and archaeological discoveries. No scholarship lives in a total vacuum. For as much as these new discoveries will influence our judgments about modern faith and archaeology, modern religious identities and views will inevitably influence the interpretation of these ancient texts and discoveries. And that is one of the great mysteries of religion and archaeology about which there is rarely any discussion. When a new discovery such as the Dead Sea Scrolls is made, it will always be subject to two levels of examination. The first, "translation," is itself a form of interpretation and not simply a neutral event. We have to hope that the process will be transparent, but it sometimes is done in a closed context. The translators almost immediately form impressions about the discovery, and their interpretations will inevitably attempt to contextualize the discovery in light of other information. All scholars, while they are not prisoners to their own ideologies, are human beings who are subject to their own backgrounds. The more they recognize this and deal with it, the better. We often say that history is written by the victors, but in reality if postmodernism teaches us anything it is that history is written by historians who may have a very wide-ranging agenda beyond the confines of the period about which they are writing. When a discovery in archaeology is made, it is always going to be subject to interpretation and comparison. What the experience of the Dead Sea Scrolls teaches us about history is that one has to be vigilant about who is writing the history and why.

Mysteries of Religion and Archaeology in Medieval Spain

4

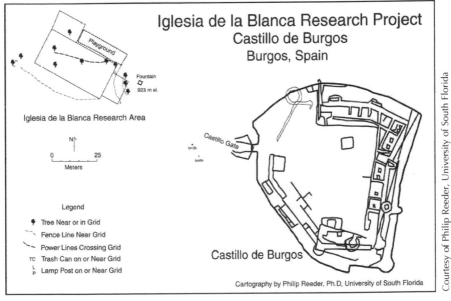

Figure 4.1. The map of the Burgos Castle and the synagogue and church of La Blanca

*And in a dream, I saw the figure of a tall man who said to
me, "why do you slumber? Hearken to these words that I say
to you and prepare yourself against the appointed season; for I
say to you, that the Jews have remained so long in captivity for
their folly and wickedness and because they have no teacher of
righteousness through whom they may recognize truth."*

—ABNER OF BURGOS (SUMMER 1295)

RESEARCH FOR THIS BOOK brought me twice to Spain for excavations that gave me a new appreciation of the complexity of the history of Europe and the Middle East. My first trip was for a project in northern Spain in Burgos, and then later I went on to southern Spain to Doña Ana Park (chronicled in chapter 2 of this book). I traveled to northern Spain in order to solve a well-known archaeological mystery. Spain had built a marvelous new museum in the north at Bilbao; attracting tourists to view the history of locations in the north of Spain became very important. In the meantime, since the 1990s, Spanish excavations and educational tours have begun to reclaim an inglorious period of Spanish history involving some of the most illustrious Jewish and Muslim populations of Europe being expelled from Spain in 1492 (during the time of the Spanish Inquisition). At this time, I learned about the single most impressive period of interaction between Jews, Christians, and Muslims, called by Jewish historians the Golden Age of Spain. This began with Jews arriving in Spain at the end of the Second Temple period (and probably in much larger numbers following the Bar Kokhba Revolt in 135 CE) and ended with the expulsion of the Jews (and most of the Muslim population) in 1492.

Diasporas from the Middle East to Spain

The dispersion of the Jewish people is usually referred to by the Greek word *diaspora*. But it is not only the Jews who have a diaspora. Any type of dispersed people over time begins to refer to their new places of residence as a diaspora. Today, for example, African Americans can refer to their communities in the Americas as a diaspora. The movement of peoples from the Middle East to other locales is a well-known part of ancient history. Some moved for economic benefits available in other locations that were no longer possible in their home countries because of famine, war, or an environmental disaster such as a tsunami or earthquake. Some moved as "new" groups moved in and pushed them out.

The ancient Judeans had been exiled by the Babylonians from their land in 586 BCE. The Temple of Jerusalem was destroyed and the Judeans moved to places in Egypt and other places in North Africa and reestablished their lives in ancient Babylonia. It is thought that some of the ancient Israelites (the so-called ten lost tribes) had earlier been exiled by the Assyrians to the far-flung places of India, Asia, Europe, and Africa. Even though I knew that many Jews were involved with ancient seafaring on the Mediterranean Sea from the Iron Age onward, the movement of Jews to Europe and North Africa is difficult to track. Archaeology does provide clues to the movements of the Jews. The first time that I investigated the Jewish inscriptions that had been found in Europe and discovered that they went back to the third century BCE, it made me realize how difficult it is to track the movement of peoples from place to place from antiquity to the medieval and modern periods. We do not always see the history of the Jews of Europe as a part of the history of Europe, but it is. I often wondered as we worked on the Atlantis/Tarshish project if the ancient Israelite sailors arrived in the port of Tarshish in southern Spain and knew that they were laying the groundwork not only for ancient Spanish history but for ancient Jewish history in Spain as well. The oldest inscriptions of Spain probably point to Jews in Spain after the second century CE, but it would not surprise me if the Israelites were a part of the earliest groups that colonized southern Iberia. Unfortunately, Spanish historians and historians who write about the history of the Jews in Spain are largely interested in the period after the rise of Islam in the eighth century or the reconquest period after the thirteenth century. The Visogothic kings conquered Spain and changed the existing Arian religion to Roman Catholicism in the sixth century CE, and a period of persecutions was initiated. Anti-Jewish measures continued right up until the Muslim conquest in 711 CE. The Muslim conquest of Spain did not take place because of the already existing Jewish communities in Spain, but the Muslim conquest was arguably made easier by the existing Jewish settlements. At first the Jews were not able to expand their communities under the Arabs. But as Cordoba, Spain, became an Islamic caliphate, the Jews of Spain increased in number and played a key role in the success of what came to be known as the Golden Age of Spain.

It is a strange part of modern historiography that the Golden Age of Spain for Jewish history is different from the Golden Age of Spain for Spanish history. The Golden Age of Spain for the Jews usually begins with the conquest of the Muslims in the eighth century and ends with the arrival of a fanatic Islamic group known as the Almohades in the twelfth century CE. The Golden Age of Spain for Spanish historians begins with the expulsion of the Jews and Muslims from Spain in 1492 (the final expulsion for Muslims is usually listed as 1609) and continues through until the seventeenth century.

Reclaiming the history of the Jews and the Muslim populations in a place such as Spain is difficult. Many of the most famous medieval churches of Spain were built upon the footprints of a mosque or synagogue. The orientation and structural design was based on Muslim or Jewish architecture and concerns. During the 1990s, throughout much of the country, beautiful buildings that served as synagogues and mosques in the Middle Ages were excavated, reconstructed, or reconstituted in a way that people could see that Jews and Muslims had lived there. The mosque and the synagogue were not rebuilt, but the footprint of the building was presented for the public to see and appreciate. Similarly, a well-known Jewish community in Burgos, Spain, had built a beautiful, early medieval synagogue near the city's main castle. The Jews seem to have been settled in Burgos by the eleventh century since they are prominently mentioned in documents from the twelfth century. In the fourteenth century, after the problems began for the Jews, a church was built over the synagogue. The church was destroyed in the Napoleonic wars in the nineteenth century, and the area is now a children's park. We went on a search to see if the footprints of the ancient synagogue were indeed still there. As we prepared for the excavations, I read up on the tragic history of the Jews in this area and realized that an archaeological project such as this serves to understand the history better. If the synagogue was still there under the church, it would tell us more about what had happened than volumes of literary accounts from the period. The history of the Jews and Christians in Spain is one that shows just how the footprints of each are left one on top of another.

The History of Religions and Archaeology

Following the developments of religions from one place in the world to another is not easy. Christianity began as a Middle Eastern religion based in a specific location, and it became a worldwide Church that is present in almost every single country on earth—which shows just how far an idea can be spread. The Jesus of the Africans is a black Jesus; the Jesus of South America appears to be an indigenous Inca who is depicted eating guinea pig at the Last Supper in Lima; and in Asia, Jesus and Mary regularly appear as if they were native Asians. Translating religious figures and places into local culture is not as easy as it seems. Often it means that one religious in-stitution is transformed into another religious institution in a short period, while other times it takes a century.

I became interested in Mary, the mother of Jesus, because of a proj-ect in Nazareth of which I was a part, but also as a natural outgrowth of my lifelong research on early Christianity. Mary is a ubiquitous person in the early Church. She is, in many respects, as important to Christianity as Jesus. But as a Jew, I was surprised just how important she is for modern Christians. They have established churches, schools, and pilgrimage sites in her name, and there have been regular sightings of her throughout the world into the current day. Throughout places as distinct as Europe and Latin America, the faithful see in Mary a direction for their prayers and deepest-held convictions for health and life. She has always been seen as a symbol of healing of body and spirit; water is associated with many of the Mary pilgrimage sites. I was therefore interested in a "Mary" project when the chance arose far from the Holy Land. This project involved a church (Nuestra Señora de la Blanca, literally "Our White/Pure Lady," a code name for Mary throughout the Middle Ages) that had been built over a synagogue in a city in central Spain, Burgos.

I serve as the director of the Maurice Greenberg Center for Judaic Studies at the University of Hartford in Connecticut. We have always been committed to taking people to places that they would not otherwise be able to go. An archaeological project in Spain was not so unusual for us. But how I came to work in Spain on a medieval church that had once been a synagogue is, in itself, an interesting story. I am primarily a Jewish historian who studies the ancient Roman period and I work in the Middle East in field archaeology. However, I wanted to stray so far to Spain because the story of the church that had once been a synagogue was so compelling and because the story of the Jews of Spain is so dramatic and heart-wrenching. It is, in my view, second only to the destruction of the Temple of Jerusalem and the Bar Kokhba Revolt of the first and second centuries CE.

In 2004, when we began this project, I was seriously ill, but I thought that it would be a good way to plan for the future in the face of an uncer-tain present. I remember that as I sat with the Spanish archaeologists in our offices at the Greenberg Center back in February 2004, I thought about how complicated this really was. To plan an excavation in a totally differ-ent country, with conditions we could not foresee, and with people we did not know, while facing a personal diagnosis that was very uncertain, seemed fraught with problems. However, planning the excavations was a wonderful distraction from my daily treatments and medical challenges. I knew that I certainly would not be able to do this project in the summer of 2004 because if things went well, that's when I would have my bone marrow transplant.

The nature of archaeological inquiry is always filled with uncertainty, and looking forward to the next discovery is something that drives archaeological teams from year to year. During my illness, just knowing that there were still many new discoveries to be made kept me going. In February 2004, as we considered the possibilities of our staff surveying a territory of roughly ten acres in a short probe excavation of a week, I knew that it would have to wait until July 2005. But I knew that we should do it, and that I *had* to do it (if I could). It drove me through many a dark moment in the recovery from my transplant. We would go to Spain, and it would end up being an important contribution to our work in archaeology.

Although it is not technically in the biblical period, our project involves the history of the use of the name of Mary, the mother of Jesus, outside of the Holy Land. We arrived in Madrid in July 2005 to do a probe excavation of the church built over the synagogue and to investigate the destroyed fortress nearby. Our group included staff and faculty from Israel and North America: Stephen Weinstein (a contractor and philanthropist from Hartford, who helped finance our expedition); Harry Jol and Jennifer Bode (University of Wisconsin); Paul Bauman and Christeen Nahas (WorleyParsons, Canada); Phil Reeder (University of South Florida); Christine Dalenta (University of Hartford); and my son Eli, age thirteen. Eli, my middle son, had been on excavations at Bethsaida and Qumran and had been an asset to the work. My three children—Yoni, Eli, and Ethan—had all had field experience at archaeological excavations in Israel starting from age ten when I would take each one to the field to have them excavate with our college students. For me, the experience in Spain was personal and professional, as most of the work has been.

An important member of our team was Stephen Weinstein, a board member from the Greenberg Center. Not only did he donate the funds to get our staff to the site, but he also had an appreciation of the work we were doing and was fluent in Spanish. If Stephen had not been living in West Hartford when I began formulating this project, we probably never would have done it. I could not have created a character like him. His passion for Spain and Jewish history is infectious, and his creative mind came in handy in the work we had to figure out. All in all, our "Mission Impossible" team was complete with a cast of scholars and staff members who made the project interesting.

As a professor of Judaic studies, I am regularly called upon to teach and lecture about Jewish history from the beginning of the Jewish diaspora in 70 CE until the modern period. One of the main questions that students ask me is how the Jews, a Middle Eastern people, ever got to Europe. The Jews spread into the diaspora of the Greco-Roman Empire in the second century BCE, but their numbers swelled to outlying communities of the Roman Empire after the destruction of the Temple in 70 CE and more exactly after the disastrous events of the Bar Kokhba Revolt in 135 CE. The Bar Kokhba Revolt was (up until the time of the Holocaust in the twentieth century) the single most devastating event in all Jewish history. Just over sixty years after the destruction of the Temple of Jerusalem and the expulsion of the Jews from Judea by the Romans after the first revolt against the Romans (in the year 70 CE), the Judeans rebelled again. This time the emperor was not taking any chances of another rebellion and decided to all but destroy any possibility of a revolt taking place in the future. In the course of three years (132–135 CE), the Emperor Hadrian felt it necessary to move twelve divisions of his Roman legions from as far away as Britain to ensure his success in rooting out the rebelliousness of the Judeans. According to the Roman historian Dio Cassius, 580,000 Jews were killed, 50 fortified towns destroyed, and 985 villages razed to the ground by conventional weapons. The Judeans were expelled from Judea, the name of Judea was changed from then on to "Palestina," and the surviving Judeans left for different parts of the growing Jewish diaspora.

There is evidence that Jews were in Europe in the first and second centuries BCE, making them one of the few continuously existing, identifiably homogeneous groups that can be studied in the history of Europe. If one wants to study Europe, one can look at the microcosm of the Jews and understand how European history developed in the Middle Ages and the Renaissance. The complex identity of the Jews of Europe allows us to understand how individual identities of different countries developed in the premodern and modern periods.

The main diaspora community of Babylonia that developed after the Babylonian Exile in the sixth century BCE and continued to develop for another sixteen hundred years was only one of the centers of Jewish learning. The Jews who arrived in North Africa, Spain, and Gaul in the Byzantine period and established communities of great importance into the early Middle Ages were different from the earlier groups that had come after the revolts of 70 CE and 135 CE. Each new layer of leadership in these communities had new titles. Instead of early rabbinic titles of the *Nasi* (a Hebrew word usually translated as "Prince") and *Av Bet Din* ("Father of the Academy") in Israel and the *Resh Galuta* (an Aramaic title usually translated as "Head of the Diaspora") in Babylonia, there was a *Geon* (a Hebrew word usually translated "Wise One"), *Nagid* (a Hebrew word that can be translated as "the Speaker"), and *Resh Kallah* (an Aramaic title usually translated as "Head of the Scholarly Gathering"). All of these titles are indicative of a very dynamic and vibrant community that sought to carve out new leadership positions to parallel a similar set of titles and positions that were present in Islamic Babylonia.

The Jews of (ancient) Visogothic Spain starting in the sixth century CE were exposed to a new and virulent form of anti-Judaism in a place where they had been quietly growing since the first and second centuries CE. Faced with expulsion, death, or conversion, the Jews in Visogothic Spain sometimes chose to follow a very unique path. They were the first group of "secret" Jews, forced to convert and maintain a double identity, being publicly Catholic and privately Jewish in the sixth and seventh centuries. Although the Jews in Spain in the Christian Byzantine period worked out compromises with a variety of local feudal and religious leaders, the situation of the Jews in Spain dramatically changed for the better in the eighth century CE. In 711 CE, Islam swept through Spain and did away with the Christian leadership that had existed from the time of the rise of the Roman and Christian empires. There is something magical about this period of Jewish, Christian, and Muslim tolerance in Spain. It was a period when coexistence flourished, albeit controlled by forces of ethnic intolerance that had been a part of Visogothic Spain and would only be matched in the Enlightenment. It was far from ideal. The Jews were "People of the Book" and accepted as a minority in the new caliphate in Spain, but it was far better than what many other Jewish communities experienced in Europe at the same time. It has always been a time that general historians like to point to as an example that history does not always repeat itself. If the Jewish Golden Age of Spain was not picture perfect or an example of utopian relations between Jews, Christians, and Muslims, it was a symbiotic relation that allowed Jewish scholarship and life to prosper in Spain. For this reason, Spain is the next closest place to Israel on earth for creative, historical Jewish life. It was the "Jerusalem of the Mediterranean," and certain cities in the north of Spain prospered more than others. The rabbis so loved Spain that they read its origins into the Bible itself, finding a reference to it in the book of Obadiah 1:20. The rabbis took an obscure place that was named in the Bible (which probably was located in the Middle East), *Sepharad*, and assigned this name to the Iberian Peninsula. By the second and third centuries CE "Sepharad" became a rabbinic name for Spain and a place of Jewish refuge after the two revolts against the Roman Empire.

Getting from Israel to Spain

My interest in Spain also derives from two personal experiences. First, I speak Spanish fluently, having served early in my career as the director of the Rabbinical Seminary of Latin America, the *Seminario Rabinico Latinoamericano* in Buenos Aires, Argentina. My wife, Eliane, is Brazilian, and she and her parents spoke Portuguese at home since they arrived in the United States in the 1970s. I have, therefore, spent most of my adult life surrounded by Spanish and Portuguese culture. When I was working at the *seminario*, I sent rabbis to Spanish- (and Portuguese-) speaking countries in Latin America, and even off to Spain. The Jews who came from Argentina to Spain were themselves escaping persecution in the repressive years of reactionary governments in the 1960s and 1970s. The Jews (as a group) were officially welcomed back to Spain only some twenty years ago. It is hard to imagine, but after being exiled in the infamous 1492 expulsion order of King Ferdinand and Queen Isabella, and even after Spain had been turned into a democratic state, the expulsion order had never been cancelled. In one of the great ironies, even though King Juan Carlos publicly retracted the five-hundred-year-old order of expulsion in 1992, Spain had begun to become a place of refuge for Latin American Jews during the rule of the infamous anti-Semitic military dictatorships of Latin America in the 1970s and into the 1980s.

The second reason for my personal interest in Spain is, as already stated, that I am interested in the "secret" of the Jewish, Christian, and Muslim *convivencia*—literally, "living together"—what we would today call "religious tolerance" or "sensitivity," which existed for a few centuries in Spain. I have spent most of my life teaching about how Jews, Christians, and Muslims can and should live together, and I am fascinated (as I think others are) about how this ancient symbiotic relationship worked.

My interest in different archaeological projects that explore the nexus between Jews, Christians, and others in antiquity has led me to become interested in the way that Jewish, Christian, and Muslim interaction works in the modern world and how it worked in the premodern world. During the late 1990s, I directed the Henry Luce Forum in Abrahamic Religions, a joint project of the Maurice Greenberg Center for Judaic Studies and the Duncan Black Macdonald Center for the Study of Islam and Christian-Muslim Relations at Hartford Seminary. Public television produced a television documentary about our work titled *The Road to Morocco: Jews, Christians and Muslims in Dialogue*. The documentary chronicles the attempts by Jews, Christians, and Muslims in the Greater Hartford area to understand each other's traditions from the inside out. We took seventy members of our dialogue groups of Jews, Christians, and Muslims to Morocco to experience one of the few places that we felt that we could safely travel to where all three religious groups' traditional life still can be found together and where the government actually was interested in promoting the life of these diverse groups for tourism. It was a very moving experience for all of us, and public television was able to capture the spirit of the *convivencia* that had earlier been found in ancient Spain. It was, by all accounts, an important source of goodwill and interest in the community. I personally invested an enormous amount of time and effort to maintain these "tri-alogues," and I felt it was rewarding and important for the intellectual life of the University of Hartford. Since 9/11, these tri-alogues have become more and more difficult to maintain, but they are an intellectual interest of mine and remain so to this day. These things came together as reasons for my choice to work in Spain at this particular site: my professional interest in the Jewish archaeology that might be found, and my personal interests and abilities in Spanish and the ancient "tri-alogue" of Spain.

Not to overstate the beautiful relations between Jews, Christians, and Muslims in ancient Spain, in the period of *convivencia* the Jews and Christians were put into a *dhimmi* (protected minority) status that enabled them to live within Muslim society with restrictions to their economic and personal lives. For example, there was a poll tax, or *jizya*, that non-Muslim males over the age of fifteen had to pay to the Muslim leadership, in addition to a community land tax. A measure of religious freedom allowed the Jews to function (as well as Christians who remained) as a community under special minority conditions. We have good documentation about this period. In some of these documents the leaders (with all of their appropriate titles) are writing about a history that was unfolding and that they knew was unique. Rabbi Hasdai Ibn Shaprut, the resh kallah, and Rabbi Samuel ibn Nagrela, the nagid of the tenth century, and the Ibn Ezra family in the eleventh century show that the situation in Spain was a place for active and positive interaction with Jews and Christians in this period. But there were also sporadic riots and fanatical rulers, such as the Islamic Fatimids in the early eleventh century, and like the uprising in Granada in 1066 that marked the beginning of the end for the Golden Age of Spain in Jewish history.

The famous period of the *convivencia* began in the ninth century and continued until the Almohades (followers of a brand of fundamental Islam) took over in the twelfth century. The Jews were ready to accept the reconquest of Spain by Christian forces in the late twelfth century and early thirteenth century because the Almohades did not foster *convivencia*.

Many of the Jews of the south in this period fled northward; the Jews of the north cast their lot with Christian leaders, who were more tolerant than the Muslim leaders of the south. The northern Christian kingdoms were now in need of this Jewish leadership to provide bridges to the local economy, trade, and other basic communal needs. Documents from this period indicate that some of the Jews moved into royal fortresses in Tudela, close to Burgos, usually under the protection of the king or local leadership. It is possible that during this period the basic framework of the Jewish quarter of Burgos, as it was constructed in its last archaeological incarnation, was finished. The synagogue and Jewish quarter near and inside the fortress city would date from the twelfth century, when Jews began to feel the insecurity of their position. During our excavation, we were lucky to have the assistance of one of the foremost experts on the Jews in this region consult with us. Professor Juan José García of the University of Burgos gave us his own insights into the Jewish community of Burgos. Although there had been Jewish life in this area from much earlier (even back to the first century CE), it was clear from the beginning of our work that the real synagogue and Jewish quarter that lay buried in this area were from the period of the *Reconquista* (literally, "reconquest"; refers to a time when the Christians were regaining control of Spain) and not the earlier period. It was a Jewish community that had already put itself under the protection of the royal family in Burgos by virtue of its location so near the fortress. In the thirteenth century we have documentation of a positive role for the Jews (and some Muslims) in Christian Spain. Judah ben Lavi de la Cabaleria achieved a high rank in Saragossa, and in Castile the physicians in the family of Ibn Waqar were close with the family of King Sancho IV. All of this created a form of the *convivencia*, this time for Jews and Christians in Christian Spain to live together in peace. This chapter is not about a single personality in Judaism or Christianity in classical Roman period archaeology, but it is about how Jewish archaeology from the earlier period affects our understanding of a place where little is known. A fifteenth-century church was built over the twelfth-century synagogue of Burgos, and this became a microcosm of the relations between Judaism, Christianity, and Islam in Spain.

The problem was that the discovery of a major church from the time after the expulsion of the Jews from Spain that had been built over the synagogue of Burgos was only one of the pieces of our work. In order to interpret why the synagogue was destroyed (on purpose or by accident), we have to understand a little about the social history of the Jews in this time period. The period following the Crusades was for many Christian countries an identity crisis. Jewish communities had been involved in helping to finance many of the Crusader campaigns in Christian communities in need of help, and this debt was a significant part of the economy. The defeat of the Crusaders at the hands of the Muslims and the return of thousands of (now unemployed) ex-Crusaders to a debt-ridden country at the end of the thirteenth century did not create an easy situation for the Jewish communities that had financed the exercise. The Jews were expelled from England by Edward I, and in France there were sporadic expulsions of Jews in different communities starting in the beginning of the fourteenth century. The sheer numbers of Jews in Spain in the fourteenth century and their place and status in all areas of the Iberian Peninsula makes Spain a unique case. Scholars do not agree as to the number of Jews in Spain at the time, but estimates range from millions (or 10 to 20 percent of the population) to 3 to 4 percent of the population. The other European Jews in need of refuge in Spain may have contributed to the situation that developed in the late 1380s in Spain.

The disturbances began in Seville on June 6, 1391. Two synagogues were converted into churches, and there were a series of murders and robberies both of very "socially and politically connected" families as well as the entire Jewish community. The murders, robberies, and taking of synagogues continued from south to north over the next four months. The numbers of victims runs from a high of ten thousand throughout the country to a low of a few thousand. But the main damage was to the property of the Jews and the mass conversions forced upon the Jews following their capture. This was a turning point in the history of religions in Europe. The Muslims retreated to Muslim enclaves in North Africa to ensure that they did not get caught up in this new wave of anti-Semitism, but the old mosques were also converted to churches.

It is clear that the synagogue and the Burgos Jewish quarter that was near the Castilo where we were working were victims of the 1391 pogroms that ravaged the area in August 1391. In other places around southern Spain, much reconstruction has been done of some of the Jewish quarters and synagogues, but not in northern Spain. The building of a church from a synagogue was not unheard of in Spain—if anything, by the end of 1391 it was an acceptable alternative to the complete annihilation of the Jewish community.

Two methods persist of appropriation by the Church of property in Spain, and both were part of our investigation in Burgos. The first involved seizing the building by force and destroying it. Once destroyed, any number of uses for the property would be suitable, but in places such as Cervera, Montblanch, and perhaps Burgos, it is possible that the synagogues were indeed destroyed and not reused. The second method of appropriation involved seizing the building and reusing or adapting it to new purposes. If it had been a building with a religious purpose such as a synagogue or a mosque, it could easily be reused or adapted as a church. This seems to be the case in the cities of Seville, Lerida, Barcelona, and Tarragona, and also in the south of the country. In fact, some of the most famous historical churches of Spain date from this same period. In Toledo, in the south of Spain, both methods are found. Many synagogues were destroyed, but others were adapted for use as churches. One finds, for example, the famous synagogue (22 meters by 28 meters) of Joseph ibn Shushan that was built in the second half of the thirteenth century, then confiscated by the Church and turned into the Church of Santa Maria la Blanca of Toledo in the fifteenth century. Two central colonnades were decorated with glazed tiles. Similarly, the synagogue (9.5 meters by 23 meters) of Samuel Ha-Levi Abulafia, minister of Pedro the Cruel, that was built in the fourteenth century was turned into the El Tránsito Church in the fifteenth century. The last form of the Church of Nuestra Señora de la Blanca of Burgos was much larger than the synagogues of this era, at 60 meters by 33 meters. It is possible that the additions were added to the original size of 40 meters by 26 meters, and it is clear that there is construction present from the thirteenth century. It was also therefore possible that the Church of Burgos was in fact the synagogue of Burgos adapted and changed to fit the needs of the church. Generally, if a synagogue were built in the Moorish design with rich ornamentation and carved decoration, one might expect that the original synagogue would contain four long arcades, a flat-beam ceiling, with horseshoe-like columns, and five bays or naves. The Burgos synagogue may have been an adaptation of the style of synagogue that was well known in medieval Europe and the Middle East. The Burgos church included five naves and rich ornamentation with examples of ceramics that were found *in situ*. The colored pieces in particular may date back to the twelfth and thirteenth centuries. In principle, therefore, it is possible to conceive of the adaptation of the synagogue of Burgos, rather than its destruction followed by the total reconstruction of a church on top of it.

The Muslims in the south had somehow maintained throughout the end of the fourteenth and fifteenth centuries a form of civil relations with the Jews. Starting at the end of the fourteenth century, the Jews were not as welcome in some of the kingdoms of northern Spain as they had been less than two centuries earlier in the reconquered territories of the Christian rulers of Spain. The differences between the treatment of the Jews in the north and south of the country in these different periods is crucial for understanding what happened next. Especially chilling are the descriptions of the pre-*reconquista* and post-*reconquista* handling of Jews in the north. Yitzhak Baer, in his monumental *A History of the Jews in Christian Spain*, describes the period before the reconquering in glowing terms:

> Bonds of friendship beyond the boundaries of communities and countries were woven between men of wealth and culture. Benvenist de la Cavallería in Saragossa, Joseph Orabuena in Tudela and Meir Alguadex in Toledo made their homes centers of culture for Spanish Jewry. The [Don Solomon] Halevi and Benveniste families in Burgos, the Matut family in Guadalajara, the de la Cavallería and Alazar families in Saragossa formed and maintained friendships with the great scholars of Catalonia—friendships that were renewed whenever opportunity offered, at weddings and the like.

Many scholars now think that the beginning of the problems between the Jews and Christians in Spain did not start in 1391 but rather more than a century before that. The year 1263 ushered in a period of disputations with the local Catholic church of Barcelona, and things were moving in a different direction before the "public disputations" period began. The disputations never seemed to resolve any theological or practical problem between the Jews and the Christians but were more an attempt to systematically answer the same series of challenges that Christians presented to the Jews in a formal attempt to achieve mass conversion. These generally ended with Jews mildly correcting the Jewish convert to Christianity who acted as the Christian interlocutor. In a famous case in 1263, King James I gave Fra Paulo Christiani, a Jewish convert to Christianity, and Rabbi Moses ben Nahman (Nahmanides) a public forum to debate the issue of Jesus's messiahship for a period of four days in the royal court. Fra Paulo attempted to prove "from our Talmud that the Messiah of whom the prophets had witnessed had already come."

Nahmanides was very specific, as was every disputation after this period. He had developed already the very modern skill that later became a hallmark of the scientific method of contextualizing historical information. He began by stating:

> Did [Fra Paulo] wish to say that the scholars who appear in the Talmud believed concerning Jesus, that he was the Messiah and that they believed he was completely man and truly God in accordance with the Christian conceptions of him? Was it not indeed a known fact that Jesus existed in the days of the Second Temple, being born and put to death before the destruction of the Temple? But the scholars of the Talmud were later than this destruction, for example, Rabbi Akiba and his associates. And those who taught the Mishnah, Rabbi Judah the Prince and Rabbi Nathan, lived at a time that was many years after the destruction; and much more remote from that event was Rabbi Ashi who composed the Talmud and reduced it to writing, for he belonged to a period of about four centuries later.

The debate continued, and as Nahmanides relates it:

> On the day appointed, the king came to a convent that was within the city bounds, where was assembled all the male population, both Gentiles and Jews. There were present the bishop, all of the priests, the scholars of the Minorites [the Franciscans] and the Preaching Friars [the Dominicans]. Fra Paulo, my opponent stood up to speak, when I, intervening, requested our lord the king that I should now be heard. The king replied that Fra Paulo should speak first because he was the petitioner. But I urged that I should now be allowed to express my opinion on the subject of the Messiah and then afterwards he, Fra Paulo, could reply on the question of accuracy.

These were real events, with real implications for the Jews of a city. In the case of Nahmanides, he obviously thought that he had succeeded in holding his own and concludes his account by saying, "On the morrow I had audience of our lord the king whose words to me were: 'Return to your city in safety and in peace.' Then he gave me three hundred dinars and I took leave of him with much affection. May God make him worthy of the life of the world to come. Amen." But it did not end there. Despite the results, the Dominicans claimed victory; when Nahmanides published his own version of the dispute, a public burning of the report was ordered and Nahmanides himself was accused of blasphemy and banished in 1264. He ended up in Israel, but he remained in contact with the families and happenings of Spain. As we shall see, these same circumstances would play themselves out again in Burgos, but this time with extreme ferocity.

It All Began in Burgos . . .

Perhaps it was destined that I would go to Burgos to find evidence of the last formal usage of the title "Teacher of Righteousness." I have made three discoveries about the Teacher of Righteousness in my archaeological work. First, we discovered what I think is the grave of the Teacher of Righteousness at Qumran in 2002. In chapter 6 of my 2009 book *Digging through the Bible*, I write about the discovery of the Teacher of Righteousness in great detail, but it is clear that our discovery in the cemetery of Qumran was worthy of world attention. The Teacher of Righteousness was the leader of the group who wrote at least some of the Dead Sea Scrolls and who challenged Jerusalem and the priests of the Temple of Jerusalem in the centuries before the destruction of the Temple in 70 CE. The views that are contained in the scrolls vary, but the most overpowering ideas that emerge from this group are their apocalyptic, end-of-the-world prophecies, which precede anything in the New Testament and lay the theological groundwork for the later book of Revelation. In a way, that would make the Qumranites' Teacher of Righteousness one of the most important religious figures in all history and probably the one that we know the least about. First, the Jews seemed to have embraced the concept of a quasi-messianic and prophetic figure such as the Teacher of Righteousness not only at Qumran but also in later rabbinic circles in which the term appears again.

As I wrote in *Digging through the Bible*, I think that the title "Teacher of Righteousness" was like the title "rabbi," passed on from generation to generation. If we learn anything from the Jewish experience it is that Jewish leadership took many different forms. The Jews who remained in the historic land of Israel created a whole subset of terms, from the *Av Bet Din* ("Head of the Court") and the *Nasi* (literally "Prince") to the Babylonian Jews' specific titles of leadership such as *Gaon*, *Resh Galuta*, *Nagid*, and *Resh Kallah*, among many others. Jews seemed to have enjoyed creating new titles that fit new roles of leadership, and the idea of a *Moreh HaTzedek* (Hebrew word for "Teacher of Righteousness") seems to have fit well with the different models of biblical and postbiblical Judaism. Many scholars did not agree with me. They thought that the Teacher of Righteousness was one person in the second century BCE and that the title was never used again. In my research, I discovered the title "Teacher of Righteousness" once again in the rabbinic literature, and in inscriptions on Byzantine period synagogues. I concluded that the title was known to Jews for hundreds of years after the Qumran settlement had been destroyed. The third time I discovered "Teacher of Righteousness" was in Burgos, Spain. Abner of

Burgos was the last and perhaps most problematic of all of the people who used the title, but his use of the term indicates that either this is a very big coincidence (the use of a very specific and unusual term) or that the title "Teacher of Righteousness" had survived nearly fifteen hundred years of use among Jews as the "true" leader of the Jews of Spain.

Abner of Burgos

Burgos (170,000 population) is located on the new A-1 route, two hours north of Madrid, and is halfway between the new Bilbao, site of the Guggenheim Museum's new branch in Spain, and Madrid. The choice for our excavations in Burgos at the site of the fifteenth-century church built over or on the remains of the twelfth-century synagogue could not have been more meaningful. The good, the bad, and the distasteful between Christians and Jews took place in Burgos. The problems can be traced back to the incitement of one individual from the city of Burgos: Abner of Burgos. He had a very mystical bent and was a Jewish scholar who converted to Christianity in 1321 and became known as Alfonso of Valladolid. Abner wrote a polemic text describing why the Jews should convert to Christianity, which he called *Moreh Tzedek*, or "Teacher of Righteousness" (in Spanish, *Mostrador de Justicia*). Now, it is a possibility that it was simply a coincidence that the title of the leader of the opposition to Jerusalem at Qumran and the leader of the synagogue (who was not the rabbi) were called by the same title: the *Teacher of Righteousness*. A former student of Abner, Rabbi Isaac Policar, wrote his own treatise countering Abner's, titled *Iggeret HeHarefot*, or the "Letter of Blasphemies," in which Policar tried to defend Judaism and criticized the motives of Abner.

It is in this period that Abner of Burgos began to convince the Spanish authorities that the Jews must be deprived of their livelihoods in moneylending and medicine and of all the autonomy that had been accorded them through the thirteenth century in Christian Spain. He died in 1348, the year of the infamous Black Plague, but his legacy in Burgos affected our understanding of what happened at the church/synagogue of Santa Maria that we were investigating. Later, thanks to Abner's efforts, priests and bishops throughout the kingdom began to agitate against the privileges that the Jews had achieved in northern Spain. Although Abner's writings may have only influenced a small part of the violence, they were a symptom of the greater problem that Jews faced in this time period. The threat was from within and from outside the Jewish community. Starting in 1390, there was a call from certain Christian leaders to destroy synagogues, baptize different Jewish groups, and institute new tax policies that created even more difficulties for the Jews. By June 1391, these official anti-Jewish proclamations were issued in many Jewish communities, from Seville to Segovia, and the Jews there were under assault. The political leaders had earlier protected the Jews from the masses, but this changed dramatically. In Burgos (as appears from records of the following year), rioters from the slums attacked the Jewish quarter several days after the proclamations were issued. The Jews left the fortress (which during the wars of the kings in northern Spain had proved impregnable until the most advanced military techniques were used against it in the nineteenth century) and took refuge in the homes of Christians situated below the fortress. Some of the Jews of Burgos were baptized and a whole quarter inhabited by apostates (*conversos*, Jews who converted to Christianity) soon sprang up. Other Jews in Burgos, who remained loyal to their faith, asked for and received from the government a written guarantee of political and economic protection. They were allowed to return to their former lives in some form. There can be no doubt but that the number of these faithful was also very small, and the others converted, embraced Christianity, and even became leaders in the Church.

Probably in July 1391, Solomon Halevi, now known as Pablo of Santa Maria, went to Paris to study Christian theology and ultimately became the bishop of Burgos (1406). His views on science and religion were extremely affected by this experience, and he attempted to use his knowledge of the Talmud, Maimonides, and other Jewish writers to validate theological proofs on behalf of the Church. His most famous series of letters involve the messianic prophecies that were fulfilled by Jesus of Nazareth, but more important, he was able to show how the Talmudic passages related to Jesus and Christianity were incorrect. Joshua Halorki, the famous ex-Jewish Burgos resident, became a key player in the entire Spanish Christian drama that would play itself out in the fifteenth century. Halorki, a former acquaintance of Halevi, entered into a polemic with Halevi over his interpretations of the Jesus passages found in rabbinic texts. Halorki was unsuccessful in bringing Halevi back to the fold and ultimately succumbed himself and converted (he became known as Hieronymus de Sancta Fide).

He played a larger role in the later disputation of Tortosa in 1413–1414, this time on the Christian side, providing sources (often counterfeit rabbinic passages) from *midrashim* (rabbinic writings) and texts that were used by the Christian disputants in ways that trivialized the rabbinic texts and were used to denigrate the Jewish religion. The treatise used as the basis of the disputation was available in Hebrew and Latin, and Pope

Benedict XIII used it as the pretext for most of the nearly two-year ordeal. The main scholars from the Jewish side, gathered together within Tortosa, included Rabbi Joseph Albo, a leading Jewish philosopher of the period, and rabbis from the north and south of the country. Although the legal obstacles to Jews were framed against "Jews and Muslims," the main target remained the Jews. The disputation of Tortosa in 1413 was the beginning of the end of any public role for the Jews in Spain. This dispute hinged upon proving from the Jewish texts, essentially the Talmud, that the Jews should legitimately accept Jesus as the Messiah. The dispute twisted and turned on scholastic understandings of the Messiah. The debate continued for months; starting in January, continuing to May 1413, when Hieronymus, the main appointed Christian disputant, submitted questions on the birthplace of the Messiah, the miraculous birth, his divinity, and the sin of Adam and Eve and its remission through the atonement of the Messiah, among others. Conversions of local Jews began in anticipation of the outcome. The disputation went on until December 1414 but continued afterward with the censorship of the Talmud. It is likely that after this time period, the Church of Nuestra Señora de la Blanca was built in Burgos in celebration of the famed dispute. The previous excavation work at the church indicates that some of the reconditioning of the structures dates from 1424. By the mid-fifteenth century, there were very few Jews left in the old Castile. Their freedoms became so restricted that by the time the Order of Expulsion came in 1492, there were very few left anyway.

The Inquisition that followed in the mid- to late fifteenth century was to ensure the "purity" of the already converted Jews (*conversos*), and it was, at first, not directed at the small groups of remaining Jews in Spain but rather the converted Jews. The Dominican, Tomas de Torquemada, was appointed inquisitor-general of both Aragon and Castile in 1483. As the Inquisition took hold in other parts of the country, Burgos was exempted from being a center of inquiry in the period following 1484. This perhaps indicates that the population of Jews was so diminished (or nonexistent) in the area that it did not present a challenge to the Church or the New Christians. In any case, by 1492, all of this was a moot point. The Order of Expulsion left only Christians in Burgos, and the Church of Nuestra Señora de la Blanca was purposely built on top of the synagogue to ensure that no memory of the synagogue would remain. The following centuries of existence for the church were cut short by the French occupation and finally the War of Independence for Spain. The French military changes to the famous Burgos church between 1808 and 1813 resulted in its final destruction in the waning days of June 1813. We began our own 2005 excavations based on the maps of the French.

The 2005 University of Hartford Excavations

As if on a Hollywood backlot, the Castillo (the city's fortress) and the church are depicted in most drawings from the sixteenth century onward as a symbol of the joint forces of Spain: the Church and the political leadership of the area. The church and the Castillo of Burgos are on top of a natural rise overlooking the city, providing a measure of importance and distance from the general population. They sit high above the cityscape of this city in Spain that is over twelve hundred years old. Our mission was to see if there were remains of the ancient Jewish community still present underneath the La Blanca church and to figure out how and where the Jews lived in relation to the medieval fortress. In the process, we discovered the secret of ancient tunnels dug into the limestone base of the Castillo that has been the subject of enormous speculation by Spanish archaeologists.

We began with a ground-penetrating radar and magnetometry survey of the church area to see if the remains of the ancient synagogue could

Courtesy of the University of Hartford Burgos Project

Figure 4.2.   The medieval *Hanukiya* (Hanukkah candelabrum) in the Burgos Castle Museum

still be found. (The church was destroyed in the Spanish war of independence against the French in 1813, and the present location is now an open children's park next to the massive Castillo.) This was done in two days. We met with the archaeologist who had excavated the church in the 1990s, Dr. Ana Maria Ortega Martinez, who showed us the remains of a synagogue that were found in a pit in the southeast corner of the excavation. A *Hanukiyyah* (medieval Hanukkah Menorah) had been found along with Jewish pottery. Ana also told us about her hunches. It was her work that had raised the possibility that the ancient synagogue could indeed still be found below the church. Although she did not excavate there, right behind the Castillo to the north, she showed us a series of burials—a necropolis, which she believed was the Jewish cemetery from the Middle Ages. The Jewish community, she said, probably lived in the Castillo after the period of the 1391 persecutions, protected by the king. She speculated that the Jewish community had to find a way of burying their dead in a time when the population of Burgos no longer wanted the Jewish community there. Their cemetery is thus behind the fortress, and she suggested it was probably connected to this cemetery with a now hidden tunnel that led directly into the Castillo.

Ana suggested we meet with the eminent Castillian historian of the Middle Ages, Dr. Juan José García, at the University of Burgos. I phoned him and he came right up. He too was excited about our excavations of the La Blanca church and the fortress. His theory was that the Jewish community was marginalized in the beginning of its stay in Burgos and lived up on top of the hill, by the synagogue. They then moved down the hill to a Jewish and Muslim quarter on the edge of the city—the suburbs—in the "good years," from the eleventh to the twelfth centuries, and then in the thirteenth and fourteenth centuries, as the situation deteriorated, they moved back to the top of the hill. It is important, he noted, that the famous historical, mythical, and literary figure El Cid (Rodrigo Diaz de Vivar) married a woman from the Burgos area and spent his "good years" in this city—perhaps an allusion to the opportunity to bring Christians, Muslims, and Jews into a diverse Spanish society in a place such as Burgos. El Cid's slogan of "Out of diversity unity" became the watchword of that time, and the Jews of the Burgos area are a part of the famous poem.

The cathedral is itself a strange amalgamation of symbols that seem to indicate that the Jews who converted to Christianity in the post-1391 era had tried to find ways to give some dignity to their ancient heritage. For example, in one of the last building phases of the cathedral, the ex-Jew Archbishop Alfonso de Cartagena built a monument for his own tomb there in the mid-fifteenth century. The Santa Maria entrance is framed by what appears to be a *magen David* (star of David). This may have been an attempt to pay homage to the Jewish heritage of the two ex-Jewish archbishops, Alfonso and his father, Pablo de Santa Maria.

So it appeared that the tenth-/eleventh-century synagogue was turned into the Church of Nuestra Señora de la Blanca, much the same way as it happened in Toledo (see earlier in this chapter). "I think it happened before the 1391 persecutions," Professor Juan José García told me. His insights were important. He had graduate students working on fourteenth-century records of Jewish properties, so he had resources to call upon for his information. To him, it seemed that the tide was already turning against the Jews in the early part of the fourteenth century in Burgos. He thanked me by giving me sixteen volumes of his research on the original documents of Burgos and its Jewish population. He knew little about Judaism, but he knew an enormous amount about the Jews of fourteenth-century Burgos. It was the first time I heard how Europeans could so easily separate the ethnic identity of the Jews from their religious identity. He was interested in our excavations, as were many others in the city.

The Castillo, or fortress, is massive. The size of a professional football stadium, it was built in the thirteenth and fourteenth centuries (and improved up until the nineteenth century) and was restored in 2003, and it is the pride of northern Spain's tourist industry. We concluded immediately that we needed to see the inner workings of the fortress. We were treated to a tour of the Castillo, now returned to all of its grandeur by the Spanish archaeologist who excavated and restored it, Silvia Rodriguez (who just happened to be our partner in the La Blanca church excavations). She introduced us immediately to an interesting mystery about the church building. There was a 70-meter-deep well (210 feet) that was constructed in the Middle Ages using very sophisticated technology, with stairs leading down. The water table was far down. To build such a well was an enormous engineering feat in the Middle Ages. Radiating out from the well were tunnels chopped away in the limestone, forming a series of outlets. When we asked her why the tunnels were there and where they led, she responded, "I think they were to defend the water, but we really do not know." Why build tunnels that seemingly go out the back of the fortress to protect the water? When we checked, it was clear that the tunnels led out the back of the fortress to the north. We were determined to figure out if there was anything important to the north. It turned out to be a simple answer. Right beyond the fortress lay the necropolis of the Jews that Ana García Martinez had pointed out to us. The tunnels were actually a secret passageway that allowed the Jews in and out of the fortress through the Jewish cemetery, without being in the sightline of the Burgos Christian mobs. They were probably built in the last period of the Jewish occupation, in the fourteenth and early fifteenth centuries, right before the Inquisition began, which ended in the Expulsion in August 1492. My interest in tunnels and hideaways of this type was sparked by a recent archaeological parallel that was found in Jewish sites all over Israel. Apparently both before and after the first and second rebellions against the Romans, Jews had begun creating specific hideaways in the villages and cities where they lived to ensure that they had places of refuge and easy ingress and exit. Many people built tunnels and hideaways, but the Jews made this into a type of ethnic marker, which when we know about the conditions of the period helps elucidate a feature that would otherwise seem very random. That is one of the reasons why our work in Spain was so important. We brought with us a whole set of different expertise and understandings that helped contextualize the archaeology in a new and meaningful way.

Our geophysical survey lasted for one week and finished on July 31, 2005. We were able to find the remains of the synagogue beneath the remains of the church and even suggested ways to excavate the synagogue without destroying what was left of the church. The Spaniards would continue with the maps if they wished to excavate the synagogue. We went throughout Spain and discovered that there was a very acute interest in excavating sites where the Jews had lived, worked, prayed, and died. In some areas where the Jews had been gone for over five hundred years, new restorations and conservation projects had popped up, and indeed many different Jewish cemeteries, neglected for half a millennium, were suddenly cared for.

The geophysics did indeed inform the literary records of the period. Two very important aspects of the synagogue presented themselves for further investigation. By mapping the water sources and one specifically deep area of the "synagogue" beneath the church, we speculated about the existence of a *mikveh* (ritual bath) in one particular area of the synagogue, based upon our knowledge of other synagogues elsewhere that in the Middle Ages would place the *mikveh* inside the synagogue if the hydrology was right. We presented our reports and maps of the subsurface to the Spanish archaeologists of the region who worked with us, and they are now in charge of future excavations. Like our later work in the Doña Ana Park, the follow-up excavations are in the hands of the local archaeologists.

Over five hundred years after the Inquisition, the Jews are returning to Spain—but they are very often not the same Jews who left. Today, Jewish

Figure 4.3.   The tunnels and burial places of the Jews near the castle

Courtesy of Philip Reeder, University of South Florida

migrations from Latin American tragedies of anti-Semitism and dictator-ships have established new congregations in some of the major Spanish cities. There are also Jewish refugees from Morocco, who often call them-selves *Mizrahi* (literally, "Eastern" in Hebrew) who arrived after finding themselves unwelcome in their own country in and after 1948 (following the establishment of the State of Israel). They were able to go "back" to Spain—despite the fact that Spain did not officially welcome Jews back into the country until the 1990s—and reestablish themselves in small numbers in Spanish-speaking congregations after 1948 (and in some cases even earlier). In 2006, I took a group of University of Hartford students to Spain to visit Jewish sites, including our excavation site in Burgos. We were surprised at how many places around Spain had established museums and sites devoted to Jewish life in Spain from over five hundred years ago. I did not want my students to leave Spain thinking that the history of the Jews in Spain had completely ended in 1492, and that there were no signs of modern Jewish life. I was happy to be able to show them that it contin-ues in small congregations in the south and north of Spain with this new generation of Jews who have made Spain their home for the first time in over five hundred years. It reminded me that this is part of the reason why I decided to write this book in the first place. History does not always fol-low clean and direct patterns. It can be what is best described as "messy"—following irregular patterns. The relations between the religious histories of Islam, Christianity, and Judaism in a place such as Spain can be uneven and not easy to track except by following the parallel tales, as I have tried to do in this chapter. There will always be "official" histories, which will compare and contrast the official channels of power in a country. But there is another history that is written by the people's actions. I am still stunned by how Spain has embraced its past by re-creating the pre-1492 Jewish sites. An excavation of a Jewish site such as the synagogue of Burgos is a part of Spanish and European history as well as Jewish history.

Writing about Jewish history in a place such as Spain is especially mud-dled since it is so influenced by conditions that were so beyond the control of the Jews. The entire experience of Spain for the Jews was bittersweet. It began as a journey from Israel in the first century CE after the destruction of the Temple in Jerusalem and continued for over fourteen hundred years with good and bad experiences. The Jews of the time of the fourteenth-century Church and during the *reconquista* thought that they would survive the violence and the "cleansing" process, and that they would ultimately straighten things out with the ruling authorities and return to living in their beloved Spain. In the twelfth century, for example, Jews in southern Spain were threatened by a fundamentalist Muslim government that ultimately forced many of them out of southern Spain into northern Spain and thus into the Diaspora. It is difficult to unreservedly characterize the Jewish experience in Spain as an example of modern tolerance and enlightenment; even the so-called "Golden Age" was only tolerant by comparison with the worst of the regimes that followed. The Jewish experience under the Christians was one of unity, disunity, and then rabid anti-Judaism, the likes of which would only reappear in the time of the seventeenth-century Chmielnicki Rebellion in eastern Europe and then in the twentieth-century Holocaust.

The history of the Jews of Spain is similar to the cultural forces I have described in *Digging through the Bible* and in the early chapters of this book. It required an enormous amount of faith for the Jews of Spain to remain loyal Spaniards from the period of the *reconquista* through the period of the Inquisition and the Expulsion. I tried to imagine whether this expulsion was better or worse than the expulsion of the ancient Judeans from Judea in the sixth century BCE or after the Bar Kokhba Revolt. In a sense, the Jews and Muslims had a choice—not a very good choice, but still a choice. They could stay and be Christians or leave and practice their own religions wherever they could. All the while, the Jews who stayed in Spain during the fourteenth and fifteenth centuries thought that the situation would turn itself around, but it did not. It was this final point that haunted my thoughts when we began our work in Poland. In Poland, during the Holocaust, the Jews had no choices.

All history changes in unexpected and sometimes unusual ways, and the lasting impact of a single period may have unintended consequences upon a later period. In Spain, we found that the resourcefulness of the Jews, Christians, and Muslims can be seen in the archaeological remains, and that the remains continue to be a force in the modern history of Spain. In every one of the archaeological treks in this book, I began by trying to help my students experience history through archaeology and to shed light upon how we can understand the interaction of different religions through the archaeological record in addition to the available textual information. Our work at Burgos and the chronicling of the horrific history of the buildup to the *Reconquista*, the Inquisition, and the Expulsion of the Jews from Spain in 1492 serve as a foreshadowing to the last and final chapter of this book, "Mysteries of Religion and Archaeology in the 'Hidden Holocaust.'"

Mysteries of Religion and Archaeology in the "Hidden Holocaust" 5

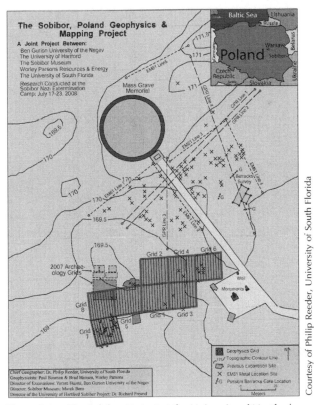

Figure 5.1.　The Sobibor Project at the University of Hartford

The night before the Revolt [at Sobibor in 1943] we said
our goodbyes and cried and then we fell asleep. I had a dream
that night. My mother came to me. I told her, in the dream,
"what are you doing here?" She took my hand and walked
through the front gate [of the camp]. She showed me to a barn.
I escaped with Samuel, but it didn't go as planned. I jumped a
fence. Grazed by a bullet I grabbed a girl for help. She pushed
me away and took a bullet and died. I don't blame her or me,
it just happened.

—INTERVIEW CONDUCTED WITH ESTHER RAAB, VINELAND, NEW
JERSEY, ON THURSDAY, AUGUST 28, 2008, BY SARAH RUTMAN,
UNIVERSITY OF HARTFORD ALUMNA

Beginning with Atlantis and Ending with the Holocaust

I WOULD HAVE WANTED TO END A BOOK titled *Digging through History* with an uplifting discovery that gives us great hope for humanity. It did not work out that way. I have worked primarily in the ancient period for the past thirty years. Although I studied the modern period as part of my undergraduate and graduate studies, I made a conscious decision not to spend my time teaching and researching topics in the modern period. In retrospect that is an absurd consideration, since everything we do in archaeology starts with the modern period and works backward. When a site is discovered, even if it has a Bronze Age foundation, it exists in the modern period and things have happened that inevitably affect the way the site is understood. You must always account for the historical layers that precede the one in which you ultimately might be interested. This requires us to work with specialists in almost every period, and every single archaeological project can be said to be "digging through history." But working on a site associated with the Holocaust in 2008 was something for which I was not fully prepared. It was a strange juxtaposition for two back-to-back projects to represent the origins of civilization and the near end of civilization—a 2008 project associated with the Holocaust in Poland and a 2009 project associated with Atlantis in Spain. I might add that both projects are still ongoing as I write what I learned from both. The two projects could not have been any more different than one another—except for the fact that we used the exact same technologies to aid the archaeologists and the same comparative methods of research in investigating both. One traced what we know about the beginnings of civilization at Atlantis through the writings of a single source, Plato, and the material culture from the site and by following the refugees and their journeys from the destroyed city. The second project illuminated what we know about one of the darkest parts of civilization at Sobibor, a Nazi extermination camp, through the writings of survivors and the material culture from the site and by following the refugees and their journeys to and from the camp. There is a strange mapping coincidence that our cartographer for both projects noticed after finishing his work at Atlantis and Sobibor. The one entrance in and out of Atlantis's concentric circle port eerily resembled the one entrance in and out of Sobibor. These two maps unintentionally represent two bookends of history.

The Unspeakable Crime: The Losses and Legacies of Sobibor and Atlantis

The chapter on Atlantis is not really a history of Atlantis nor is this chapter intended to be a complete history of the Holocaust. In one short book like this I did not have the space to fully outline the achievements of Atlantis nor could I trace the cultural and technological losses of a place like Atlantis. The inhabitants of Atlantis did not expect that they would suddenly have their entire tradition wiped out. I suspect that Plato was moved to write about Atlantis because he realized the loss to civilization and needed to describe the rise and fall of this place. The story of Atlantis has inspired generations of writers even until our own period for the same reason. History is replete with examples of devastation for us to study and attempt not to repeat the same mistakes. Plato's *Timaeus* and *Critias* are not just idle fascinations with the tale of an ancient civilization that is no more. He wrote his works to memorialize and quantify the loss by compiling details about architecture, people, religion, political system, art, and the advances of each. He also told a moral tale. Plato had a supreme sense of hope that by writing about how it began and how it ended he was providing future generations with a cautionary narrative about the fragility of civilization. Part of the reason why this book ends with the Holocaust is not because we have an idle fascination with the Holocaust but because, like Atlantis, the Holocaust provides a cautionary tale about how fragile our civilization is even in the modern period.

Like our search for the refugees from Atlantis, each chapter in this book has focused on some aspect of lives lived from ancient to modern periods. In the chapter on divine footprints we saw how people attempt to mark the appearance of the divine in their lives with concrete and physical reminders of their encounters with a transcendent force in the universe. The Atlantis chapter showed us how ancients tried to preserve their religious heritage by memorializing their ancient past in later architecture and iconography. The Dead Sea Scrolls chapter showed us why the scrolls were significant—not only because they were from an ancient group but also because they were hidden in the hopes that they would provide literary signposts for the future. The ancient people who hid the scrolls did not retrieve the scrolls themselves but they instead provided generations to come with a meaningful religious experience. As we have seen, the scrolls have influenced us. But as much as the scrolls have influenced our modern religious views, we, in turn, have influenced the interpretation of these scrolls with our own modern religious orientations.

In the chapter on medieval and premodern Spain the focus was on how the archaeology informs us about the religious interaction between the Jews, Christians, and Muslims who lived for over a thousand years in Spain and the sudden and almost inexplicable expulsion of the Jews and the Muslims in the fifteenth century. The expulsion of the Muslims and Jews from Spain is documented not only in the literature of the period but also in the destruction of the physical institutions of the Jews and Muslims of Spain. The final chapter on the Holocaust helps us better understand how civilization nearly came to an end as the violence and the planned destruction of the Jews (and other "undesirables") spiraled out of control into systematic and now technologically advanced extermination. The focus in preceding chapters has been on how archaeology can be used to study history through its enduring religious edifices and cultural remains. In this chapter we use archaeology to study the history of the period through the evidence of the institutions and technologies used to destroy cultural and human remains.

This chapter imparts firsthand knowledge of what happened in Europe in the 1930s and 1940s. It provokes the reader to understand why the Holocaust is the ultimate cautionary tale of history. The chapter gives a short history of the Holocaust to show not only what was destroyed but also how it was carried out. If we are to understand why the loss is important, we must understand more about the legacy. First, the Holocaust is not just a "genocide." Genocide is a horrible and unspeakable crime of humanity wherever it occurs, an attempt by one or multiple groups to wipe out another ethnic group, often through systematic violence that pits one group in society against another. The Holocaust was a form of genocide but was different, first because it was preceded by such a long and winding history of systematic violence against Jews. In addition, unlike other genocides, which are often not carefully planned and executed, the Holocaust was planned very meticulously using the highest levels of technological advancement and was executed by people who stood in the center of civilization in Europe. In many ways, the sophisticated technological innovations present at Atlantis that were used to advance their society are an interesting counterpoint with the Holocaust, which used technological innovations in the service of the extermination of the Jews and other undesirables. I learned working on this book how human genius and achievement can be used in the service of great good and great evil.

A Short History of the Holocaust

I could begin the history of the Holocaust in the nineteenth century with the rise of modern anti-Semitism—but I will not. Some histories of the Holocaust begin with anti-Judaism doctrines that were a part of European life from the late Roman period until the modern period. Some histories trace a direct line between the types of anti-Judaism doctrines that resulted in the expulsion of the Jews from Spain in 1492 to the Holocaust. It is true that the "purification of the blood" that the fifteenth-century Spanish implemented in the Inquisition and Expulsion were markedly different from the early anti-Judaic polemics that functioned from the Byzantine period onward. While early anti-Judaic polemics called for the Jews to accept the norms of Christianity against long-held Jewish views, the purification of the blood of the fifteenth century seemed to imply that there was little a Jew could do to be a part of Christian Europe. In the case of the Spaniards, many of the Jews who remained in Spain from the late fourteenth century cleansing and conversions were "infecting" both "old" and "newly professing" Christians. The problem was not just Judaism, the religion—it was also the Jew. They used terminology that would become amplified in the Holocaust. Even if Jews "converted," these "new" Christians were somehow "infecting" the purity of the race and religion. This idea that the undesirable could never make himself or herself acceptable through a religious conversion made possible the nineteenth-century European anti-Semitism. It was this form of anti-Semitism that made the very existence of the Jews an anathema. The Holocaust would not have been possible but for these earlier steps. For the purposes of this book, the Holocaust refers to the period between 1933 and 1945, in which the Jews and other people deemed by the Nazis in Germany as undesirables (homosexuals, gypsies, and Jehovah's Witnesses, among others) were first disenfranchised of their legal and human rights, dispossessed of all their businesses, trades, property, and assets, and then interned within concentration camps and ghettoes, mostly ending with their systematic destruction in methodically created extermination camps with specialized gassing facilities.

The Holocaust began in Germany and later spread to the countries the Nazis conquered. A debate erupted among historians in the 1980s over the origins of the Final Solution, divided between "intentionalists" and "functionalists." The intentionalists saw the Final Solution as the direct outcome of Hitler's policies and the long-term goal of the Nazi party before its rise to power. Functionalists argued for a "twisted road to Auschwitz" that was an outcome of either bureaucratic or structural developments, and not fully planned from start to finish.

I am an "intentionalist-functionalist." My view of history from Atlantis to the Holocaust has taught me that we have to beware of chains of events that, although not directly connected, are indirectly linked. As I stated in the first chapter, history is messy. It is rare to see that all of the factors line up to cause a single event. But after viewing the documents for the planning of the extermination camps and how the architects drew up these plans as a part of a "Final Solution of the Jewish Problem" formulated by the Nazis in the early part of the 1940s, it is hard not to trace the steps backward and see them as anything but planned. When the Nazis realized that they would be unable to "export" the undesirables to another location, nor were they able to have them killed through more conventional means (starvation, deprivation, firing squads, etc.), they came up with the diabolical Final Solution. Extermination camps were not the first step. They were the last step in a series of events that sealed the fates of millions and revealed much of what our civilization is capable. Most of the undesirables were not combatants, nor can they be categorized as dissidents in a search for rationalization. The victims were the very old, the very young, the weak and infirm, as well as those who were fit to serve in the national army on behalf of the state but were instead exterminated. The placement of extermination camps in far-flung areas of Poland, such as Sobibor (not in the heart of Nazi Germany), and mostly staffed by ragtag groups of local or regional enforcers (and not by Nazi soldiers), was far from accidental. It was a calculated attempt by the Nazis to spread the responsibility for the

Final Solution through the conquered Polish and Ukrainian populations and draw upon the deep-seated popular enmity in these areas toward the Jews.

Near the end of the war, many of the concentration camps (the jails for the Nazis' prisoners, which were located throughout Europe) were hurriedly converted into makeshift extermination camps—the Final Solution had become too large of a task even for the well-planned "official" extermination camps. Most people who went to extermination camps received numbers. The meticulous records kept about the transport of the victims to the camps represent one of the many ways that we may calculate those who were killed. The Sobibor camp is famous because it was one of the "planned" extermination camps of the Final Solution. It is also famous because on October 14, 1943, the inmates staged a successful rebellion that almost upended the Nazis' entire plan for the extermination of all the undesirables in all the camps.

1943

In August 1943, the Treblinka extermination camp in Poland was the site of a successful rebellion in which seventy prisoners escaped. However, it also resulted in the immediate killing of fifteen hundred prisoners. Then, on October 14, 1943, there was a successful rebellion at Sobibor. These two uprisings caused fear among the Nazi officials, who became afraid that other camps would rebel and chaos would break out in the well-oiled "Final Solution of the Jewish Question," mapped out in a meeting known as the Wannsee Conference that was held in Berlin in January 1942.

There had, in fact, been many successful small rebellions, both at Sobibor and other camps, but nothing had matched the scope of Sobibor's October 1943 rebellion. Up until the 1943 rebellion, it is estimated that up to 250,000 Jews had been transferred and killed at Sobibor. The rebellion is important because survivors of the rebellion told their story after the war and gave the kind of detail of life and death at the camp that informs us about how an extermination camp worked. Also, just over half of the six hundred prisoners present in the camp on the day of the rebellion escaped (some died in the minefields and some died in the weeks and months following) but only forty-seven of those escapees survived the war. The survivors of the Sobibor rebellion are unique because, unlike the survivors at other camps liberated in 1945, the Sobibor survivors felt very empowered by their act of rebellion and after the war

felt that this was a particularly important message for the Jewish people
in the post–World War II era.

The attempt to kill all of the Jews in Europe began in earnest in the
summer of 1942. The Jews and other undesirables realized by summer
1942 that their transport to and internment in these camps was different
from the earlier roundups. By summer 1942, inmates at a majority of the
extermination camps that were becoming operational realized they were
going to be killed soon after arrival, but they did not immediately rebel.
Many were weak, disoriented, and debilitated by the time they reached
the camps. The immediate selections gave some reason to hope that they
might live. Most of the Jewish inmates were not trained in military tac-
tics, nor were they able to plan an uprising. Why was Sobibor different?
It seems that the Jews who arrived at Sobibor in the summer and early
fall of 1943 in this far eastern part of Poland were different from the Jews
who had been transported to other parts of Poland. Some were captured
(Jewish) Soviet soldiers, and they were trained to fight back. But by the
time the rebellion broke out, nearly 250,000 Jews had been exterminated
at Sobibor.

The operation that brought Sobibor to functional efficiency was something that had nothing at all to do with Sobibor. "Operation Reinhard"
was named for Reinhard Heydrich, one of the Nazi architects of the
Final Solution. Heydrich died as a result of wounds suffered in an attack
by the Resistance movement in June 1942. In his honor, the stepped-
up exterminations at Treblinka, Bełżec, and Sobibor began. "Operation
Reinhard" officially ended after the Sobibor rebellion in October. Almost
any precipitating cause might have been used as a subterfuge for the pace
of the extermination, but the use of Reinhard's name gave Nazi officers
a pretext for the extermination camp's work. After the rebellion, the
Nazis made every attempt to cover up what had happened there. Between
October and December 1943, search parties rounded up as many rebels as
they could and shot them in the forests. They closed and exterminated the
labor camp at Luta, Poland (near Sobibor), and unfortunately, even Polish resistance fighters who were fighting the Nazis turned in some of the
Jewish rebels. Within ten weeks of the Sobibor rebellion, the Nazis began
the great deception of hiding Sobibor from the Poles, from the rest of the
Nazi hierarchy, and from other extermination camps by covering the camp
installations. The great irony is, of course, that in the Nazi attempt to cover
over the camp in the middle of the war, they inadvertently preserved evidence. Sobibor, unlike other extermination camps, presents a unique opportunity for understanding the mechanisms of the Final Solution. Other

Figure 5.2. The map of Poland projects

Courtesy of Philip Reeder, University of South Florida

camps were used right up until 1945, and following the liberation were badly preserved because of the rampant disease. Many camps at the end of World War II were thoroughly destroyed, dismantled, or burned out of fear of being discovered by Allied forces. As the Russians overran the camps in 1944–1945, many of these facilities in their sector were reused when possible for housing political prisoners. Sobibor, however, was different. It lay covered with dirt in the middle of a dense forest in what was a very unforgiving part of the country on the border with what is today the Ukraine. In many cases, all we have left are the memories of survivors who were in these camps and whatever physical evidence remains at the site. In the case of Sobibor, we have an abundance of information both from the memories of the survivors and at the site. In our Sobibor documentation project we used both.

Archaeology of the Mind:
Survivors as "Living Books"

In addition to the physical excavations of an archaeological site there is also a cultural archaeology of the people who lived at a site, their written materials and recollections that are often preserved in different literary forms, and the people who lived in the area at the same time who, although they did not live at the site, were indirectly connected to it. The ability to analyze these people is often in the realm of psychologists, but I call this "archaeology of the mind." In the case of Sobibor (and most of the Holocaust), an "archaeology of the mind" needs to be done as one sifts through the written and oral testimonies for information that links them with the camp. The idea of people as "living books" is a concept rooted in ancient religious folklore. What began as oral testimony and emerged into written texts over the centuries is what connects our project with ancient literary texts and modern archaeology. From Asia and Africa to South America and indigenous tribes around the world, we find that there were people within the group who were designated as "living books" and who kept the collective memory of people alive. They often possessed prodigious memories or they were a small part of a larger narrative (of many different "living books") that may never have been written down. Even the best of these "living books" are people with their own personal narratives woven into the collective memory of a significant event or place. In order to understand the narrative, we are forced to compare and contrast the memory with other pieces of evidence. It is an analysis that draws upon historical criticism and psychology.

The founding father of modern psychological analysis, Sigmund Freud, was very aware of the connection between the archaeology of the land and its relationship with the archaeology of the mind. While visiting the Rodin sculpture museum a few years ago in Paris, I came upon an exhibition of the antiquities of Sigmund Freud. The breadth and extent of the collections of antiquities of these two giants of the twentieth century, Freud and Rodin, was amazing. It was a powerful visit, both because it showed me how important material culture is for understanding the human spirit, but also because it demonstrated how material culture enlightens the artist about the past and inspires his or her own contemporary work. Rodin used figurines and statuettes of the Greeks and Romans to inform his own work of sculpting modern statues and designs. Freud used the figurines and material culture of the past to unlock the secrets of the mind of his patients. One could sense why the Rodin Museum had put Freud's figurines together with the sketches and statues of Rodin. It showed how two moderns reflected upon the past and learned how to think about the present. It appears, for different reasons, that both were ardent collectors of antiquities over most of their lifetimes. I could understand why Rodin saw archaeology (especially ancient figurines) as an important source of inspiration for his own sculpting, but I was surprised by Freud's lifetime devotion to collecting thousands of pieces of ancient religious life, given his sense that religion was more an illusion than a reality. What motivated Freud to seek out the most ancient pieces of ancient societies? What did he see in these small objects? Freud himself saw his process of unlocking the secrets of the psyche as a type of "archaeology of the mind." He saw the search for the understanding of the human psyche as similar to the type of search that goes on at an archaeological site, complete with a stratigraphy. Just as the archaeologist interprets the site in light of the artifacts buried there, so too the psychiatrist interprets the mind of a subject in light of the artifacts of one's life buried in the psyche of the individual.

I have never forgotten that aspect of archaeology—that all archaeology begins with human beings, their search for meaning, and the artifacts that define their lives. Because of that, I always try to investigate the people behind the artifacts. At ancient sites that means "listening to"/reading carefully the words on a written page and comparing the manuscripts. At more recent sites, it means talking to indigenous people who preserve in an oral history a part of the key to unlocking the site's secrets. Physical anthropologists look carefully at the bones and remains of a person. Cultural anthropologists want to know more about their subjects. An archaeologist who ignores the human narratives, especially in the modern period, is always going to lack a part of the site's story.

Over the past few years I have had students interview and take testimony from survivors of the Holocaust. Most of the work that we do on our University of Hartford projects begins by interviewing survivors. Students film hours of testimony of survivors, often asking similar questions in different ways to help unlock mysteries of *how* people remember things, which is just as significant as *what* they remember. Memory is a very fragile part of the human psyche. A trauma that happened last year or decades ago is remembered in a different format than a memory of a race won or the marriage of a child. Many of the traumatic memories are suppressed in order to allow people to continue with their lives. The harrowing memory sits between active and passive memory and often is compressed into manageable "clips" that have been well processed by the person in order to preserve their own dignity (or the dignity of the person they are remembering).

I use "hidden" in this chapter's title because in many ways, part of our project involves unlocking the "hidden" memories of survivors that will add to the information that has been gathered on the Holocaust from the "active" memories of the survivors. These memories are "hidden" because they are embedded deep in the psyches of the survivors and can perhaps be understood when we introduce stimuli (artifacts of the period) that were a part of their traumatic experience and will spark a memory. The idea that memory is constructed in independent images that are transformed into a narrative is complex and multilayered, and neurobiologists are only beginning to comprehend it. The psychological archaeology of examining human memory has become a major part of Holocaust studies. Researchers have concluded that the type of traumatic experience that is embedded in the memory of a Holocaust survivor must be carefully retrieved. It is not as easily accessed as a pleasant childhood memory might be. The memory of the Holocaust survivor is a carefully constructed reality that incorporates elements that protect the spirit of the individual at the same time that the memory recalls insights or impressions of an event. I remember assigning a class the book by Professor Lawrence Langer titled *Holocaust Testimonies: The Ruins of Memory* (1991), based upon the hundreds of testimonies at the Yale University Fortunoff Video Archives. Most of the students who read the book were shocked that instead of focusing on the heroism and personal narratives, Langer tries to understand the types of memories and selves that the survivors created. The self that they could live with was different from the sum of the parts of their memories.

We have had students interview survivors and write up the testimonies as part of classroom assignments. At our annual Holocaust Teachers' Workshops, we have all different types of testimonies presented, examined, and analyzed by middle and high school teachers and skilled university professors in order to teach how testimony of observers/participants in historical events can help us define history. An important example of this occurred when my colleague, Dr. Avinoam Patt, and I organized a conference on Sobibor at the University of Hartford in the fall of 2008 after we returned from doing our work there in the summer. We invited Mrs. Selma Engel to participate in our conference. She is a survivor of the Sobibor rebellion and now lives in Connecticut. She sat for hours of filmed interviews about her experience, and her memory of the event was invaluable in our research on Sobibor. I will never forget the moment that I showed her slides of some of the artifacts that had been discovered at Sobibor. For example, we showed her small glass vessels that resembled perfume bottles, which had been found near the foundations of what looked like the footings of buildings. Archaeologists often puzzle over the meaning of ancient artifacts—in this case, we knew these artifacts were perfume bottles. What were they doing in the area where we were working? How did they get there? Were they smuggled perfume bottles that the victims held onto even as all of their possessions were taken from them—or something else? I remember seeing Selma perk up as I showed her artifacts that had been discovered in the excavations done by Yoram Haimi in previous years and then showed her artifacts and personal effects that had been discovered in our own work. I asked her about the glass bottles and the artifacts, and for one brief moment I could see that these artifacts stimulated a memory of events that had happened in a real place in a real time almost seventy years ago in Europe. Selma commented to me that these were the types of perfume bottles that she knew from shower and bathroom facilities. We wondered if these were artifacts from the Nazi facade of "showers" used to bring the Jews quietly to the gas chambers. Only future excavations will reveal more about the camp and the location of all the facilities, but it is that combination of a personal narrative and archaeology that this book is really all about.

The fact that the Nazis told the Jews that they were going to "showers" is a well-known part of the history of the extermination camps. Fifty years from now when there are no more survivors to talk about their memories of the camps we will only have the written accounts, disparate video clips that archives around the world have collected from survivors, and the artifacts left in these camps. Increasingly, archaeology (together with this literature and testimonies) may be an important way of understanding what happened during the Holocaust. These artifacts can provide more help if they are investigated (together with the literature and the testimonies) while at least some of the survivors are around to provide greater context.

Thanks to the books and testimonies of the survivors of Sobibor we have a variety of memories of what the entire experience of Sobibor was like. The systematic extermination followed a very regular pattern that the books and testimonies outline. The Jews arriving at the Sobibor camp would have been greeted by the company commander delivering a speech about how this was a "resettlement" camp and announcing that they were going to learn a new trade. First, everyone was urged to get undressed so that their clothes could be disinfected, and they could take a shower for the health of everyone in the camp. The Jews had been kept in squalid conditions in cattle cars for often hundreds of miles (as they were transported from their home country to a concentration point and then on to an extermination camp), and the idea of a shower made their movement from the trains to the camps much easier. Throughout, the Nazis assumed that the harrowing conditions and quick transitions would allow the subterfuge to play itself without the possibility of a rebellion.

Part of Selma Engel's testimony is chronicled in Leonard Felson's article in the July 2010 *Reader's Digest* titled "Secrets of Sobibor." (Leonard Felson had accompanied us in our work at Sobibor.) When we met with Selma, she mentioned how unfortunate it was that we were too late to interview her husband Chaim Engel. Chaim, she told me, had passed away a few years previous to our interview, and he remembered many more details about the inner workings of the rebellion and about the Sobibor camp. She also said that but for Chaim's courage, she would never have survived the camp life, the rebellion, the escape, or the years after spent on the run. According to Selma, Chaim was the reason she survived. But it was Selma's memory of the perfume bottles that revealed another aspect of what we called "the hidden Holocaust" that this chapter will investigate. Unlike many of the other chapters, in which historians are dependent upon one or two narratives, documents, or events that have been passed down over hundreds and sometimes thousands of years, the history of the Holocaust is still being written. Archaeology works best when there are comparative narratives and sites to help understand the material culture. Sobibor was a planned extermination camp that followed a very specific model, and having these comparative sites and the different narratives is one of the best ways of using archaeology in the writing of history. Elements of history are hidden when we do not consider the details of narratives or fail to make comparisons between material culture and historical narratives. Unfortunately, it requires historians to be more sensitive to the material culture and archaeologists (who collect and interpret these items) to be more sensitive to the historical narratives. Those perfume bottles reminded me that without Selma's recollections, these objects would not be as meaningful. Our project and the public conference we had at the University of Hartford after returning from Sobibor were opportunities to have a survivor evaluate the evidence that we had of the rebellion to help us reconstruct the "crime scene." It is rare in archaeology to have a person who lived at the site you are working on who can give greater meaning to the archaeologist's interpretation of the material culture.

A biblical archaeologist lends authority to the Bible and other ancient written materials, which are then compared to the material culture from the same time period. The written word is illuminated by the material culture, and the material culture is illuminated by the written word. Today, thanks to visionary institutes of Holocaust studies worldwide (which began work when many more Holocaust survivors were alive), the analysis of survivor testimony that has been carefully collected and archived (and/or filmed) can be analyzed by future generations of researchers. In our study, we combined the testimonies of survivors, bystanders, and perpetrators together with an investigation of the material culture from an extermination camp and a nearby labor camp. This type of research, which involves archives and specialists in material culture, has become the next generation of Holocaust studies, especially as survivors have begun to pass. With the material culture found at camps together with the testimonies we come closer to understanding more about what happened at Sobibor.

One of the great mysteries of religion and archaeology is what we will discover about the Holocaust once all of the data have been assembled. Will they help us understand more about why the Holocaust occurred if we unravel more about how and what happened? I fear that we might understand less and less about the Holocaust as we know more and more about what happened. Even focusing on one camp, the amount of data is mind-boggling; what I hope is that as we learn more about the details of the camp, we will understand more about the people who were there. One thing is certain: Once we no longer have survivors to interview and we are left to only rely upon the written and filmed testimonies that many have left, it will be infinitely more difficult to fine-tune our work.

I included the words "hidden Holocaust" in the title of this chapter for a number of reasons. First, the stories of perpetrators, bystanders, and most of the victims are rarely known. When I ask my students what they know about the Holocaust, they usually tell me the story of Anne Frank (often without knowing that she perished in a camp). The hidden part of history is that which we more than likely ignore or never take the time to learn. In discussing the "almost" hidden Holocaust of Sobibor, this chapter gives the reader a way to understand the hidden histories. The Nazis tried to hide the entire Sobibor extermination camp after the prisoner insurgence because they feared that the story of rebellion at Sobibor might empower other Jews (and non-Jewish prisoners—the Nazis also rounded up homosexuals, political prisoners, gypsies, and Jehovah's Witnesses) to rebel and make the concentration and extermination infinitely more difficult for them.

Another reason I use "hidden" is because in many ways our project involves unlocking the hidden memories of survivors that will add to the information that has been gathered on the Holocaust from the "active" memories of the survivors. These memories are "hidden" because they are embedded deep in the psyches of the survivors and can perhaps be understood when we introduce stimuli (read: artifacts of the period) that were a part of their traumatic experience and will spark a memory. The idea that memory is constructed in independent images that are transformed into a narrative is complex and multilayered, and neurobiologists are only beginning to comprehend it. The psychological archaeology of examining human memory has become a major part of Holocaust studies. The memory of the Holocaust survivor is a carefully constructed reality that incorporates elements that protect the spirit of the individual at the same time that the memory recalls insights or impressions of an event. The other major element in survivor memory is the collective Jewish memory, usually infused by the religious texts and ideas that are taught as a part of their early education. Buried in the collective Jewish memory is the idea that Jews were not historically known as victims but rather as rebels, which played a key role in the importance of Sobibor.

Connecting the Dots: From Jewish Rebels in Antiquity to Jewish Victims of the Modern Period

This chapter is not only about our work in Poland, nor is it just about our attempts to document the life and culture now lost in Poland. It also discusses how one goes about reclaiming a hidden or almost forgotten history. Part of what discoveries do is fill in missing or forgotten pieces of history. Often one trend prevails and a new discovery will suddenly allow us to rewrite our understanding of history. In this chapter I aim to show how the rebellion of Sobibor demonstrates a missing facet of Jewish history—Jews as rebels.

I have spent the better part of three decades writing about revolts by the Jews in antiquity, and I was always troubled hearing my students' view that the Jews have *always* been "the victims of history." Where and when, I wondered, did this view begin? The story of Sobibor fits more closely with most of what we know of the history of the Jews from the biblical period through the Middle Ages. For many modern readers, it is strange to think of the Jews as rebels, but that is what the name "Judea" came to mean to much of the Roman world by the end of the second century CE. Today it seems a little incongruous, but in the second century CE, crushing the forces of the tiny province of Judea became the unlikely obsession of the greatest superpower of the time, the Roman Empire. It is what motivated the Romans to create one of the oddest and yet ubiquitous artifacts of antiquity that I have ever encountered: a coin that circulated in the farthest reaches of the Empire. The coin is found from the far-flung western provinces of the Empire to the southern frontiers in North Africa and all throughout the Levant. It circulated in areas where there were few Jews and in regions where the knowledge of Judea was nil. It was a special issue coin that simply read "Judea capta," meaning "Judea has been captured," and it usually featured a Jewish female figure (symbolizing the nation of Judaea, or Judah—a feminine noun in Hebrew) seated at the right of the coin in a position of submission (or mourning) at the base of a palm tree (which itself was a symbol of the nation of Judea and is also found on the Bar Kokhba Revolt–era coins), with a victorious Roman soldier standing over her to the left. The symbolism would have been unmistakable to anyone in the Empire: If you rebel, you will be defeated by the might of Rome and lose what sovereignty you have, just like Judea. This coin seems to have circulated for a long while after the Jews were no longer a power, and in areas where the people had never even met a Jew; its symbolism was still powerful even when the symbols were not fully understood. It helped make a small people much more important than they ever really were.

For twenty-five years in the first century CE, at least forty-eight different types of "Judea capta" coins were issued in gold, silver, and bronze in different denominations throughout the Roman Empire. This small and relatively unimportant people in a relatively minor part of the Empire (Judea) had a coin issued to ensure that other peoples in the Empire would not rebel like the Jews. The coin was intended to be a warning for these other, larger peoples within the Empire that if they did rebel, their fate would be the same as that of the Jews. But publicity of this sort is a double-edged sword. For a coin such as this to be meaningful, all of the other people who used and handled these coins throughout the Empire had to know that the Jews were rebels and that their defeat was a significant victory. Although the Romans wanted to remove the image of the Jews from history, they inadvertently made them much more important to Roman history. The obscure history of Jewish rebellion ironically became far more important than it would have been had the Romans just decided to allow the matter to drop. This is an example of what I call the "unintended consequences" of history. The ruling government tried to get rid of the Judeans and ironically kept the embers of rebellion fresh in Judea. By the time of Hadrian's defeat of the Judeans' Second Rebellion against the Romans some sixty years later in 135 CE, it was unclear to the Romans how to undo the "Judean = Rebel" urban myth. (An "urban myth" is one that persists often beyond the reality of any real data to substantiate it.) So when the Emperor Hadrian defeated the Jews in the Second Rebellion, he decided to remove the name of Judea from history. He simply changed the name of the country so there was no rallying cry for Judeans in the diaspora. He literally erased Judea from all further references in any Roman document and changed it to another old/new name known in Greek and Roman sources: Palestina. Borrowing on the biblical name "Philistine," he re-created the ancient name of the country that was still known in his own time; Judea became Palestine—a change that resonates all the way to the twenty-first century.

But something of the original meaning of the "rebel" Judean/Jew persisted. In the Bible and throughout much of medieval Christian writings, the Jews were known as a "stubborn" and "stiff-necked" people, based upon the way that many read the texts of the rebellious Israelites in the desert of Sinai in the books of Exodus and Deuteronomy, and also because they stubbornly refused to accept Jesus as the Messiah. There are many examples of how the Jews were rebels in societies from Egypt, Israel, Babylonia, India, Europe, and North Africa to the farthest reaches of Russia over the past two thousand years—so why did my students in the twenty-first century see the Jews as history's perpetual victims? It is because people rarely look beyond the short history that they know. This is the historical memory of the Jews that made the rebellions of Sobibor and the Warsaw ghetto so meaningful.

A Short History of Biblical and Jewish Rebellions

In *Digging through the Bible*, I wrote about the revolt of the Israelites against the Egyptians, led by the "ultimate" rebel, Moses, and his rebellious brother and sister, Aaron and Miriam. I discussed how the whole idea of Abraham and his religious rebellion against the very traditions that he was born into in Mesopotamia implies that rebellion was in the DNA of the ancient Israelites. I want to be clear about this. Whether we can prove that each and every person and event is historically accurate in general and in detail is not the question. The fact that the Bible is filled with examples of rebellion tells us that the writers of the Bible were intensely interested in portraying the Jews as rebels. When one looks at King David's family, for example, the writers are not at all embarrassed to write that there were rebellions against his rule. David's own rebellion against his father-in-law and king, Saul, shows us that the Jews/Israelites did not only engage in rebellions against the "outside" world; questioning authority, even the legitimate authority of the Israelites, was a view that spanned the generations and families of ancient Israel. The prophets of ancient Israel did not accept the status quo and spoke frankly to kings and priests about actions they thought were immoral or unjust. The Bible tells us that after King Solomon died, the ten northern tribes of Israel did not feel compelled to stay with the southern tribes. They felt that it did not suit their political and religious interests, and they rebelled against the House of David and established their own kings, priests, and religious institutions. The religious rebellions of the Judean kings Hezekiah and Josiah in the eighth and seventh centuries BCE against the religious norms of their own day and people are examples of just how profoundly acceptable the idea of rebellion was. The biblical prophecies of Ezekiel and Jeremiah are religious rebellions in the sixth century BCE and allowed the ancient Judeans to survive (and some say "thrive") during their exile from the land of Israel by continuing to worship their Judean God outside the land of Judah.

If Jews had just accepted the status quo of their circumstances, history would have passed them by. Instead, they rebelled against the common wisdom of the day when necessary and forged a new path. I remember the first time that I read a book in Hebrew that confirmed my suspicions that the Jews were mutinous. *In the Footsteps of Rebels and Kings*, by Beno

Rothenberg and Yohanan Aharoni (published in Hebrew in Tel Aviv in 1960), changed my attitude about the Jews. Aharoni had spent the 1950s and 1960s as a professor of archaeology at Tel Aviv University in the heyday of the beginnings of Israeli archaeology. The enterprise that Aharoni and others like Yigael Yadin and ultimately many other Israeli archaeologists were engaged in was good science and state building. In the post–World War II era, they were interested in turning back the clock to the ancient Israelite and Jew who was *not* a victim of history and the Holocaust. Some criticize Israeli archaeology from this period because it seems to have placed too much attention on heroism and courage (and on sites that celebrated these qualities) over commemorating the defeats and victimization of the ancient Jews. I think that this was a healthy corrective to the theme of victimization present in the ghettoes of medieval Europe and the ever-present specter of the Holocaust in post–World War II Israel. The idea of the Jewish rebel was reborn in the archaeology of Israel in the 1950s, and we have rarely looked back.

One of the most significant discoveries of archaeology of the Greco-Roman period that emerged in post–World War II Israel was a new understanding about how an obscure and highly problematic rebellion of the Jews in the second century BCE affected Greco-Roman history in general and Jewish history in particular. I do not think that it is an accident that the Maccabees became a major symbol for the nascent modern State of Israel. Through the Jewish holiday of Hanukkah, most people have a passing familiarity with the second-century BCE revolt of the Maccabees against the Greek Seleucids that was led by the Hasmonean family of Judah Maccabee. In general, people know about the miracle of the oil in the Temple (which lasted for eight days) but hear almost nothing about the rebellion. In the past sixty years, archaeology in Israel has revealed just how traumatic this entire rebellion was for ancient Jewish history and its ripple effect in making rebellion a policy of Jewish history. The Hasmoneans, a family of Jewish rebels, dislodged not only the Greek Seleucids from Israel but also the ruling Jewish families and religious officials of Judaism at the time of the rebellion, and replaced them with Hasmonean family members. This major event was not just about external oppression but also about collaborators and culture assimilators, and it turned religious and political Judaism upside down for the next three hundred years. Many Jews by the first century CE wondered if Judaism in Jerusalem was in the hands of the rightful leadership. The splinter groups known as the Pharisees, the Sadducees, the Essenes, and the Zealots were all able to stake claims to new and different models of leadership in the period from the second century BCE to the first century CE. Some might say that without the successful and problematic rebellion of the Maccabees, the followers of Jesus would not have had the impetus to create the movement that they did. The discovery of the Dead Sea Scrolls and of many other second and first century BCE sites in Israel and the diaspora showed that the Hasmonean rebellion had a ripple effect upon Jews and Judaism in many different places.

By the first century CE, Jewish rebels and rebellions abounded in Israel and the diaspora. The circle of Jesus, the Zealots, the Pharisees, and the Sadducees in many ways can all be seen as continuous parallel circles of external and internal rebels and rebellions. In 66 CE, the Great Jewish revolt (called the First Revolt and led by the Zealots) against the Romans broke out, and the pendulum of history began to swing against the Jews. The Second Revolt against the Romans in the second century CE, led by Shimon Bar Kokhba, and the coalescing of the Christians as a separate group, shook the foundations of Judaism. In these revolts, Jews were placed under difficult circumstances, and instead of acquiescing and adopting a passive attitude toward their oppressors, or continuing with the status quo, some decided that they needed to revolt in order to remain Jews. It is in this way that Christianity is really the result of the Jewish rebellions of the first and second centuries CE. We find that the early Christians remained a sect of Judaism until the middle of the Bar Kokhba Revolt, and then suddenly we find that by the middle of the second century the Christians are a very distinct religious group, separate from Judaism. Many think that it was this second rebellion that convinced the early Christians that this was not the way to usher in the "kingdom" that Jesus had spoken about.

This is also a way of understanding the development of Islam as well, some four hundred years later. In the seventh century CE, Muhammad rebelled against the norms of Arabian idolatry, and it is no wonder that his earliest followers were Jews seeking liberation. These rebellions resulted in totally different religious traditions, but within Judaism, the trend toward religious rebellion continued throughout the Middle Ages. For almost two thousand years (from Abraham to the rabbis), the Jews seem to have been well known as insurgents in the ancient world. However, then the rabbis and rabbinic literature created a different definition of the Jews. Rabbi Judah the Prince, for example, removed all mention of the Maccabees and their rebellion from his major literary work, the Mishnah, even though the Jews continued to celebrate Hanukkah. The rabbis began to emphasize a different "back story" for Hanukkah that did not emphasize the rebellion. Instead of a story of a rebellion force and a military victory, it became about the triumph of the spirit and the famous miracle of the oil cruse (a very famous motif in the Bible and rabbinic lore associated with the prophet Elijah). By the third century CE, rabbinic Jews were only reading about rebellions in the far-off past of the Bible (and even many of those they reinterpreted!). There was almost no mention of the rebellions of the Zealots and the Maccabees to be found in rabbinic texts. The Jews still read about the rebellions in the synagogue in the weekly pentateuchal episodes in the desert, but each of these rebellions were tempered by prophetic readings that deemphasized the violence and wars in favor of the ideals of spiritual and moral victories. The rabbis, who ultimately were responsible for the canon of the Hebrew Bible (and the decisions about what prophetic section should be read with what pentateuchal reading on any given Shabbat), created a Judaism that favored a more spiritual message over a history of rebellions. Some scholars even think that the rabbinical influence may have extended to the outright censoring of works such as the ancient book titled *The Book of the Wars of the Lord*, which is cited in the book of Numbers 21:14 (but which never found its way into the Jewish canon). This was a complete reorientation for Greco-Roman Judaism, and its consequences lingered into the premodern period.

Up until the twentieth century, we read little about successful rebellions of the Jews in rabbinic literature, but accounts of successful Jewish rebellions are known from a variety of other sources. We have to look very carefully in non-Jewish literature, rabbinic polemic literature, and *geniza* fragments of written material (such as the Cairo Geniza in the Ben Ezra Synagogue mentioned in chapter 3) that included thousands of fragments of correspondence and nonlegal Jewish literature. Some of the most famous Jewish mutinies show that despite rabbinic attempts to curtail the information flow to the general public, Jews continued to rebel for a variety of new reasons. In the sixth century CE, for example, the Jewish leader Mar Zutra (II) rebelled against the Persians and established a short-lived independent Jewish state in what is today a part of Iraq (it was then still called Babylonia). He and many of the leaders of his rebellion were deposed and executed, but the group apparently went to the mountains in what is today Dagestan, Azerbaijan, and Chechnya and became known by the locals as "mountain Jews" of the Caucacus. Often my incredulous twenty-first-century students ask me if I really believe that Jews were given to this type of "rebellious" behavior and I say that the stories are so unusual and so dissimilar to the "official" history of the Jews told in the Crusades that these stories seem more authentic than not. The Jews of Babylonia who revolted against the ruling government(s) and were being discriminated against in the aftermath of these rebellions, moved to a new part of the Empire and served the new leadership in a community of semi-independence far from the center of Judaism.

Far from being victims of history, during the early Middle Ages we have excellent examples of ongoing mini-rebellions that continued to define the Jews as rebels. This ongoing tradition of messianic or quasi-messianic leaders who initiated rebellions includes figures like the twelfth-century CE David Alroy from Kurdistan, a figure in France in the eleventh century, and even one in Spain in the twelfth century. Little is known of these rebellious Jewish groups that were led by quasi-messianic figures, but one of them caught the attention of the famed twelfth-century rabbinic scholar, Rabbi Moses, the son of Maimon of Cairo (better known by the Greek variant of his name, Maimonides). In his letter to the Yemenite Jews (*Iggeret Teman*) he indicates that the rabbis were troubled by the ongoing pattern of simmering Jewish rebellions that had an eschatological bent. The movements of rebellions were not only Jewish movements or even just religious rebellions; they were usually mixed rebellions that included Muslims and Christians who were trying to work out their own "end of days" scenarios. This pattern of rebellion was not found throughout Europe, to be sure, and the Crusades show how some Jewish communities acquiesced in the face of violence. The idea of active Jewish rebellion was tempered by the idea of passive (nonviolent) Jewish martyrdom (*Kiddush HaShem* in Hebrew) and became a part of the norm for European Jews.

This defiant pattern seems to have changed for the Jews starting in the fourteenth and fifteenth centuries with the *reconquista* and final expulsion from Spain in 1492. The Jewish spirit of resistance became less frequent and nearly disappeared until the premodern period. It was replaced by histories that included expulsions, ghettoes, *dhimmis* (non-Muslims living in a Muslim area), the toleration of small groups of Jews in some countries, and their victimization in others.

By the nineteenth century, the Jews had become known as victims rather than rebels. Through the pogroms of the seventeenth century in Poland, the nineteenth-century rise of anti-Semites in Germany, the czarist cantons of Russia (a situation in which Jewish boys were forced into the Russian army and made to serve many years, while having to endure constant attempts by superiors to convert them to Christianity), and the Dreyfus case of France (a situation in which a French Jewish military officer was accused and convicted of treason, despite overwhelming evidence that he was innocent), the Jews were seen as the pariah of choice for many different groups in Europe. The victims of the nineteenth century were introduced to new ways of victimization in the twentieth century, as communism and socialism fought bitter battles in Europe with the Jews squeezed into one ideology or another. The millions of Jews who became part of the Soviet Union, Germany, and the rest of Europe in the twentieth century served valiantly in the armies of Europe in World War I, and it was this legacy of Jewish soldiers that indirectly led to the success of the rebellions in the period of the Holocaust. At the same time that the Jews were trying to become full members of the new twentieth-century entities in Europe, Zionism was trying to reimagine modern Jews in their own land serving their own ideology. The Jews of Europe were neither victims nor rebels by the time the Nazis seized control of Germany. But during the darkest days of the Holocaust a new rebel emerged who would be the model for the two most famous rebellions during the Holocaust: Sobibor and the Warsaw ghetto.

Documenting the Rebels of the Warsaw Ghetto and Sobibor

The year 1943 was the year that reinvigorated the idea of rebellion for the Jews. The October 1943 Sobibor rebellion would probably not have happened but for the earlier example of the Warsaw ghetto uprising. By 1943 there were upwards of three hundred thousand to four hundred thousand Jews concentrated in a densely populated walled ghetto in Warsaw. Starting with an insurgency in the Warsaw ghetto in January 1943 and ending in May 1943, a poorly outfitted group in the ghetto rebelled against the Nazis in the single greatest example of rebellion in the Holocaust. I would like to think that part of this rebellion was a result of the influences of Jewish history, but it is also a result of the mix of Jews who were by then concentrated in the Warsaw ghetto. Many of the stories about the two famous revolts of the Holocaust at the Warsaw ghetto and Sobibor are available to us because of the commitment of survivors and historians to telling the tales of the rebellions. I make mention of one historian in the Warsaw ghetto because his work is unique. Dr. Emanuel Ringelblum is perhaps the single most important figure for the history of the Holocaust, because he kept meticulous notes in the Warsaw ghetto, which were found after the war. Dr. Ringelblum is an example of how history is not necessarily written by the victors but rather by those with enough forethought to preserve it. His story is chronicled in the 2007 book *Who Will Write Our History? Emanuel Ringelblum, the Warsaw Ghetto, and the Oyneg Shabes Archive*, by my colleague in Hartford, Dr. Samuel D. Kassow. Since Professor Kassow teaches history at Trinity College in Hartford, I had heard many lectures about Ringelblum, and Kassow always makes his story come alive. I also have learned that Ringelblum was another form of "rebel": the historian.

Emanuel Ringelblum was trained as a historian of Polish Jewish history from the late Middle Ages to the eighteenth century. As the Nazis moved into Poland in 1940, Ringelblum wondered whether the history of the Jews would end there. The fear that he had is, I think, a fear that Jews have had throughout history—that their world would end with them and that they bore the responsibility for recording and saving their history. He wanted to make sure to send a "message in a bottle" to the people who would survive the war about who the Jews of Poland were and what the Warsaw ghetto was like. His group, Oyneg Shabes, assembled the available records and buried them, just like the authors of the Dead Sea Scrolls did in the caves around Qumran. Oyneg Shabes (literally, "the Happiness of the Sabbath," presumably because they met on the Sabbath) was the name of a traditional Jewish religious gathering after Friday night or Saturday services when Jews would get together to socialize. It was a good cover for the history-collecting group in the Warsaw ghetto, since they gathered at the risk of their lives. Their gathering on the Sabbath was tolerated by the Nazis. Instead of words of the ancient Torah/Bible, the life of the Jews of Poland was their study. Ringelblum originally thought he would come back, retrieve his records, and write a history of what happened in the ghetto. Like the latter-day Essenes (who are assumed to have written some of the scrolls), Oyneg Shabes collected, together with dozens of volunteers, tens of thousands of pieces of evidence of the life and culture of the Jews of Poland in essays, posters, art, and other written programs. As the Final Solution was being implemented (and became known to the people in the ghetto) and the Treblinka and Chelmno death camps were up and running in 1942 and early 1943, Ringelblum and his cohorts prepared their "message in a bottle" in three milk cans and ten metal boxes, which were buried in three different locations in the ghetto.

Despite the fact that Ringelblum and many of his volunteers did not survive the war, much of his work did, and it was rediscovered. At almost the same period that the Dead Sea Scrolls were found in caves near Qumran, Ringelblum's archives were found in post–World War II Warsaw. I include this story and the story of the Warsaw ghetto uprising in this book because they are not well known, nor is Ringelblum's valiant effort to preserve these documents of the life of Polish Jewry before and during the destruction of this thousand-year history. Ringelblum did not know about the Dead Sea Scrolls, but he did know that Jews in exile had, for centuries, written their histories in order to ensure that they were preserved. In much the same way that the rabbis of the Mishnah wrote down their "oral" history in order to preserve it after the Bar Kokhba Revolt's disastrous conclusion in the second century CE, so too Ringelblum thought that if he did not collect this history it would disappear. By collecting and then burying all of this evidence, Ringelblum performed the ultimate act of defiance against the Nazis: the preservation of Jewish history.

This is very similar to what we wanted to do in Sobibor—collect all of the extant information about what happened there and write a micro-history of the Holocaust by way of a "total" site project at the camp and its environs. Sobibor has been written about by survivors, historians, and writers who culled their information from firsthand accounts of the rebellion that broke out there on October 14, 1943. The most important part of the numerous written accounts is that they complement one another, as survivors and researchers began to talk about their lives starting after the war. Alexander Pechersky, for example, who was the leader of the rebellion in 1943, wrote about his recollections in the 1946 Yiddish publication *Emes* in Moscow. Herschel Cukerman wrote about his own recollections in 1955 in Yiddish in Tel Aviv. There were Polish researchers in the 1950s and 1960s who wrote short reports about the camp and the events that happened there. In 1968, Shlomo (Stanislaw) Szmajzner published in Portuguese his own view of the rebellion in *The Hell of Sobibor* in Brazil. The *Yizkor* book of Włodawa (the nearby village), published in Israel in 1974, was an important source of information about who the Jews around Sobibor were before they were deported. None of these writers were interested in the material culture still available at the site or at the satellite sites from Włodawa to Luta, but their accounts of the rebellion and the life at Sobibor are important for our comparisons with the material culture found at these sites.

Authors began to write about Jewish resistance in a number of post–World War II publications, and they provided us with a context for understanding why Sobibor was different from other camps. As I mentioned earlier, before the Sobibor rebellion there were other rebellions that took place in the extermination camps in 1942, in transports, transport sites, and ghettos. Yuri Suhl (*They Fought Back*, 1967) and many others wrote about the Warsaw ghetto uprising and other acts of resistance. The 1980s introduced a number of different types of works specifically on Sobibor—for example, Miriam Novitch's *Sobibor Martyrdom and Revolt* (1980), Richard Rashke's *Escape from Sobibor* (1982), and Yitzhak Arad's *Belzec, Sobibor, Treblinka: The Operation Reinhard Death Camp* (1987). These researchers and writers used the firsthand accounts of the rebellion survivors to write social history. The survivor literature continued to be written into the 1990s and most recently in publications initiated in Poland as part of a new attempt by Poland to document in readable English collections aspects of life at So- bibor and the Holocaust: Thomas Toivi Blatt's *Sobibor: The Forgotten Revolt* (1997) and *From the Ashes of Sobibor* (1997); Kalmen Wewryk's *To Sobibor and Back: An Eyewitness Account* (2008); Kurt Ticho's *My Legacy* (2008); and Andrew Zielinkski's *Conversations with Regina* (2008).

How We Went from Mount Sinai to Sobibor

Most of the written accounts (and even social histories) of the events at Sobibor (and the Holocaust in general) usually lack one aspect: the material culture from the site. My colleague at the University of Hartford, Professor Avinoam Patt, was involved with the dissertation of PhD candidate Robin O'Neil in the Department of Hebrew and Jewish Studies at the University College London in 2008 titled "Belzec Death Camp and the Origins of Jewish Genocide in Galicia." What made Robin's arguments so compelling was that he included details of the excavations conducted by Dr. Andrzej Kola, director of the Archaeological Faculty at the Nicholas Copernicus University in Poland, from 1997 to 2000. This work at Bełżec, although problematic, is important for directing the work at Sobibor. These camps were constructed from a master plan, so that although it was altered to lo- cal conditions and materials, certain basic elements of architecture may be compared from the excavations at Bełżec to help locate elements (barracks, gas chambers, areas for burning, etc.) at Sobibor.

When I met Robin in London in 2008, he explained his own misgiv- ings about the use of the type of archaeology that was done at Bełżec. His misgivings are a litany of the types of excesses that archaeologists all over the world have been accused of: excavating the graves of the dead, un- earthing bones, fat, and a variety of different human remains (burned ash and fragmentary pieces of cored materials). In the case of Bełżec, however, Jews felt victimized a second time. First, there was the extermination camp that had to be summarily evacuated and disinfected following the libera- tion of the camps in 1945 without the possibility of proper and dignified burials for the dead, and now here was an archaeologist digging through the very remains that they had been unable to properly rebury. Robin published articles about the excavations in *East European Jewish Affairs*, and his dissertation specifically shows the problems with standard archaeologi- cal methods in an extermination camp. I tried to reassure him that our method of mapping the subsurface would obviate the excesses that he and others had noted. He recognized just how different the documentation of an extermination camp would be if you first had competent geophysicists (with archaeological background) mapping the subsurface before any excavation was done.

The idea of using archaeological techniques in excavating an extermination camp was not new. Beginning in the 1980s, Chelmno, an extermination camp west of Warsaw and north of Lodz, was excavated by Dr. Lucia Nowak, director of the Konin Regional Museum in Poznan, Poland. The excavations were done in three phases from 1986 into 2004 and used standard archaeological methodologies. The publication of her work in the symposium proceedings from 2004 includes many of the personal items discovered. I saw them on display at the Imperial War Museum in London. In addition, her work draws from the personal accounts in her second volume, *Chelmno Witnesses Speak*, also published by the Konin Regional Museum. The need for systematic excavations began in the communist era after looters began searching areas around the camps, both in the forest and at the actual camp sites. In 2001, Professor Dr. Andrzej Kola began work on Sobibor after having worked at Bełżec using standard archaeological methods that included drilling, exploratory boreholes, and standard excavation methods. Therein lies part of the issue and why our work was so important. Archaeology requires that one actually finish the work at a site and write a final report in order to ensure that future builders know exactly what may and may not be built there. Kola's initial forays at Sobibor were greeted with interest, but criticism from the Bełżec excavations meant that Sobibor would be even more problematic. His work at Sobibor in 2001 was as problematic as his work at Bełżec (for a short analysis of the problems, see Avi Weiss's article at www.hir.org/amcha/belzec.html titled "A Monumental Failure at Belzec"). Yoram Haimi's new excavations at Sobibor on behalf of the Ben Gurion University of the Negev together with Yad Vashem in Jerusalem are different.

We formulated this Sobibor project on the model of other archaeological endeavors that we had done in the past. But how we came to work in Sobibor the year after our work at Har Karkom in 2007 is itself unusual. In 2007, while working on Har Karkom in southern Israel, I came to know about one of the supervising regional archaeologists of the Israel Antiquities Authority by the name of Yoram Haimi. Haimi is a well-trained archaeologist of prehistoric Israel who lives in the south of Israel and teaches parttime at Ben Gurion University of the Negev in Beer Sheva. Yoram knows the Negev region as well as anyone. He is from a Moroccan Jewish family, and I came to know about him from two sources—one professional and the other personal. When a member of his extended family in Connecticut told me about Yoram's interest in excavating a unique site associated with his family, I naturally assumed that it was something very ancient and in the south of the country. I was wrong. When I met Yoram for the first time, he told me how his family history had been touched by the Holocaust. Most people do not know that while people speak about the six million Jews who were killed in Europe during the Holocaust, not all of the Jews who died in Europe were European (Ashkenazic) Jews. Over the years I had met many Sephardic Jews from Greece, for example, who had told me their own stories of the Holocaust. In countries like Greece, Morocco, Egypt, and Turkey, Jews were hunted down, interned, and exterminated. They were not all of European extraction but are generally called Sephardic or Eastern (Mizrahi or "Oriental") Jews, and many of them ultimately fell victim to the Holocaust as well, serving in far-flung labor camps or in extermination camps like their European compatriots.

Yoram's connection to the Holocaust was different. I contacted him, told him I would be in Israel working on our excavations at Yavne (in the south of Israel), and invited him to discuss his new excavation idea. In

Courtesy of the University of Hartford Sobibor Project

Figure 5.3.   Yoram Haimi at Sobibor

January 2008, I met him at the Ben and Jerry's Ice Cream Parlor across the way from our archaeological site in Yavne. He showed me a PowerPoint of his work at Sobibor. It was a moving story that begins with his personal connection to the site: his two Moroccan uncles, Isaac and Maurice Ben Zaquen, died there. They were residing in Paris when World War II broke out, and on February 9, 1943, they were arrested by the Nazis and sent to the transit camp of Drancy outside of Paris. Like many other detention centers throughout France, Drancy was created in 1941 and was under French Vichy control (which worked with the Nazis after France's surrender) until it was finally taken over completely by the Nazis in July 1943 as part of the mass extermination program of the Final Solution. From the documents that Yoram showed me from the Nazi researcher Serge Klarsfeld, it is clear that his uncles were on the lists of deportees from France to Sobibor on transport 53 on March 25, 1943. Out of seventy-five transports of trains to Poland, seventy-one transports took Jews to Auschwitz, and four were sent to Sobibor. His uncles were sent to Sobibor and were never heard from again.

Excavating a place where you have a personal connection is one of the most daunting tasks an excavator can undertake. For most of the excavations that we have dealt with in this book, there are at least a few degrees of separation between the excavators and the site they are working on. There are ethnic, cultural, and often religious considerations involved in the excavations I chose to highlight in this book, but this was very personal for Yoram. Even for my colleague, Professor Avinoam Patt, whose great-grandparents were transported to Sobibor for extermination, Sobibor was more than just an academic question. This is not as rare as you might think. Increasingly in the past fifty years in Africa, the United States, and Latin America, indigenous peoples with vested cultural interests have been trained in archaeology and have begun to excavate sites that are associated with their families and extended families' or clans' history—but Sobibor was more than just a burial site. It was the equivalent of a crime scene.

When Yoram discussed with me how he wanted his project to be done in a systematic and dignified way that would allow him to avoid all the pitfalls of earlier attempts at understanding other extermination camps, I knew that our techniques would help ensure his success. I explained to Yoram what our process of high-tech subsurface mapping could do that would allow him to map the area in a dignified and systematic way, and point him in the right direction to excavate only those areas where architecture and artifacts could be found. Most important, it would help him avoid disinterring the bones of people who had died there. One of the archaeological techniques that had been employed previously was using coring equipment to bore holes in the ground and take samples of the bones, fat, and ash in order to determine where bodies were buried. Using the geophysical subsurface mapping techniques, this was no longer necessary. The techniques we were using could determine where bodies were buried and avoid disturbing the burials. It could be done in a way that would make Jews feel that the Jewish value of *kavod hamet* (dignity of the dead) could be maintained at the same time that good science was being done. Today, following twenty years of legislation (and court challenges to local practices) all throughout the world, archaeologists are very careful not to excavate graves and burial sites except in a very controlled and supervised manner with a specific scientific goal. In the period before the legislation, many ancient and premodern burial sites were disturbed in the name of science without religious officials having too much control over the situation. In the nineteenth and throughout most of the twentieth centuries, there were attempts to have physical anthropologists scientifically analyze bones and burials through techniques learned in the forensic sciences in order to understand how ancient and premodern people lived, ate, and died. It was a valiant effort to help us understand how people had developed. Bones and burials were measured and categorized, and data were collected. Often following this, bones and burials were then put on display in museums to introduce the general public to the particulars of ancient peoples and to demystify death. I remember as a child going to museums and seeing these burial sites and the bones.

Even the display of burials and bones of ancient and premodern peoples is no longer a part of most museum collections today, which re-create the particulars of burial and bones without using the real bones. Jews, in particular, are, and have always been in the long tradition of Judaism, very sensitive to the display (and even touching) of bones and burial sites. It is not only in the period of the Holocaust that Jewish burials have become important. It is an issue that goes back as far as the earliest parts of the Bible itself. In the book of Genesis, one of the first great acts of compassion of the patriarch Abraham for his wife Sarah is to find an appropriate and dignified burial site for her after she dies. The concept of *kavod hamet* was one that became a part of every Jewish community throughout the world. The extermination camps, where so many Jews died in such a short period of time under such extreme conditions, are as holy to Jews as the biblical burials of their ancestors.

Full Documentation

After Yoram Haimi and I agreed to work together at Sobibor, I told him that if we could get our licenses for our work in Poland, we would try to do at least two additional and important subprojects. Raising funds for a project of this size in a short period of time is not easy. A geophysical survey of this magnitude would require a large team of people and require processing and analysis of the work long after the end of the initial research in Poland. I set out to find a donor who would understand the importance of this work. Second, I told Yoram that since we were working at an extermination camp, we needed to proceed carefully, by first doing the geophysics. This same team had been involved in the work at the cemetery of Qumran, perhaps the most ancient Jewish cemetery of Israel, and we knew how problematic working with burials could become. There we had documented every one of the 1,213 graves using geophysics. We would pursue good science, do some of the "truth-testing" of the geophysics mapping, and provide maps and follow-up consultations for his excavations. Our Sobibor project would go beyond the camp and involve talking to the survivors and Polish locals as part of the documentation process. I thought filming our work would be a good way to record it, and I set out to find a film producer who would understand the importance of this story. I am happy to say that almost immediately I found the right donors and the right television producer to document the work.

In the course of planning, I spoke with a film producer who had worked on one of my earlier television documentaries. When I told him the story of Yoram and the site, he was so moved that he agreed to make arrangements to film the work. The details of the area, the survivors, and the work at Sobibor together would tell a story about how science can help put the pieces together. The work we would be doing would be contributing to the field and to the history of the period, the story was compelling, and the archaeologists were themselves extremely passionate about the work. It was one of the most inspiring projects on which I have ever worked.

Gary Hochman is the television science documentarian who had developed our PBS *NOVA* program *Ancient Refuge in the Holy Land*, about the Cave of Letters on the Dead Sea that rebels had used over a long period of time. The work that we did in the cave from 1999 to 2002 involved the story of Jewish rebels almost eighteen hundred years before Sobibor. These rebels revolted against Roman rule in Judea and used the cave as a place of refuge after they escaped from the Romans. It is a heartrending story that I chronicle in my books *Secrets of the Cave of Letters* and *Digging through the Bible*. While working in the cave, we found the bodies of nineteen rebels

Courtesy of the University of Hartford Sobibor Project

Figure 5.4.   Documenting Sobibor

interred there. At the time it was difficult for me to fathom how the bodies of Jewish men, women, and children who had died such a long time ago were preserved so well in this Dead Sea cave. The writings and personal effects of the people were also found, and for the first time we could understand how these rebels thought about their lives and we could document their deaths. The Sobibor story is eerily similar to this story, except this time it happened less than seventy years ago, and they left us writings and personal effects that at least some of the survivors could still explain.

When I explained to Gary Hochman that this was a story about how science would help us document the history of the Holocaust, he agreed to help us. It is not easy to work in the field and document ancient events, but Gary is a thoughtful and thorough television producer. He has created other documentaries about less sensational and well-known events, and in this case he saw the information of Sobibor and the other places that we would be surveying in Poland as both a human interest story and a science story. He documented our scientific work at Sobibor in meticulous detail (a geophysical survey of the camp in preparation for further excavations there) and combined it with testimonies and the heartrending story of Yoram Haimi.

One of the film clips of the documentary that goes beyond the scientific work is from the Ben Gurion University 2009 excavations in the areas that we had mapped out in 2008. In it, Gary captures the essence of the documentation process. Yoram brings the workers to see the stones dedicated to his own family members that are placed along a walkway which commemorates the dead. The group lights small candles to serve as a memorial of their own visit to the site. As Yoram, a strong Israeli who has lived through Israeli wars and terrorist attacks and most recently the Hamas shelling from the Gaza Strip, begins to tell the workers about his own loss, his tear-filled account helps the workers understand how this is more than just a scientific project for him. It is a personal journey of faith and archaeology.

Digging through Personal Histories

As a student of history, I have taken multiple courses on the Holocaust; Sobibor's place in this history is well known. As a historian of the ancient period, I never thought that I would ever research a project in the modern period, but in this case, it was a project that I felt we could do and do well. In every excavation, you must dig through different periods. You cannot ignore one stratum and move on to another. Every layer of human activity at a site is important, up to and including the last and uppermost level, so even at our most ancient sites, we have modern historians and modern material culture experts evaluating the finds. In many ways, I knew we could do this at a place like Sobibor: evaluate the overall culture and history of the period and the region and use that to help understand the material culture at the site. Thus was born our Sobibor Documentation Project.

Building a project that is primarily based in the modern period requires people with specific modern history backgrounds. I am happy to say that I had one of the best modern Jewish historians of the Holocaust at the University of Hartford, and he was the person to whom I turned to fill in the history of the period. Dr. Avinoam Patt is the Philip D. Feltman Professor of Modern Jewish History at the University of Hartford. His parents are Israelis and he was brought up in Texas, but his family directly suffered in the Holocaust. His great-grandparents ended up in Sobibor. He was interested in researching the background information on Sobibor, he knew many of the modern research languages, and it was personally and professionally important for him to work on the project. When I hired him at the University of Hartford, I told him that I wanted to have a colleague with whom I could work, but I never expected that we would ever work on the same project. In retrospect, I cannot imagine ever doing this project without a person at my own university who could help me understand all of the historical questions on a day-to-day basis. In my thirty years of teaching, I have never before had a colleague like this, so it is an odd coincidence that Avi would be available precisely at a time when I would need his services.

I also had personal experiences with the Holocaust. Today nothing remains of the dynamic Jewish life where my own family came from in Europe except the cemetery and a group of plaques. I have often thought about the accidents of history that allowed me to be born in 1955 in the United States, where I was able to grow up and live to go and work all over the world without too many restrictions on my personal freedoms. I have wondered how it would have been for me if I had been born a generation earlier in my family's Polish village of Zhitomir. Would I have lived or died, collected historical references in a ghetto, survived in the forest, rebelled against the Nazis with the resistance fighters, or died of starvation or gassing in a camp? This is something that I am sure haunts many modern Jewish academics born after the Holocaust.

How Was a Systematic Extermination of Your Neighbors Tolerated?

One of the biggest questions that my students ask about the Holocaust is how a systematic extermination suddenly became acceptable in places like Germany and Poland where the Jews had lived for almost a thousand years. In fact, this is one of the reasons why we talked to non-Jewish Poles who lived near Sobibor during the extermination period when we were in Poland. I wanted to understand how they tolerated such an extreme behavior. Were they complicit with the Nazis because they agreed to the policy, or were they forced into submission? I never got my answer to that question but it is clear that some of them (like Jan—see below) felt a sense of guilt for being a part of the mechanism. The construction, existence, purpose, and finally the closing and dismantling of Sobibor were justified by the rubric of "Operation Reinhard." The idea of systematic extermination of noncombatants is what makes the Holocaust so horrific. This idea of systematic extermination in Germany had been pioneered by the Nazis in the late 1930s through a little-known project, called simply "Aktion T4." The T4 Project, a state-endorsed euthanasia project, was formulated at Tiergarten Street #4 in Berlin and instituted as policy in 1939, resulting in the deaths of thousands of severely disabled people and other "undesirables" in Nazi Germany in anticipation of the extermination camps. By 1940, what had been learned from the T4 Project was now ready to be expanded for a larger population. Even after the project was officially ended, the "research" that it provided laid the groundwork for the extermination camp model of the Final Solution. By the summer of 1941, the use of carbon monoxide from a running van into an airtight room occurred to those involved with the T4 Project. After a few experiments on ill and infirm ghetto detainees, Red Army officers, and incurables, the method was approved. Within weeks, there was a shortage of vans to conduct the rising number of prisoners, so separate gas chambers at camps, which were fully dedicated to this purpose, were created. The idea of killing people on such a massive scale while removing the direct contact between the perpetrator and the victim made the program easier to implement. The three camps, Bełżec, Treblinka, and Sobibor, were the models for this work. Bełżec came first, followed by Sobibor and Treblinka. Their layout was similar in terms of the placement of the various areas of activity: there were three, or perhaps four, separate camps or sectors within the larger extermination camp. Camps I and II were living barracks and workshops, Camp III was for the gas chambers, and, depending on the type of burning facilities available, Camp IV was used for burning and burial of the remains.

Sobibor's location was a key to its success. It was in an isolated area, even though it was on a railroad link to Włodawa. The ability to keep a low profile for the camp was paramount, and the dense forest provided a measure of protection. Locals were needed to help move larger groups from the railroad cars, and the close proximity to places such as Luta and Włodawa was important so that many of the victims' possessions could be sold at local markets. Physical topography was important for the camp size, and the existence of rivers and valleys helped determine how the camp was laid out. On October 14, 1943, most of the rebels went out the front gate because it represented the only clear road in and out of the camp. The remainder of the camp was fortified and there were not clear exit routes through the forests. The chaotic exit resulted in 318 participants escaping, with only 47 surviving the war to tell their stories. Based on the trials of surviving SS (after the war), their testimonies, and those of prisoners of Sobibor, survivors created a map of what they remembered the camp to look like. They were even able to reconstruct a chronological history of the daily life of the camp. Each of the different survivors (including the SS and Ukrainian guards who were tried in court) who wrote their own personal account was participating in the collective and private memories of the others. These multiple sources formed a body of data.

Most historians and literary scholars are familiar with this type of work from the ancient period through the modern period. We have multiple versions of the lives of the famous people in antiquity (Alexander the

Great, Julius Caesar, Jesus of Nazareth) and multiple versions of famous battles of the Byzantines, the Crusaders, Napoleon, the Civil War, and even World War II. A historian looks at the different eyewitness testimonies and is able to create a more synoptic reading of the elements that are similar or different in each of the accounts. In the case of the different Sobibor survivor accounts, maps of the camp had been drawn from memory, and they did not match each other in small but crucial elements. The need for a map that was based upon a combination of the survivor maps and our subsurface mapping would be a major part of our contribution to the Sobibor documentation project.

The University of Hartford's Sobibor Documentation Project

The documentation about the Sobibor camp was collected from a variety of literary accounts written down at various times after 1945, the evidence of the archaeology and geophysical survey, and oral testimonies. We had enough details to compare with the material culture from the regional sites we were looking at: Włodawa, Luta, and Sobibor. The Sobibor camp was located near Sobibor village, in the eastern part of the Lublin district of Poland, close to the Chelm Włodawa railway line. It is possible to see where this is all located and the proximity to the border in the map in figure 5.2.

My team comprised members from Canada and the United States (plus our two translators from Poland and one volunteer from England, Deborah Rozansky), including Sarah Rutman, a senior student in archaeology from the University of Hartford; my son, Ethan; our cartographer, Philip Reeder of the University of South Florida; our chief geophysicist, Paul Bauman of WorleyParsons, Inc.; and his assistant geophysicist, Brad Hansen from WorleyParsons. Paul Bauman had earlier worked at another firm that loaned us the equipment every summer for our work. That company, Komex International, was a gas and oil exploration/geophysics company that was ultimately bought out by the larger company WorleyParsons. Tad Dibrowski was a Polish-born hydrogeologist who cofounded Komex in the 1970s. Tad had helped Paul every year with our requests for time and equipment for our excavations in the late 1990s and early 2000s. We included the name of the company, Komex, in most of our films, articles, and books because they were so generous. When Paul went to Tad to tell him about our work in Sobibor, Tad was immediately engaged. He told Paul that he had a direct connection to Sobibor, and not only did he help Paul in making his arrangements, but he also offered the services of his sister, Zofia Zinserling, as a personal translator for our project. Tad's father had been a businessman in the area of Sobibor in the late 1930s and early 1940s. He provided building materials and agricultural supplies in the region, especially feed and some of the construction materials. Tad's father was hired to help build the personal stables for the infamous Odilo Globocink, who in 1942 was hired by Heinrich Himmler to head "Operation Reinhard." Tad even remembers seeing Globocink, who was ultimately in charge of the building of Sobibor. The fact that Tad had such a close connection with the camp of Sobibor was one of those unusual coincidences that continued to occur throughout our work. Tad's father ultimately died in a reused, post–World War II concentration camp located in Majdanek, Poland, which was used as a prison under the communists. It was a bittersweet irony that his company was now responsible for uncovering the camp at Sobibor—a small type of redemption of a lost history. For Tad and Paul, there was now a personal connection that stretched from Canada to Israel and back to Poland.

As Paul related this story to me back in 2008, I remember thinking that this is one of the ways that the interconnections between people work, although some people deem such things as just an odd coincidence. Tad's father died in what had been an infamous concentration camp in Poland, and people from Tad's company were recovering the history of an extermination camp in Poland. It was an indirect and unintended form of retributive justice that neither I nor Paul could have anticipated. In 2010 I finally met Tad in Calgary and thanked him for the different excavations with which his company (Komex and later WorleyParsonsKomex) had helped us. He bent down (he is a very tall and large man with a huge grip) and said, "No, thank you, for giving us the opportunity to do this work." This is one of the divine footprints of history: finding people who can help at precisely the moment that you need their assistance. This has been one of the great "coincidences" of our work.

Not only was our project at Sobibor intended to provide research data for future excavations, but we also had an educational project that is a part of the Maurice Greenberg Center for Judaic Studies at the University of Hartford where Avi and I teach. Every year we present to area educators new research on the Holocaust at a teachers' workshop. Finding opportunities to teach about new research on the Holocaust motivated both Avi and me to go out to the field and to help make this documentary about the work. We also brought two student workers from Hartford to help the geophysicists, and they learned more about the Holocaust in the field than anything we could ever teach in the classroom. One was a major in Judaic studies, Sarah Rutman, who had been on almost all of our other excavations; she had worked with the geophysicists before and knew her way around excavation sites. Her family's history was also linked to the Holocaust, and her work in Sobibor was more of an education about history, archaeology, and Judaic studies than any course could give her. She also learned in the field about the Holocaust in a way that we could not really teach in a classroom by meeting people in Poland and interviewing refugees in the United States. In addition, I brought my own twelve-year-old son, Ethan. Ethan had been with me on excavations since he was ten years old and had also worked with the geophysicists, but some of my colleagues questioned my judgment in taking a youngster to work at an extermination camp. Some of them came out and asked me whether I thought that the gruesome nature of the task might traumatize him for the rest of his life. I had decided to ask him whether he wanted to come to Sobibor with me following our work in Israel, where he worked on the Bethsaida excavations. Almost everywhere I went, from meetings with the chief rabbi to the work at Włodawa, Luta, Sobibor, and Otwock, Ethan was with me. He asked lots of questions and made me think that this was an experience that he would only fully understand years from now. He regularly would sit in the meetings and negotiations with his iPod on, listening to music. But whenever he was called upon to do work, he turned off the iPod, put it away, and focused on the task at hand.

Włodawa and Luta, Poland: 1940–2008

The first part of our project was spent gathering as much information as we could about the site. We began our work in Poland in the city of Włodawa, because I wanted to see if we could understand what the relationship was between this city and the building of Sobibor. We were also interested in seeing what the level of Jewish culture and interaction was in a town close to Sobibor. It is estimated that over two-thirds of all the businesses of Włodawa were owned or run by Jews before the war. The Jews were a large percentage of the population of this city. We came away with a deeper understanding of how well everyone in Włodawa must have known Jewish culture and how most non-Jews in Włodawa must have known Jews. It was, of course, on the main train route to Sobibor. I knew that everyone in the city would have seen the trainloads of Jews passing through on the train line, and I wanted to know what was left of the historic presence of the Jews there. The director of the Sobibor

Figure 5.5.   The Włodawa synagogue restoration

Museum, Marek Bem, was responsible for the restoration of the synagogue and study house that sat in the middle of Włodawa. Marek was very proud of how well the restoration had been done. It had not been destroyed during the war because it was an example of excellent architecture and was well built. The moment that we arrived in Włodawa, I knew that I had been transported back to the pre–World War II time. Little had changed in Włodawa—except that the village had been mostly Jewish before 1939 and now there are no Jews and a beautifully restored synagogue and study house. In a strange twist to my interest in Włodawa, almost two years later, as I was finishing this book, I met the granddaughter of a Jewess who left Włodawa on the eve of the Holocaust; her stories provided me with a background about the city that added to my own interest in what made the change over from a Jewish city with a proud past into a non-Jewish city with a reborn proud past. In my work in Spain I had had a similar insight. Most of the restored areas of medieval Jewish presence in Spain had taken on local importance despite the fact that there were no Jews in these cities. In one of the two Jewish restaurants I visited in Segovia, Spain, I asked about why the Jewish sites had local interest, and the restaurant owner said that it was just their unique touristic theme.

When I visited with the chief rabbi of Poland, Rabbi Michael Shudrich, on the Sabbath before we began our work at Sobibor, he told me that to understand the whole story, going to the places around the camps was as important as going to the camps themselves. The restoration of the Polish sites was done to attract Polish and non-Polish tourism, but also to educate Poles about their own history. I began to see how problematic it must be for modern-day Poles to view their own history in this way. It might be slightly comforting for Poles to see Jewish tourists from families connected to Włodawa coming to visit in much the same way that modern Spaniards view Jewish tourists coming to see the sites of medieval Jewish remains. For Poles, making sure that the World War II stories of Polish citizens are known and written up has become a form of national therapy.

In creating our own Sobibor project at the University of Hartford, however, I decided it would be important to find and interview a local Polish family who lived during the period and hear a firsthand account. I found a source in an unexpected place. While sitting at a table in KwaZulu province in South Africa finishing this book, I met Libby Lenkinski, whose grandmother was from Włodawa. She told me about her grandmother, who had kept many letters and photos of her life in Włodawa from before the war, as well as letters from her relatives that continued up until the war. This type of documentation is very important for the understanding of not only Sobibor but also the area around Sobibor, which included Włodawa and also Luta. As the World War II survivors are passing away, so too are the people who lived in the areas where the Nazi Holocaust functioned. The testimony of the people who lived through it and survived, both Jews and non-Jews, is very important to understanding the "rest of the story." Whoever knew what was going on is as valuable as the testimonies of the victims.

The Luta Field

Thanks to the chief rabbi of Poland and our other translator, Lukazc Biedka, a psychiatrist from Warsaw, we were able to make an appointment to visit with a local farmer, Jan, who wanted to tell his own Sobibor story. He lived in Luta, a small town a few miles outside of Sobibor. Jan had seen the labor units from Sobibor working in the field by the Bug River, and he also had seen the laborers killed in the field nearby after the rebellion. He knew what was happening, like many of the people, and he remembered it all. When we decided to bring our equipment to work in the Sobibor camp, we were asked to do a few different tasks in the few days that we

Courtesy of the University of Hartford Sobibor Project

Figure 5.6.   The Luta burials in the field

were in Poland. One was to survey the field in back of Jan's home. We learned that it had been a killing field for the Nazis after the rebellion at Sobibor, and for sixty years he did not speak about it.

Jan wanted to tell his story because of a young girl that he met before the war. She was a Jewish child, and he knew that she had been taken away as the Nazis planned and built the Sobibor camp. The details of Jan's story illuminate the "Hidden Holocaust," the reverberating effects of the events of the time. Jan knew that his classmate had been taken away; he had a soft place in his heart for her and he did nothing. He was a young man some sixty-five years ago, and he had a cart and horse. Carts like those Jan described were used at the camp, probably to bring the weak and the invalids directly to the gassing chambers, especially in the early months of the camp's work. (Later it seems that there was a light-gauge rail system that brought the weak and infirm directly to the gassing chambers, but this probably was not operational in the earliest period.) Jan was told to bring his horse and cart to the Sobibor camp in 1942. He says that he did not know exactly why he was being pressed into service, but he was a teenager and was fearful of not listening to the Nazis and their Polish surrogates.

Courtesy of the University of Hartford Sobibor Project

Figure 5.7.   Jan, Lukazc, and Freund in Luta

When he arrived at the camp, he says that he was overwhelmed by the smell of the burning of the bodies. He says that he fell from his cart, and when he awoke he was alone. This experience made him remember it all.

The Camp: The Hidden Holocaust and the Survivors

The facts of the Sobibor revolt were recorded by a number of survivors. While there are conflicting pieces of information in these accounts, all celebrate the role of Alexander (Sasha) Pechersky in its success. I should point out that Holocaust deniers exploit even minor differences in survivor accounts to create the impression that these testimonies are untrue. Indeed, the fact that there are minor differences gives them greater credibility for historians, who regularly must dig through conflicting accounts of events that happened as recently as 9/11. If all of the accounts were exactly the same, it would seem that they were all drawing off of one another. Instead, each has a new element that only someone who had been there could have added. The fact that there are multiple and complementary attestations to the role of Sasha Pechersky in the rebellion makes him come alive as a person. He was a Jew molded by the tradition of Simeon Bar Kokhba in the face of the Second Rebellion in 135 CE. Pechersky was born in the Ukraine in 1909, was brought into the Red Army, and by 1941 was already a junior officer. As the Nazis progressed in their battle to take Leningrad, the inevitability of Jewish military personnel being taken as prisoners increased. Jews in the Soviet Army distinguished themselves as combat officers and were taken as POWs when the Nazis were pushing through the Soviet Union in 1941. In October 1941, Pechersky was captured by the Nazis. After a failed escape attempt from a POW camp, it was discovered that he was Jewish, and he was sent to a labor camp in Minsk. By September 1943, he was transferred to Sobibor. Sobibor camp resistance leaders recognized Pechersky's expertise as a combat officer and began assisting him in his plan to lead a prisoner uprising, which involved luring guards into an isolated area and killing them. Then, as the rebellion was in full swing, Perchersky addressed the prisoners and told them to break through the barbed wire and escape across a minefield. This plan allowed only a fraction of the inmates to escape, but in the end it yielded results for large groups of prisoners to be liberated. Pechersky survived Sobibor and joined a unit of partisans, which, like other partisan groups of the period, conducted small raids upon isolated Nazi units. He was active until he was injured and arrested by the Soviets, charged with collaboration with the Nazis, and sent to a gulag after the war. He was only released after his role in the Sobibor rebellion became international news.

Another Sobibor survivor, Thomas Toivi Blatt, was very young during the rebellion. He investigated and wrote about its history, and the results are found in his two books, *Sobibor: The Forgotten Revolt* and *From the Ashes of Sobibor*. His story of the revolt was told in *Escape from Sobibor*, the award-winning Chrysler Corporation film special of 1987. His documentation was invaluable for understanding the different characters and what actually happened on that October day in 1943.

As mentioned, in addition to our excavation work, we collaborated to preserve video footage about Sobibor for the University of Hartford. Gary Hochman, the producer leading the video documentation, followed one of the eight surviving rebels, Philip Bialowitz, who now lives in New York, back to Sobibor. Bialowitz and his brother were in Sobibor. The Bialowitzes' hometown was Izbica, Poland, a small *shtetl* (village) on the way to Lublin in eastern Poland. During the war the Nazis located a transit camp there and then shipped off many of the inmates to Bełżec and Sobibor. Bialowitz's story of growing up as a Polish youth in Warsaw and

Courtesy of the University of Hartford Sobibor Project

Figure 5.8.   Philip Bialowitz at Sobibor in 2008

later in Lublin is chronicled during his interviews with Gary Hochman for the documentary *Hidden Holocaust*. It traces his own attempt to come to terms with his treatment before, during, and after the rebellion. During the film, Gary took Bialowitz back to his hometown and then to visit the farm family that sheltered Bialowitz following the Sobibor revolt. Most enlightening in the documentary is the moment when Bialowitz returns to Sobibor and has a chance encounter with the son of one of the Nazi guards who was killed during the revolt. As I look at the footage, I think that it is one of the most insightful moments in the history of our work at Sobibor—two grieving people together at a small memorial on the site, connecting in a positive way: one an adult who barely knew his father but wanted to make amends for what he did, and another a man who has spent his life thinking about what happened to him. In the footage you see the two of them standing in front of the cement ash mound at Sobibor as Mr. Bialowitz intones the words of the ancient Jewish prayer the *Kaddish* (the mourner's prayer). Mr. Bialowitz wrote a memoir (with his son Joseph Bialowitz) titled *A Promise at Sobibor: A Jewish Boy's Story of Revolt and Survival in Nazi-Occupied Poland* (2010) so that his story could be told from the perspective that he had as a child.

Mapping the Sobibor Camp

The life of an inmate at Sobibor was well known and shared by the different survivor accounts. The railroad is the constant in the area. There were four "sectors" or camps, and each was laid out to ensure that each group that came in did not know what was going on in all of the locations. Even as we worked each day on the excavation site, we could hear the whistle of the train as it came in on the spur that leads into the forest in front of the camp to this day. In March 1942, a new spur was built from the main Włodawa branch, which ended at a concrete ramp (still visible in 2008). The ramp is opposite what had been Sobibor's station house. The different camp sections had numbers and designations with the purpose of hiding what was going on inside. According to the accounts, there were three buildings in Camp I that were used by the administrators to make it seem like a labor camp: the station house, the forester's house, and even a two-story post office.

During our work in Camp III in the summer of 2008, we found many scattered pieces of brick in a concentrated area at the end of what has since been confirmed as the *Himmelfahrsstrasse* (German for "the road to heaven"—the code word for the way to the gas chambers), near a large number of personal artifacts, along a route filled with barbed wire and a piece of what appeared to be a light rail system for helping transport those people who could not walk to the gas chambers to the site. The ground-penetrating radar (GPR) seemed to reveal the outer contours of the footings of a building. The excavations will tell much more. The comparisons with the Bełżec camp reveal the similarities as well. At Bełżec, there was a light rail system that led up to a twelve-foot-square gas chambers building that could hold up to 180 people at one time. At Bełżec there was a small door leading from a porch from the light rail system that ran along the length of the building. There was an area for removing the gassed bodies opposite the entrance. The motor that produced the deadly carbon monoxide gas would have been right next to this building. At Bełżec there were pipes that conducted the gas to the building. There were large and deep burial pits. A narrow gauge light railway was used to bring those who could not walk to the gas chambers. It would have led from the main railway station at the front gate to the burning and burial areas. As Yoram

Haimi's excavations followed the trail of artifacts, the comparison with Bełżec was even more significant.

Artifacts of Life and Death:
Some Insights Gained from Our Work

"Artifacts" is a word that I use throughout the book to describe items with varying measures of importance that were used by people in their daily lives. Throughout this book I have tried to elucidate the power of artifacts to illuminate and inspire. The "key of Peter" story that I reprised in chapter 1 was important because that key symbolized the most important theological expression of Christianity by one of the most important Roman Catholic figures of the twentieth century. The key in its original first-century context was just an iron door key for opening a wooden door. Artifacts (and even replicas of original artifacts that are scientifically validated) provide an insight into the past that texts do not.

In chapter 2 we examined two small artifacts, the Astarte figurines that we found in the Doña Ana Park, in the larger context of the ancient world. What struck me about the figurines was their connection with the pan-Mediterranean and Near Eastern religions and cultures. The discovery of such tiny items in the midst of a vast swamp, while remarkable, is not unprecedented. Who used these items, when, and why did they end up in the mudflats while most of the ancient contours of the city are buried beneath thousands of pounds of sediment? In the same chapter we discovered that the warrior-steles with the concentric circles of central Spain hinted at the lives of people who had lived before them on the coast and were creating this signpost to remember their past. It shows us how the ancients were continually trying to send us a message across history to tell us about who they were and what they believed was important.

In chapter 3 we investigated perhaps the most famous artifact of the twentieth century, the corpus known collectively as the Dead Sea Scrolls. Eleven caves that ring the ancient site of Qumran were filled with the scrolls that electrified the public's imagination for the past sixty years. During our investigation of the cemetery, the bathing facilities, the rooms, and the defensive tower of Qumran and the caves near the settlement we came to understand just how archaeological artifacts (including the Dead Sea Scrolls themselves) tell us about lives committed to religious ideals that were lived under duress and constantly threatened with extinction. The scrolls are artifacts that accidentally emerged from caves along the

Dead Sea after World War II and the Holocaust (1947), and so in trying to contextualize their significance in this period we must not ignore how people understood the sudden appearance of the scrolls. As you have read, many people (including scholars) looked at the timing of these events as significant. The amount of scrolls materials aside (nine hundred separate manuscripts), it was also a unique "message" of divine retribution (*The War Scroll*, for example) in the scrolls that shook the post–World War II Jewish and Christian worlds in a way that no other single artifact has ever done. While the scrolls are inevitably linked to a small and rather insignificant group (in the long history of the world) in an obscure location and in a very specific time period, the scrolls' impact goes far beyond that of almost any other artifact of the twentieth century. The scrolls remind us of just how much history we do not yet know and how quickly our understanding of history can be changed by one discovery.

The medieval church of Burgos, Spain, that we investigated in chapter 4 is an example of another artifact that tells us much about the relationship between Judaism, Christianity, and Islam in the Middle Ages. "How," we might ask, "did humanity move from the Golden Age of Spain to the forcible transformation of synagogues and mosques into churches and the conversion of Jews and Muslims to Christianity in the space of a few hundred years?" When someone asks me what we can learn from history, it is not only to ask what went wrong but also to ask what went right. When we consider whether or not Judaism, Christianity, and Islam can live together in the modern world, we need look only at the Spanish experiment to learn sobering lessons about what works and what does not and why. A large artifact like a church that has been transformed from a synagogue or a mosque tells us a lot about the past and the future. One of the most famous artifacts from this period that I saw in a museum in Israel taught me about how a single artifact can encapsulate an entire historical period. The artifact was a key brought from Spain by the families of the refugees of the 1492 expulsion from Spain. The large medieval door key from the home of the refugee from Spain became a family heirloom that was passed from generation to generation and hung with pride on the wall of the home (and remembered in songs). They kept the key to their home in Spain as a measure of their faith. Akin to an amulet, it was their attempt to maintain faith in their ultimate return even as they lived in Morocco or Turkey, and it symbolized their faith in some future divine judgment. The key of Bethsaida and the key of Spain are very different keys, but they both help us understand religious ideas with enormous staying power.

Perhaps the most poignant artifacts of Sobibor were also keys. The artifacts along the *Himmelfahrsstrasse* tell us much about what the victims thought awaited them at the end of the road in 1942 when the camp opened, and through October 1943 when the rebellion took place. It is the many small artifacts that I thought were the most meaningful. There were many small keys (of differing sizes) that were probably used to lock luggage, perhaps homes, cupboards, and unknown locks. They tell us much about the state of mind of the victims. They appear to be haphazardly buried along the way to the gas chambers. It is suspected that many of these small keys fit the locks of the suitcases that the prisoners arrived with, containing what was left of their lives. They were obliged to leave the suitcases as they left the trains on their way to "disinfection." These small artifacts and all of the artifacts that are found in scientifically controlled excavations hold a unique meaning for archaeology, especially when they are accompanied by written testimonies that can be compared. Throughout this book I have tried to emphasize that this is why we must take any textual information available about a site seriously (but often not literally) as we excavate.

Burials: From Qumran to Sobibor

When I arrived in Warsaw from Israel in July 2008, I made my way to speak to the chief rabbi of Poland, an American-born, Polish-speaking man named Michael Shudrich. He and I had been students together in New York in the 1970s, and he was one of the few people who could give me insights into some of the problems I might have working at Sobibor, based upon his thirty years of experience in Poland. We met with many of the people at his synagogue, which is a composite of modern Poles and refugees from former Soviet countries who arrived in Poland looking for Jewish life. One of the most important things that Rabbi Shudrich explained to me was the problem that had plagued other scientific teams in their work at extermination camps. It was a problem that was not uniquely Jewish, but it was an issue that has become for many archaeologists a great matter of sensitivity: how to excavate, and not violate, the sacred space of the dead.

I alluded to the importance of the issue of the dignity of the dead in many of the projects that we undertook in my book *Digging through the Bible*. This is not just a passing issue. It is for many people the crux of the problem of archaeology. In the past two hundred years, archaeologists and anthropologists have dug up the remains of Native Americans, indigenous peoples, and a host of ancient and modern burials all in the name of science. The remains of ancient peoples sat in our leading museums, and people came to see these rather ghoulish scenes that were re-created in the form of dioramas and reconstructed native scenes to educate the public about ancient traditions and customs. In the 1960s and 1970s, more and more groups began to petition the learned societies of archaeology and anthropology to abandon this desecration of burial sites. Museums took the original bones and remains from public areas of museums, and sometimes substituted casts of the bones that looked for all intents and purposes like the originals. Attempts were made to rebury in dignified places designated by the affected groups. The burial mound was seen as a holy place that needed protection and veneration. The Israel Antiquities Authority has set very specific guidelines for those who are involved in the discovery of burials. These strict regulations are monitored by religious and ultra-religious bodies of Jews specifically because they have seen the kind of desecration that has happened to Jewish burials all over the world during the past few hundred years. While we were working in the cemetery of Qumran, religious activists sat and watched our work for hours as we moved with the GPR over the 1,213 individual graves and carefully catalogued what was in each grave. This type of noninvasive archaeology gives scientists some of the information they need to assess the site without having to open each grave. Without this technique, the graves of Qumran look just like randomly placed stones. With the GPR of each grave, we could see if there were grave goods (usually special items and pottery—items that were buried in the grave), the depth of burial, and indeed if it was (or was not) a grave.

In Israel, archaeologists are very careful not to excavate graves not only because of Jewish concerns but also because it leads to a denigration of the profession of archaeology. The Jewish concept of *kavod hamet* (literally, the dignity of the dead) has always been a deeply rooted tradition within the Jewish people. In Jewish law, this concept is invoked to ensure a speedy burial after death (often by waiving some ritual responsibilities) as well as proper care of the dead and the burial place. It also prohibits certain actions, including autopsy (except in rare cases) and limits the possibilities of removal and excavation of corpses, bones, and even ashes of burned remains. This law is carefully maintained in a place such as Israel. However, Poland has, for all intents and purposes, as many Jewish burials as any other place on earth, and the strictures for the care and treatment of the burials of Jews is not always as well known to non-Jews. That is why our work with a noninvasive method was so important in a place like Poland.

A Geophysical Death Camp Survey

We used three different techniques to map the subsurface at Sobibor: an electromagnetic high-resolution metal detector and terrain conductivity meter, ground-penetrating radar, and electrical gradiometer together with GPS-linked mapping. The EM61 metal detector is able to detect any shallow mapping for both ferro- (iron and steel) and non-ferromagnetic (copper, lead, gold, etc.) metal in the near surface. This is a very sophisticated metal detector and allowed us the opportunity to go over the surfaces where the GPR had identified something but needed further verification. The EM61 we used had a maximum depth of investigation of 3.5 meters below ground surface. The instrument can locate a metal object as small as a bolt or nail in the top few inches of earth, and something as large as a single fuel drum at its full depth of investigation of 10 feet. At that depth, the instrument cannot identify an object as small as a single coin, but it can give information on something as large as a railroad track.

Since there were no formal crematoria at Sobibor, metal tracks were used to construct a frame (according to testimonies) upon which they burned the bodies. Generally, an EM61 mapped anomaly will preserve the approximate shape, size, and aspect ratio of the buried target. For instance, a buried box will produce a rectangular anomaly, and a buried pipe or barbed wire will

Figure 5.9.   Paul Bauman with the ground-penetrating radar

Courtesy of the University of Hartford Sobibor Project

produce a long, linear anomaly. However, the geophysical footprint of the EM61 mapped anomaly will generally be somewhat larger than the footprint of the object itself. The greater the depth of burial, the larger the size of the EM61 mapped anomaly. In the case of the Sobibor surveys, the EM61 data that was collected in the open field were positionally coupled to GPS. Data positioning accuracy should be within 10 cm of the positional accuracy of the grid itself. Precise grid locations were surveyed in by Dr. Phil Reeder of the University of South Florida, and he produced an easily readable and changeable map that could easily be published and sent to other specialists around the globe for evaluation.

The EM38 terrain conductivity meter measures the electrical conductivity of the subsurface (i.e., terrain conductivity) to depths of 2–4 feet. EM38 is particularly well suited to identifying small, pieces of metal near the surface. Objects as small as a nail can be located up to 2–4 feet below the surface; it is important to compare and contrast all of the different techniques (EM 61 and GPR). The main advantage of this type of measurement is being extremely accurate in deciding where and why to dig.

Ground-Penetrating Radar: Limitations and Possibilities

Finally, it was decided to use GPR and not the original proposal of ERT at Sobibor. Yoram's initial work at Sobibor indicated that artifacts were buried only up to 6 feet below the surface, where GPR is most effective. We also had a concern that ERT would be slightly invasive (metal electrodes are pounded into the ground for the electrical charge). GPR seemed to be the best choice for the work. Since we worked in Poland in 2008 we have seen that other groups have begun using GPR, even at death camps that have already been restored.

We used a type of GPR setup that is dragged along the surface of the land as opposed to a unit that was on what looked like a lawnmower. Easily maneuverable, the GPR unit from WorleyParsons was the technology of choice in Luta, Sobibor, and Otwock. It did not disturb anything below ground, and it was the most noninvasive technique that would provide high-quality results. GPR is a high-frequency electromagnetic technique that uses the propagation and reflection of radar waves to map subsurface interfaces. In general, any change in soil texture or moisture content will create a radar reflection. Discrete objects—made of stone, cement, wood, plastic, metal, and so on—will also create distinct radar reflections. Higher frequency GPR transmitting antennas provide greater (finer) resolution, but less depth of investigation. The depth of investigation was generally 6 feet (2 meters) and sometimes deeper.

Low-Altitude, High-Resolution Aerial Photography of Sobibor: Getting the Big Picture

In almost every excavation that we have done, balloon photos have revealed a view that we could never have gotten so quickly and easily. It is an inexpensive and often logistically efficient means to see the big picture of a site. Often, there are sensitive issues that require difficult negotiations to get airplane or helicopter fly-over photographers. Using helium weather balloons was one of the great solutions to the vexing problem of getting the big picture when it comes to archaeology.

At Sobibor, we could see the killing fields where the ash and cremation formed a very clear, defined, nonforested area. Low-altitude aerial photography from helium-filled weather balloons allowed us to photograph and measure the size of the area of the mass burials in the open field. These are defined by deeper green hues in the vegetation. This conclusion is supported by coring activities by previous archaeologists in 2001 (see discussion of Dr. Andrezj Kola's excavation earlier in this chapter), according to

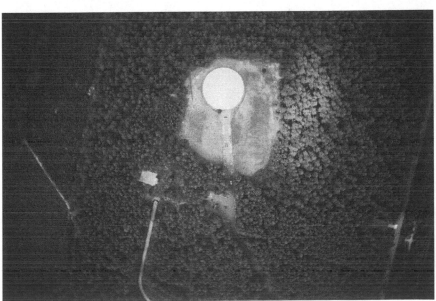

Figure 5.10. The aerial photograph of Sobibor

Courtesy of the University of Hartford Sobibor Project

Marek Bem, the director of the Sobibor park and museum. This conclusion was also supported by the processing of several GPR profiles that were done over the top of the areas.

In the field, there is a large cement circle (which is made up of the ash that was collected from the area). This is the most prominent monument at the site. However, not all of the ash was collected into the circle, only the layers above the ground level. The cement circle used to have a clear viewing panel in the front of it, which featured some of the bones together with a view of the ash layer so that people could know what was inside. According to Bem, this viewing panel was removed after complaints about the rather ghoulish nature of the arrangement. This cement circle is the place where most people who visit the camp come to pay their respects. Jewish groups view this site as the place where a memorial service should be conducted—in effect, it is the memorial at Sobibor. Also, the aerial photographs appear to show very clear areas of the contours of the Sobibor camp, which can easily be distinguished from surrounding forest by the subtle but clear change in tree canopy height and homogeneity. Magnetic gradient data in the open field has identified a number of buried metal anomalies in the field, which are relatively close to the surface. One anomaly that was particularly large in magnitude and in area was identified at the junction of two tentatively identified mass burials. According to Bem, this anomaly may indicate the locations of steel rails used in cremating human remains. The EM38 shows close to the surface indications of buried metal to the southwest, south, and southeast of the circular monument.

One of our objectives was to get a perspective of how big the camp was in the middle of a forest. A looming question that is asked by Holocaust deniers regards the size of the camp, based upon the small maps by the survivors, which are not drawn to scale. One of the Holocaust denier Internet sites asks, "How could 250,000 people have been put to death in such a small area?" In reality, if one has the full perspective of the camp, it is ample room for a systematic extermination machine. These subcamps took up more than twenty acres of Sobibor, and the camp's areas were all divided up into the standard quadrants. Aerial photographs would prove this. We did have some photographic comparisons to go on, thanks to random photos that were taken of the camp in 1944. First, a researcher, Alex Bay, provided us with a photograph from the U.S. Naval Archives taken in 1944 (before the camp was covered with heavy forest). This was invaluable, but only if we could get the same perspective from our work. The fact that we were in Poland on the border with Ukraine made for an interesting question of getting aerial photography in an easy and effective way. Fly-overs of planes and helicopters would have required enormous challenges. We turned to the balloon solution. Approximately 350 aerial photographs were taken from cameras mounted on the tether of helium-filled balloons. Photographs were taken from elevations varying from 20 meters to approximately 400 meters above ground surface. The majority of photographs were taken with the camera lens looking directly downward, though some shots were taken at oblique angles. All digital photographs were delivered, unedited, to the museum and the archaeological team before our departure from Sobibor.

GPS Mapping

With the exception of the magnetic gradiometer, all external GPS data were collected to pinpoint the locations of everything that was found for future excavators and Polish architects to reference as they work at the camp in the future. Part of our work was not only to prepare a map for future excavations but also to avoid some of the problems that had befallen other camps when officials decided to put up memorials in the camp. GPS, a technology that most people realize is an invaluable tool for traveling, has become the best friend of architects, archaeologists, and geologists. It provides exact locations that will not change with the dynamic vicissitudes of land recovery, memorials, climate, and long-term land use. The antenna for the GPS is designed to provide improved coverage in wooded areas, or in the vicinity of buildings and other sources of interference with the GPS signal. GPS data were corrected to a nearby Polish base station.

Some of the Results from Our Sobibor Project

Most of what was found was left in the ground for the systematic excavations to record *in situ*. As in other sites, everything that will be found belongs to the site, and director Marek Bem told me that he is interested in creating a museum at Sobibor for displaying the artifacts. But "truth-testing" of our equipment required us to do small excavations at the moment that large metal artifacts were found close to the surface. In the area of the field surrounding the monument to the rebellion, the sensors were mounted on backpacks and relatively high off the ground (up to four feet). What we see below surface can indicate a variety of different objects, which are called anomalies. Since we did not dig up every anomaly, we can only theorize as to what is below the surface, although after hundreds of hours

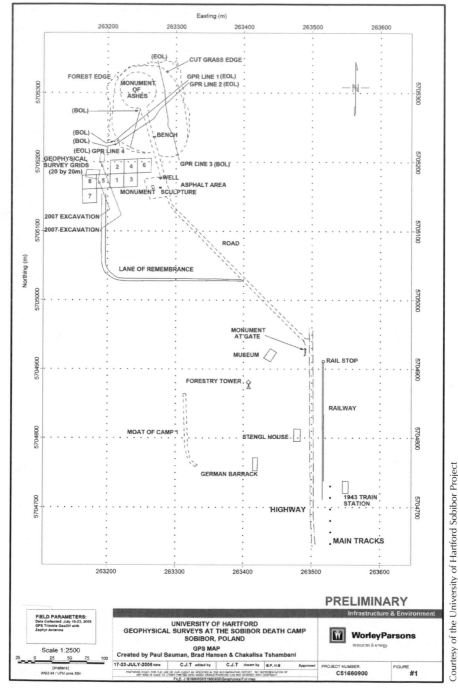

Figure 5.11. The geophysics results

Courtesy of the University of Hartford Sobibor Project

of observing objects using these sensors, it is possible for me to be more specific about what is buried in one location or another on the basis of what the geophysicists say about them. The anomalies that we found likely indicate very large pieces of metal (in contrast to nails, bolts, small pieces of wire, etc.). The most prominent anomalies in the open field are related to known features, including rebar (steel rods) used in the construction of the monument, walkways, curbs, and metal in the benches along the walkway leading to the monument. However, a large-magnitude anomaly was identified in the middle of the open field in the eastern central portion of the plot, in proximity to the trees but far from the monument. It is hypothesized that this area of buried metal may be related to rails used in cremating human bodies. Several (say five) discrete areas of buried metal are also identified in the southwest quadrant of the plot, and several others in the southeast quadrant. We can confirm that there is a large amount of buried metal under grids 1, 2, 3, and 4. The data also confirm that at least a significant percentage of this buried metal is iron and steel (rather than non-ferromagnetic metal), and that a noticeably large amount of metal is buried in a north-south trend on the west edge of grid 1 (east edge of grid 5). What this metal is may be determined by excavation.

Of particular interest are the large number of finds, very specifically aligned, in grids 5, 7, and 8. It seems that the eastern portion of grid 5 may be related to a previously existing foundation of a building (either an excavation of the building or foundation debris of a building). Here is where it is important to read the accounts written by the survivors in tandem with the work that has been done by Yoram Haimi, together with the geophysics. Near the building, the EM61 high-resolution metal detector has identified hundreds of small to medium-sized metal objects scattered in the area of grids 1 through 8. Some of this buried metallic debris appears to form distinct geometric patterns, which may be related to former buildings, camp infrastructure (narrow gauge rail, fences, etc.), or other unknown sources. This is why excavations are so important to uncovering the final story of Sobibor.

From Sobibor to Otwock

As we left Sobibor on the last day of the dig to go to Otwock on our way to the airport, we knew this was just the beginning of the work. Yoram and his students and volunteers who would excavate the site would have an easier task thanks to the geophysical survey, but more important I think is that those who have loved ones buried there can rest assured that no effort was spared to locate and isolate the areas where the dead are buried. This was the main goal of our work. In doing so I think we contributed to the field and to the history of Holocaust research. Our work in Poland did not end at Sobibor, but the idea that the work goes on and is being documented in a film that tells the larger tale of how the survivors and collaborators think about the Holocaust is especially important.

On our way to the Warsaw airport, we unloaded our equipment and did one more subproject related to the Holocaust in an area that is on the outskirts of the city, a hamlet known as Otwock, some fifteen miles southeast of Warsaw. Although I do not want to give too much information on the family burial we were searching for, I think it is important to say that this was a part of the mystery of the "Hidden Holocaust." Rabbi Shudrich made a personal petition for us to use the GPR to help find the missing burials of a family that was shot in the middle of the war and buried on the spot. The area was forested, with bungalows lining the muddy roads that led through the forest. Our team arrived and we began our work by listening to the testimony of the family who knew the story of the killings. After they indicated where the burials were thought to be, we began our work.

Figure 5.12.   Paul Bauman and the rabbi at Otwock

Courtesy of the University of Hartford Sobibor Project

Otwock was historically well known because it is so close to Warsaw and was at one time a resort area. In Otwock a *Judenrat* (a Jewish administrative council for a community in Nazi Germany, appointed by German officials) was established in October 1939, and in December 1940 about fifteen thousand persons were crowded into a ghetto that was created for those who were outside of the Warsaw ghetto. The Otwock ghetto was liquidated in the late summer of 1942. Presumably the killing of this one particular Jewish family that we were looking for happened either directly before the liquidation or in the dragnet that was set up for those who evaded the liquidation (although there was a question after the war about the killing and the courts apparently did not list the killing as taking place during the war). During the ghetto's existence, about two thousand residents died of hunger and typhus. During the liquidation of the Otwork ghetto about eight thousand residents were sent to Treblinka and Auschwitz, and about four thousand persons evaded deportation. But most were ultimately caught and shot. We were looking for one family in Otwork who had been gunned down and buried in a very specific location.

We were investigating one particular case from this ghetto and one particular testimony of someone who was there that day and was able to direct us to the general location where the crime happened. On the day we arrived, Rabbi Shudrich had brought someone from the burial society of Poland as well as a rabbi from Israel who was an expert in the whole religious legal question of what should be done when bodies are located in an undignified burial location and need to be disinterred for burial in a dignified location. This rabbi is involved in a group that handles the reinterment of bodies in Israel. This group is very meticulous in their work. They usually will interview the family and determine if there is a very specific reason why a person will be disinterred and then reinterred in Israel. Moving a body from an undignified place of burial qualifies as a reason, which was the case of the Otwock research. The rabbi from Jerusalem brought his divining sticks. We brought our GPR. Only once before had I seen divining sticks. They have been used by people all over the world to locate hidden graves up until the modern period. Here we were, in a suburb outside of a modern town of Warsaw, watching a religious authority from Jerusalem use a technology that has provided spiritual leaders with a measure of certainty about where an ancient grave was located. Divining rods are used by spiritual leaders with particular sensitivity to be directed to their unmarked target. The geophysicists watched in fascination as the rabbi moved from place to place in the area where the women had said the murder had taken place. His divining rods moved from side to side, then suddenly crossed to indicate where the bodies might be buried. We went over the same area with the GPR. It was a case where faith and archaeology met to solve a mystery. At the end of the day, we said our good-byes to the rabbis at Otwock, gave them copies of the printouts of the research to study and act on, packed up, and went to the airport. It was time to go back to the United States and Canada and prepare for our next project.

Acknowledgments

THIS IS A BOOK ABOUT HISTORY and the writing of history, but it is not a history book. This is also a book about archaeology and how archaeological research contributes to our understanding of history, but it is not an archaeology textbook. It is a book about major issues and mysteries of how religion and religious faiths interact in history, but it is not a religious handbook. Mostly this is a book about my own encounter with topics from the beginnings of civilization at Atlantis to the near end of civilization during the Holocaust.

Over the past thirty years I have collected the results of research projects I have participated in that I feel add to the understanding of history and archaeology. The book was written for the general public, who may not be trained historians, scholars of religion, theologians, or archaeologists, but rather interested readers. This is an introductory-level book on how I think archaeology can help us understand history better, if we can track how archaeological work has enlightened us in a few key periods over the past four thousand years. I chose a number of examples that I have firsthand knowledge of. I included a bibliography at the end of the book for the reader's reference. I alluded to many of the different views held by others about each event or site. While I attempted to bring in some of the other major theories and information on some of these sites, I presented my own theories and information from sites of which I have firsthand knowledge.

I did not thirty years ago intend to write this book. It began to take shape as my own interests and research in the history of the world and Jewish history began to coalesce. Over the past decade I began noticing connections between what I was teaching and researching in different time periods. The chapters in this book parallel my own research and scholarly presentations at professional societies over the past decade. The fact that I am able to write a book with the title *Digging through History: Archaeology and Religion from Atlantis to the Holocaust* is largely because I stand on the shoulders of many teachers and pioneers in different disciplines of research, and because in each project I was working with a group of specialists who allowed me to participate in their research.

I am indebted to my fellow field archaeologists, geoscientists, historians, religion and Bible scholars, filmmakers, Judaic studies faculty, donors, and volunteers who have worked with me over the past twenty-five years and contributed to my own knowledge base. I hope I will acknowledge most of the people who made contributions to the present work, but on the chance that I miss some of you, many other names and affiliations can be found in the numerous publications, papers, press releases, documentaries, and interviews that led up to the writing of this book over the past decade. In particular, I would like to thank the geoscientists, archaeologists, and historians in all of the locations where we have worked. The role of WorleyParsons Inc. in Canada, for all of the work supervised by the geophysicist Paul Bauman, is of special note. Many of the projects were facilitated because of the work of Paul and his assistants from WorleyParsons over the years from the sites in southern and northern Spain, Poland, and Israel, and they will be mentioned by name below. I would like to acknowledge the following for their special friendship and work: in Poland, the archaeologists of record, Yoram Haimi and Isaac Gilead of Ben Gurion University, Israel, and Marek Bem and Wojciech Mazurek of the Sobibor Museum; in Spain, Dr. Sebastian Celestino of CSIS Badajoz, Spain, and Dr. Ana Garcia Martinez and Dr. Juan José Garcia of the University of Burgos; in Israel, Dr. Hanan Eshel of Bar Ilan University, Magen Broshi, emeritus of the Israel Museum, Dr. Dan Bahat of Bar Ilan University, Dr. Danny Syon of the Israel Antiquities Authority, Dr. Michal Artzy and Shalom Yanklowitz of Haifa University, and Dr. Adolfo Roitman of the Shrine of the Book at the Israel Museum in Jerusalem. Some of our work was done in Israel together with Dr. Carl Savage of Drew University and Dr. Rami Arav of the University of Nebraska at Omaha, who during the past twenty-five years has tirelessly worked on the Bethsaida Excavations Project with me and some twenty other directors to unravel the mysteries of Bethsaida on the northeast shore of the Sea of Galilee and was always there to answer many of my questions. Rami has been a veritable encyclopedia of information and he never tired of listening to my archaeological insights and together with my colleagues at the University of Hartford (and the University of Connecticut), Avinoam Patt, Hazza Abu Raia, and Maha Darawsha, have helped form my ideas about the long duration of human history that spans more than the Middle East.

The ideas and many versions of the chapters in this book have been presented over the past thirty years at professional conferences of the American Academy of Religion, Association of Jewish Studies, and the Society of Biblical Literature (regional, national, and international conferences), and American Schools of Oriental Research, and I am thankful for the feedback I received at these conferences.

This book is intended for nonspecialists in archaeology, religion, history, and biblical studies and is not intended to take the place of the more academic tomes that are also available. I will use this book in my survey of history course that covers the period from the Bronze Age (3000 BCE) until the modern period. I have always alluded to the Holocaust at the end of the course, not because I see it as the end of history, but because after presenting the whole scope of major events I think that an event like the Holocaust can be properly contextualized. We have separate courses at the university on modern history and the Holocaust, but my course is a survey; this book is intended for this course and my course on Bible and archaeology.

Any errors that have occurred in the reporting of the data in this book are my responsibility alone. The results presented here, however, are data that I, as well as other scholars, have collected, lectured on, presented at conferences, and published. All the information I used in the book was reported to me either orally or in writing through interim reports, lectures, and conferences in geology, geography, religion, history, and archaeology. I also gave my own translations based on the Revised Standard Version of the Bible.

Writing about Archaeology for the Public

This volume is a hybrid, as are my books *Digging through the Bible* (2009) and *Secrets of the Cave of Letters* (2004); even the four volumes on Bethsaida (*Bethsaida: A City by the North Shore of the Sea of Galilee*, ed. Arav and Freund, 1995, 1999, 2004, 2009) follow a precedent that was started by Yigael Yadin in the 1960s (in Hebrew and later in English) in books on Hazor, Masada, and Bar Kokhba. These books contain archaeological data researched by scholars but written primarily for the public.

These types of hybrid books and exhibition catalogues (see the bibliography for many others) have engaged the general public in thinking in a serious and informed way about the Bible, history, and the archaeology that has been uncovered in the past half century. *Digging through History* is unique because it includes a critical methodology of the Bible and history, covers different biblical periods, then continues its trajectory into the modern period. It addresses most of the major questions I have been asked by students and lecture attendees around the country. Unlike other works I have read, this book also covers the topics within each of the different historical periods, from the beginning of civilization until the "almost" end of civilization in the Holocaust (I calculate almost five thousand years). The book does not begin with the Bible, but with a question from outside that is parallel to the rise of civilization in the Middle East—Atlantis. This is a continuation of the book I published in 2009, *Digging through the Bible*, but it goes beyond the Bible and covers a much wider swath of human history.

Over the past twenty-five years—since the excavations at Bethsaida began—I knew that I was engaged in an enterprise that was interesting to the general public. Thanks to television documentaries, many of our discoveries were directly brought to the public. UNO-TV, at the University of Nebraska at Omaha, made three documentaries (*The Lost City of Bethsaida*, *Return to the Cave of Letters*, and *The Road to Morocco*), which slowly brought the results of our excavations to a larger and larger public. These led to many other television documentaries, including *Kingdom of David*, *The Fifth Gospel*, Biblical Archaeology Society's *An Archaeological Search for Jesus*, NOVA's *Ancient Refuge in the Holy Land*, CNN's *After Jesus—The First Christians*, and the *National Geographic* special titled *Finding Atlantis*. The wide interest in our documentaries convinced me that we were engaged in an important enterprise that needed a written volume to tell "the rest of the story."

It has been an education for all of us involved in the Bethsaida Excavations Project Consortium housed at the University of Nebraska at Omaha (UNO) and the other projects that we directed through the University of Hartford. The projects in the south of Spain included many different local universities and specialists, but mainly we brought our own group of geophysicists led by Dr. Harry Jol, Bryan Frenz, and Jennifer Bode of the University of Wisconsin, Eau Claire; Paul Bauman, chief geophysicist, and his assistants Christeen Nahas, Brad Hansen, Jennifer M. MacDonald, Laurie Pankratow, and Dan Parker from WorleyParsons in Canada; and our cartographer, Dr. Philip Reeder of the University of South Florida, whose tireless work deserves special acknowledgment. In the south of Spain there were many different teams of Spanish archaeologists, geologists, historians, and researchers. Special help on the underwater work was provided by Professors Claudio Lozano Guerra-Librero and Juan Antonio Morales of the University of Huelva. In Doña Blanca, we are indebted to Dr. Diego Mata of the University of Huelva, and in the Doña Ana Park and Cancho Roano, the principal investigator, Dr. Sebastian Celestino Perez, was of the Institute of Archaeology (CSIC). Juan J. Villarias Robles of CSIC, Angel Leon Conde of FUHE, Antonio Rodriguez Ramirez of the University of Huelva, Victorino Mayor Herrera of the Institute of Archaeology, and Enrique Cerrillo Cuenca of CSIC were also listed as major contributors to the work there. A very good large team of experts spent much time acquiring licenses and analyzing the results following the work that was done in the field. The filming teams of Associated Producers, organized by executive producer Simcha Jacobovici, were an enormous help in the field in Spain. I want to acknowledge the first year's team of Kelly, Michael, and Igal, and also the final team, which included Javiera Quintana, Kathryn Liprott, and director and writer Graeme Ball, who created the documentary *Finding Atlantis* that appeared on the National Geographic Channel.

In the north of Spain, Burgos, we included a totally different set of local universities and specialists than we did in the south of the country. The director of ArchaeoSpain Inc. was our partner, together with our regional Spanish archaeologists, Silvia Pascual, Gerardo Martinez, and Dr. Ana Maria Ortega Martinez, who excavated the area in the 1980s, and the well-known historian of the region, Dr. Juan José Garcia, who provided historical background to the Jewish history of the medieval period in Spain. Working in Israel and Spain as a foreigner is not easy even for those of us who speak Hebrew, Spanish, and Arabic. Many local people helped us with the logistics and special documents that were used and mentioned in the individual chapters. In Burges, Professor Harry Jol ran the GPR projects.

The site maps that I have included in this volume are all the work of Professor Phil Reeder of the University of South Florida. His maps have become the standard for archaeological work, and he has pioneered a new, scientific methodology for working in caves and land sites. The geophysics teams included many people whom Paul Bauman brought from Worley-Parsons and earlier from Komex Inc. in Calgary, Canada: Laurie Pankratow, Jen MacDonald, Rob Passow, Eric Pascal, Christine Nahas, Chris Pooley, Dan Parker, and Brad Hansen. In the case of Poland, volunteers who helped with the work on-site and off included Deborah Rozansky, London; Sarah Rutman, University of Hartford; Len Felson, *Reader's Digest*; Professor Avi Patt, University of Hartford; Lukazc Biedka, Warsaw, a translator at the site and especially at the Luta project; Rabbi Michael Shudrich, the chief rabbi of Poland; Wojciech Mazurek, regional archaeologist of Sobibor, Włodowa, Poland; and Zofia Zinserling, Warsaw, translator.

Most of what I am writing about here has been presented in many different scholarly publications and conference presentations over the past decade and in books. In the case of Bethsaida, Yavne, Nazareth, Qumran, and the Cave of Letters it was extremely difficult to have a foreign university (especially one in Nebraska and later at Hartford) administrate, excavate, and publish the results of excavations in some of the most important locations of Israel. We have done this by making most of the results available to many scholars even in a "raw" state. From lectures at national and international conferences and articles in the popular and more scholarly publications to books, CDs, websites, documentaries, and so on, the information has been made available to other scholars to comment on. Four or five dissertations have utilized our results, and many books and articles by other scholars often use the information gathered by our teams without any citations. When I moved to the University of Hartford from the University of Nebraska at Omaha, the University of Hartford embraced the excavation projects as a natural extension of the Maurice Greenberg Center for Judaic Studies. The president, Walter Harrison, and the then chair of the regents, Arnold Greenberg, made sure that we had the funding and the administrative support we needed. The administrative assistant, Susan Gottlieb, made sure that the work of all these excavations was properly administered. Susan and her husband, Phil, deserve special honor in the creation of this book. Phil Gottlieb is one of the most informed and finest docents at our Museum of Jewish Civilization, which houses the antiquities collection on loan to the university from the Antiquities Authority of Israel since 2003. The curator of the museum is DreAnna Hadash, who also was the illustrator in residence for this book and helped arrange the photos. I also want to thank Phil and Susan Gottlieb, who read the early drafts of the book to make sure they were meaningful for the public and corrected them.

In addition, I want to fully acknowledge the editing of this book by Mary Brady of Haverhill, Massachusetts, and Professor Emeritus John T. Greene of Michigan State University. Mary gave me the type of technical assistance that a book like this requires, while John understands how the general public reads a book that is about disparate ideas—textual information, archaeology, and religion. My book *Digging through the Bible* was also aided by John's careful reading and corrections. In my twenty-five years of working with John in the field, I have discovered that his erudition in writing and in the field is only surpassed by his kindness to students and colleagues alike. His friendship and keen eye for detail made both of these books better. I also need to thank my colleague Professor Avinoam Patt, the Philip D. Feltman Professor of Modern History at the University of

Hartford and an excellent scholar of the Holocaust, who read many of the chapters, but especially the chapter on the "Hidden Holocaust." Professor Emeritus Fred Strickert of Wartburg College read the book manuscript and made many helpful suggestions on the entire manuscript, as did Professor Jerome Hall, a marine archaeologist at the University of San Diego (especially regarding Atlantis, Tarshish, and the Dead Sea Scrolls). Professor Ruth Fine, the Salomon and Victoria Cohen Professor in Spanish and Latin American Literature, and chair of the Department of Romance and Latin American Studies at the Hebrew University in Jerusalem, helped edit the chapter on Spain. As in the case of *Digging through the Bible*, I want to thank my general editor Sarah Stanton, Jin Yu, Patricia Stevenson, and others at Rowman & Littlefield, who have also helped shape the manuscript and the bibliographies, indexes, and reference guide.

Most of what appears in this book has been filmed by a number of different film producers and companies, and I am grateful to them. The materials on and about Atlantis in Spain were filmed by Associated Producers of Canada. The film producer, Simcha Jacobovici, shared with me footage from much of the work and helped me understand more about what we had accomplished. Gary Hochman, the director/producer of the NOVA episode *Ancient Refuge in the Holy Land*, has filmed many of the excavations that are mentioned in the book, and he continues to work on documentaries that incorporate our work at Sobibor, Har Karkom, Qumran, Yavne, and Nazareth into future documentaries. He has shared raw footage with me that has enriched my understanding of what happened at sites that I was working on. Filming in a foreign country is not easy. Filming an archaeological site and resolving difficult historical and archaeological questions in a fifty-six-minute production requires skill and a more-than-rudimentary grasp of multiple cultural and religious histories, textual traditions, and archaeology. Simcha's and Gary's great strengths are in their ability to understand that the material culture, the literary sources, and the oral sources are all telling a complex story that does not emerge on its own. Although I feel that books educate, I have come to appreciate that the medium of film has the ability to educate millions in a way that often is more intelligible than words on a page. Unfortunately, I have come to understand that these documentaries can only accommodate part of the larger aspects of science and that this book is a necessary complement to whatever documentary is made. This was another reason for me to write a book like this that has an overarching view of history and incorporates complex histories and literary traditions in a way that I think tells "the rest of the story." Even this book is only a part of the rich details, and I have included other books and articles in the bibliography for those who want to continue their search for answers. Much additional information on Atlantis, the Holocaust, Spain, Sobibor, Qumran, the Cave of Letters, Har Karkom, and Yavne is available on a variety of websites at links at the University of Hartford's Greenberg Center's site (www.hartford.edu/greenberg).

The sponsorship of most of our archaeological work at the university has come from the Maurice Greenberg Center for Judaic Studies, founded in 1985 by a substantial gift from Arnold C. and Beverly Greenberg of West Hartford, Connecticut. The Maurice Greenberg Center for Judaic Studies is a department of Judaic studies in the College of Arts and Sciences at the University of Hartford (offering three different bachelor of arts degrees and a joint master's program with the University of Connecticut). It is also an academic center of excellence at the university, which together with the university's Museum of Jewish Civilization provides the students, staff, faculty, and general community of Greater Hartford ample opportunity for all types of cultural and academic events and exhibitions related to Jewish life and civilization every year. Thanks to the generous donations of the founding donors of the Greenberg Center, one of the significant areas of research of the center has been biblical archaeology. The Greenberg Center is responsible for helping identify donors to underwrite some of the costs of these excavations through the donations of benefactors of the university. I would like to acknowledge the development office, Barbara Starr, Rachel Kimmelblatt, and Rise Roth, who have been instrumental in making our excavations a priority for funding. I would like to personally acknowledge some of the donors and funding sources who made most of the excavations possible: John and Carol Merrill for funding the Cave of Letters and Qumran excavations (thanks to the good offices of Hershel Shanks at *Biblical Archaeology Review*); Barnea Selavan and David Willner of Foundation Stone of Jerusalem for the development of a Tel Yavne Prototype Excavation Project; William and Judy Freund for the funding of the Yavne and the Sobibor projects; Joel and Sue Grae for the funding of our Har Karkom Excavations Project at the University of Hartford; Steven Konover and the Millie & Irving Bercowetz Fund at the University of Hartford for our ongoing archaeological projects in Israel; and finally Stephen Weinstein for funding our Burgos Excavations Project. Stephen, our contractor on-site in Spain and philanthropist on the Burgos project, was the perfect person for this work, and he helped in the excavations. This is the best type of philanthropist, one who wants to see the work through and is not afraid to get his hands dirty. He is also a Spanish-phile, and his language skills helped us through tricky situations.

Judy and William Freund have made our excavations and documentation projects at Yavne and Sobibor possible. Judy and Bill (who are not my relatives, but I believe we are biologically related in some larger realm) are donors who came to our son's bar mitzvah at my excavations site, Bethsaida, in Israel; helped fund our excavations; and even helped edit my book *Digging through the Bible* and parts of *Digging through History*, because they were part of the audience that I was writing for: educated readers. I was glad that Judy was able to read an early draft of this book before her passing. Judy fled with her family from Germany to Haifa in August 1933, and she arrived not knowing Hebrew to a place that was filling with Jewish immigrants who were just beginning to flee Hitler's Europe. She went to the Reali School in Haifa, perhaps one of the best Jewish schools in Israel at the time, and she was imbued with a love of the land of Israel. Bill's family left Germany later; in 1949 they met again and ultimately married and built a life in the United States—Bill as an economist and Judy as a mother, wife, volunteer, and tireless worker on behalf of many causes. Bill and Judy funded projects from two edges of Jewish history, from the first century CE (Yavne) and the twentieth century (Sobibor). Judy passed away as I was editing this book. I dedicated this work to her, in part, and I will miss the many hours of discussions about archaeology and life that I enjoyed in our times together.

Many of our donors and supporters, like Stephen Weinstein, Margie Scribante, John and Carol Merrill, Barnea Selavan and David Willner, William and Judy Freund, and SusAnna and Joel Grae, not only helped fund projects but also came to the site to visit and often worked at the excavations. This type of dedication makes research a public and a very personal event. In this regard, I need to acknowledge the thousands of volunteers who have participated in these excavations and who have contributed ideas to my own thinking in those long hours of excavating, pottery readings, and lectures. Another acknowledgment is necessary for the University of Nebraska at Omaha's International Studies and Programs and its dean, Thomas Gouttierre, who through thick and thin has helped the Bethsaida Project and the Cave of Letters Project, and my own dean of the College of Arts and Sciences at the University of Hartford, Dr. Joseph Voelker, who also continued to support our efforts during difficult years in Israel. Mostly these last acknowledgments are for the people who do not receive mention in the course of the book, people like Amir Drori, former director general of the Israel Antiquities Authority, who actually encouraged us to return to the Cave of Letters and Qumran. Director Drori, who had himself excavated in the Cave of Letters with Yadin, intimately understood the importance of our work, and we are indebted to him for his consultations. The present director general of the Israel Antiquities Authority, Shuka Dorfman, encouraged this work as well, because he has the vision to realize that the technological advances that we used in the Cave of Letters could be used in many other archaeological contexts. I would also like to acknowledge the input of Uzi Dahari, Hava Katz, Gideon Avni, Jon Seligman, Baruch Brandl, David Amit, Orit Shamir, Orna Cohen, Shalom Yanklowitz, Yardena Alexandre, Danny Syon, Peninah Shor, and Donald Ariel, all of the Israel Antiquities Authority, for a variety of research, permits, insights, and consultations that they provided in the course of the excavations.

Over the years I have come to know personally a few people who have contributed to my own knowledge base and have passed away and deserve my special thanks: Hanan Eshel, Yigal Shiloh, John Rousseau, Father Bargil Pixner, Yizhar Hirschfield, Amir Drori, and staff members Phyllis Stetser and Pinchas Porat. Their presence at conferences and on sites, as well as their friendship, will be missed.

Our thanks to our neighbors and friends in our "Israel home" at Beit Yigal Allon Museum on Kibbutz Ginosar. Special thanks to Katy Bar-Noff, Ada Yardeni, Bill Scheinmann, Shai and Judith Schwartz, Director Nir Rottenberg and Director Emeritus Nitza Kaplan of the Beit Allon Museum, and the staff of the Beit Allon Museum, especially Marina Banai, who made our work there much easier over the past eighteen years. Maintaining an office and permanent laboratory space at Beit Allon has enabled most of our archaeological activities in Israel to continue uninterrupted. It is more than just storage, restoration, and research space. Over the years, Kibbutz Ginosar has made the pottery restorers and staff members who have stayed for extended periods feel like a part of the kibbutz family and has made our foreign visitors comfortable at the Nof Ginosar Hotel. It has become a much-appreciated hospitality.

I am completing this book as the University of Hartford's Maurice Greenberg Center for Judaic Studies is celebrating its twenty-fifth anniversary. Every year I have been able to take students to excavate and experience what I was experiencing in the field thanks to the generosity of our donors. It has been a blessing for me and my family to have been here now for nearly fifteen years, contributing to the history of Judaic studies at the University of Hartford.

Finally, my personal history helped me write about general history. My stepfather, Howard Berkowitz, always used to say that he was born on a tragic day—April 14, 1912, the day the *Titanic* sank. I discovered after he passed away that he was born on April 10, but his account had become his way of placing himself in a known history when he met someone new. My mother, Beatrice, used to celebrate her birthday on New Year's Eve for most of my life. Only much later did I learn that she was actually born on January 1 and her family had her birthday officially changed to December 31 so she could attend elementary school earlier. My mom always celebrated her birthday on New Year's Eve because she knew that we would always be celebrating her birthday. My uncle, Aaron Stovitz, added a middle name when he was serving in the armed forces in World War II. He told me that he added it because it bothered him that when they did morning roll call they would always say "Aaron 'middle name' Stovitz" because he had no middle name. So he created a middle name and used it as his official name for the rest of his life. Judy (Steinberger) Freund, who passed away as I was finishing the editing of this book, had a similar story that she told me. She and Bill Freund were not family but, as you will see in the pages of this book, our connection was very profound. Judy's Hebrew name was not in fact Yehudit (Judith), but rather Yiska. Judy and her family arrived in Israel in the 1930s escaping the Nazis, and when she went to enroll in her school they asked her what her Hebrew name was. She told them Yiska, and they told her that this was not a Hebrew name. They told her to come back when she had a Hebrew name. In point of fact, however, Yiska is a Hebrew name. It is an obscure name of a woman in Genesis 11:29, but it was not a well-known name. So Yiska changed her name to Yehudit, and she was enrolled in her Haifa school.

I tell these four vignettes because I am dedicating this book to these four people who have been a part of my own family and personal history, and their lives stretch back only about one hundred years. What these four stories demonstrate is one of the great principles of history writing. History is not neat. When you try to make everything fit into a neat series of events that follow a straight line, you will find that you are not always writing about history. Things happen and people decide to change their own history because of unanticipated reasons. People and circumstances are uniquely fluid. You can try to track them with evidence like archaeology and personal narratives, but the more we try to have texts and rules (especially rules that come from different periods) imposed upon the material culture and personal narratives, the more problematic the comparison becomes. History follows a whole series of twists and turns, and it is generally not as neat and linear as most history books portray it. You just have to be prepared to follow a story line or artifacts where it takes you. Rediscovering or recovering a lost history has become a lifelong pursuit of mine. I have always been interested in figuring out how and why an incident in history unfolded and its impact upon society. I have done this through an examination of material culture and literary and oral sources. This book is an attempt to show how I came to understand a few incidents and places in history through the lens of archaeological work that I had been involved with. It is not at all comprehensive, but it spans the very beginnings of history to my own time and will serve to introduce the reader to events, texts, methods, and people that have influenced history through their writings and lives.

My personal history includes a thanks to my wife, Eliane, and my children Yoni, Eli, and Ethan, who gave me the freedom to go and pursue these expeditions over the past decade, often at the expense of not being at home. And I cannot end a book about history without writing a continuing thank-you to my bone marrow transplant donor, who shares a genetic history with me that few others on the planet do. These past eight years since my bone marrow transplant have been the most physically challenging of my life and have given me a perspective on human history that perhaps I would never have had but for my encounter with my own mortality. Continuing to go to excavate after a transplant has been challenging, but I am thankful to have medical and family support. I continue to acknowledge my bone marrow donor, Steve (Shlomo Hackel); the staff and founders of the "Gift of Life" Bone Marrow Foundation and Dana Farber Cancer Institute; and my transplant specialist, Dr. Robert J. Soiffer, who keep me in "working order" to do these projects.

Dr. Richard A. Freund
Director and Professor
Maurice Greenberg Center for Judaic Studies
University of Hartford

Bibliography

Dead Sea Scrolls, Qumran, and Archaeology of the Land of Israel

All of the books edited by Hershel Shanks, publisher of *Biblical Archaeology Review* (www.bibarch.com), are highly recommended.

Shanks, Hershel, ed. *Ancient Israel: A Short History from Abraham to the Roman Destruction of the Temple.* Upper Saddle River, NJ: Prentice Hall, 1988.

———, ed. *Christianity and Rabbinic Judaism: A Parallel History of Their Origins and Early Development.* Washington, DC: Biblical Archacology Society, 1992.

———. *In the Temple of Solomon and the Tomb of Caiaphas.* Washington, DC: Biblical Archaeology Society, 1993.

———. *The Mystery and Meaning of the Dead Sea Scrolls.* New York: Vintage Press, 1999.

———, ed. *Understanding the Dead Sea Scrolls: A Reader from the Biblical Archaeology Review.* New York: Vintage Press, 1993.

Shanks, Hershel, and Benjamin Mazar. *Recent Archaeology in the Land of Israel.* Washington, DC: Biblical Archaeology Society, 1985.

The Hebrew University's Orion Center's website includes an extensive bibliography of recent research on the Dead Sea Scrolls (http://orion.mscc.huji.ac.il/index.html).

The Israel Antiquities Authority's website has information on many sites excavated in Israel and related publications (www.antiquities.org.il).

Amiran, Ruth, and Zeev Goldman. *Archaeological Discoveries in the Holy Land.* New York: Bonanza, 1967.

Arav, Rami, and Richard A. Freund. *Bethsaida: A City by the North Shore of the Sea of Galilee.* 4 vols. Kirksville, MO: Truman State University Press, 1995, 2000, 2004, 2008.

Avi-Yonah, Michael. "Archaeology." In *Encyclopaedia Judaica*, vol. 3. Jerusalem: Encyclopaedia Judaica, 1971.

de Vaux, Roland. *Ancient Israel.* 2 vols. New York: McGraw-Hill, 1965.

Dever, William G., ed. *A Manual of Field Excavations.* Jerusalem: Hebrew Union College, 1970.

Freund, Richard. *Digging through the Bible.* Lanham, MD: Rowman & Littlefield, 2009.

———. *Secrets of the Cave of Letters.* New York: Prometheus, 2006.

Leakey, Mary. *Disclosing the Past: An Autobiography.* New York: Doubleday, 1984.

Mazar, Amihai. *Archaeology of the Land of the Bible, 10,000–586 B.C.E.* New York: Doubleday, 1990.

Meyers, Eric M., and James F. Strange. *Archaeology, the Rabbis, and Early Christianity.* Nashville, TN: Abingdon, 1981.

Rousseau, John J., and Rami Arav. *Jesus and His World: An Archaeological and Cultural Dictionary.* Minneapolis, MN: Fortress Press, 1995.

Thompson, Henry O. *Biblical Archaeology: The World, the Mediterranean, the Bible.* New York: Paragon House, 1987.

Yadin, Yigael. *Bar Kokhba.* New York: Random House, 1970.

———. *Masada: Herod's Fortress and the Zealots' Last Stand.* New York: Random House, 1966.

———. *The Message of the Scrolls.* New York: Random House, 1957.

Spain, Atlantis, Tarshish

Albright, M. W. F. "New Light on the Early History of Phoenician Colonization." *Bulletin of the American Schools of Oriental Research* 83 (1941): 14–22.

Bendala, M. "A Thorny Problem: Was There Contact between the Peoples of the Sea and Tartessos?" In *Encounters and Transformations: The Archaeology of Iberia in Transition,* ed. M. Balmuth, A. Gilman, and L. Prado-Torreira, 89–94. Monographs in Mediterranean Archaeology 7. Sheffield, UK: Sheffield Academic Press, 1997.

Berlitz, Charles. *Atlantis: The Eighth Continent.* New York: Putnam, 1984.

———. *Mystery of Atlantis.* New York: Grosset & Dunlap, 1969.

Brennan, Herbie. *The Atlantis Enigma.* London: Piatkus, 2000.

Castleden, Rodney. *Atlantis Destroyed.* New York: Routledge, 1998.

———. *Minoans: Life in Bronze Age Crete.* New York: Routledge, 1990.

Cayce, Edgar Evans. *Mysteries of Atlantis Revisited.* San Francisco: Harper & Row, 1988.

Cayce, Hugh Lynn, ed. *Edgar Cayce on Atlantis.* New York: Hawthorn Books, 1968.

Celestino, S., N. Rafel, and X-L. Armada. *Cancho Roano* 6 (The Sanctuary-Palace). Badajoz: CSIC, 1996.

———. *Cancho Roano* 8. Merida: CSIC, 2003.

———. *Cancho Roano* 9. Merida: CSIC, 2003.

———. *Culture Contact between the Mediterranean and the Atlantic: Precolonization* [Spanish], 11, Rome and Madrid, Consejo Superior de Investigaciones Cientificas. Madrid: CSIC, 2008.

———. "New Light on the Warrior Stelae from Tartessos." *Antiquity* 80 (2006): 89–101.

———. "Precolonization and Colonization in the Interior of Tartessos." In *Colonial Encounters in Ancient Iberia*, ed. by M. Dietler and C. Lopez-Ruiz, 229–51. Chicago: University of Chicago Press, 2009.

Chamorro, Javier G. "Survey of Archaeological Research on Tartessos." *American Journal of Archaeology* 91, no. 2 (1987): 197–232.

Chapin, Henry. *The Search for Atlantis*. New York: Crowell-Collier Press, 1968.

Collins, Andrew. *Gateway to Atlantis: The Search for a Source of a Lost Civilization*. New York: Carroll & Graf, 2000.

Cross, F. M. "The Old Phoenician Inscription from Spain Dedicated to Hurrian Astarte." *Harvard Theological Review* 64 (1971): 189–95.

de Boer, Jelle Zeilinga, and Donald Theodore Sanders. *Volcanoes in Human History: The Far-Reaching Effects of Major Eruptions*. Princeton, NJ: Princeton University Press, 2002.

Donnelly, Ignatius. *Atlantis: The Antediluvian World*. London: Sidgwick & Jackson, 1970.

Doumas, Christos. "The Minoan Eruption of the Santorini Volcano." *Antiquity* 48, no. 190 (1974): 110–15.

———. *Thera, Pompeii of the Ancient Aegean: Excavations at Akrotiri, 1967–79*. New York: Thames and Hudson, 1983.

Dunbavin, Paul. *Atlantis of the West: The Case for Britain's Drowned Megalithic Civilization*. New York: Carroll & Graf, 2003.

Ebon, Martin. *Atlantis: The New Evidence*. New York: New American Library, 1977.

Elat, M. "Tarshish and the Problem of the Phoenician Colonization in the Western Mediterranean." *Orientalia Lovaniensia Perodica* 13 (1982): 55–69.

Ellis, Richard. *Imagining Atlantis*. New York: Knopf, 1998.

Gill, Christopher. "The Genre of the Atlantis Story." *Classical Philology* 72, no. 4 (October 1977): 287–304.

Gomez Toscano, Francisco. "Proto-Historical Occupation between Guadiana and Guadalquivir: The Myth and the Reality." *SPAL* (2002): 151–59.

González de Canales, Fernando, L. Serrano, and J. Llompart. "The Earliest Evidence of Phoenician Presence in the South of the Iberian Peninsula" [Spanish]. *Mainake* 28 (2006): 105–28.

Gutiérrez-Mas, J. M., C. Juan, and J. A. Morales. "Evidence of High-Energy Events in Shelly Layers Interbedded in Coastal Holocene Sands in Cadiz Bay (South-West Spain)." *Earth Surface Processes and Landforms* 34 (2004): 810–23.

James, Peter. *The Sunken Kingdom: The Atlantis Mystery Solved.* London: Pimlico, 1996.

Kühne, R. W. "A Location for 'Atlantis'?" *Antiquity* 78, no. 300 (2004).

Lipinski, E. "Tarshish." In *Theological Dictionary of the Old Testament,* ed. G. J. Botterweck, H. Ringgren, and H.-J. Fabry, 15:790–93. Grand Rapids, MI: Eerdmans, 2006.

Manning, Stuart W. *A Test of Time: The Volcano of Thera and the Chronology and History of the East Mediterranean in the Mid Second Millennium BC.* Oxford: Oxbow Books, 1999.

Marinatos, Spyridon. "The Volcanic Destruction of Minoan Crete." *Antiquity* 13 (1939): 425ff.

Plato. *Critias.* In *Timaeus, Critias, Cleitophon, Menexenus, Epistles,* translated by R. G. Bury, 255–307. Cambridge, MA: Harvard University Press, 1929.

———. *Timaeus.* In *Timaeus, Critias, Cleitophon, Menexenus, Epistles,* translated by R. G. Bury, 41–43. Cambridge, MA: Harvard University Press, 1929.

Rexine, John E. "Atlantis: Fact or Fantasy." *Classical Bulletin* 51 (1974–1975): 49–53.

Schulten, A. *Ancient Geography and Ethnography of the Iberian Peninsula* [Spanish] I. Madrid: Consejo Superior de Investigaciones Cientificas, 1958.

———. "Atlantis." *Ampurias* 1 (1939): 33–53.

———. *Tartessos.* Hamburg, 1922. 2nd ed., Madrid: Espasa Calpe, 1945.

Stemman, Roy. *Atlantis and the Lost Lands.* Garden City, NY: Doubleday, 1977.

Sullivan, Robert. *Atlantis Rising: The True Story of a Submerged Land Yesterday and Today.* New York: Simon & Schuster, 1999.

Tsirkin, Ju. B. "The Hebrew Bible and the Origin of Tartessian Power." *Aula Orientalis* 4 (1986): 179–85.

———. "The Phoenicians and the Tartessos." *Gerion* 15 (1997): 15–25.

Vitaliano, Dorothy B. "Atlantis: A Review Essay." *Journal of the Folklore Institute* 8 (1971): 68–76.

———. *Legends of the Earth: Their Geologic Origins.* Bloomington: Indiana University Press, 1973.

Wilson, Colin, and Rand Flem-Ath. *The Atlantis Blueprint: Unlocking the Ancient Mysteries of a Long-Lost Civilization.* New York: Delacorte Press, 2001.

Zangger, Eberhard. *The Flood from Heaven: Deciphering the Atlantis Legend.* New York: Morrow, 1992.

Qumran, Qumran Cemetery, and the Dead Sea Scrolls

Allegro, J. M. *The Chosen People: A Study of Jewish History from the Time of the Exile until the Revolt of Bar Kocheba (Sixth Century B.C. to Second Century A.D.).* Garden City, NY: Doubleday, 1972.

———. *The Dead Sea Scrolls: A Reappraisal.* Harmondsworth, UK: Penguin, 1964.

———. *The Dead Sea Scrolls and the Christian Myth.* London: Westbridge Books, 1979.

———. *The Treasury of the Copper Scroll: The Opening and Decipherment of the Most Mysterious of the Dead Sea Scrolls; A Unique Inventory of Buried Treasure.* Garden City, NY: Doubleday, 1960.

Cross, F. M., Jr. *The Ancient Library of Qumran and Modern Biblical Studies: The Haskell Lectures, 1956–1957.* 3rd ed. Minneapolis, MN: Fortress, 1995.

———. "The Manuscripts of the Dead Sea Caves." *Biblical Archaeologist* 17, no. 1 (1954): 2–21.

———. "The Old Testament at Qumran." In *The Ancient Library of Qumran,* chap. 4. New York: Anchor Books, 1961.

Cross, F. M., and S. Talmon. *Qumran and the History of the Biblical Text.* Cambridge, MA: Harvard University Press, 1975.

Freund, R. "A New Interpretation of the Incense Shovels of the Cave of the Letters." In *The Dead Sea Scrolls: Fifty Years after their Discovery,* Proceedings of the Jerusalem Congress, July 20–25, 1997, 644–60. Jerusalem: Israel Exploration Society in Cooperation with the Shrine of the Book, Israel Museum, 2000.

———, M. Broshi, H. Eshel, and B. Schultz. "New Data on the Cemetery East of Khirbet Qumran." *Dead Sea Discoveries* 9, no. 2 (2002): 135–65.

Steckoll, S. H. "Preliminary Excavation Report in the Qumran Cemetery." *Revue de Qumran* 6 (1968): 323–36.

Taylor, J. E. "The Cemeteries of Khirbet Qumran and Women's Presence at the Site." *Dead Sea Discoveries* 6 (1999): 285–336.

History of Judaism

Alon, G. *The Jews in Their Land in the Talmudic Age.* Cambridge, MA: Harvard University Press, 1989.

Avi-Yonah, M. *The Jews of Palestine: A Political History from the Bar Kokhba War to the Arab Conquest.* Jerusalem: Magnes Press, 1984.

Baron, S. W. *A Social and Religious History of the Jews.* 18 vols. New York: Columbia University Press, 1952–1983.

Guttmann, A. *Rabbinic Judaism in the Making: The Halakhah from Ezra to Judah I.* Detroit, MI: Wayne State University Press, 1970.

History of Spain, Medieval

Ashtor, Eliyhau. *The Jews of Moslem Spain.* 3 vols. Philadelphia: Jewish Publication Society, 1973, 1992.

Baer, Yitzhak. *A History of the Jews in Christian Spain: From the Age of Reconquest to the Fourteenth Century*, translated by Louis Schoffman. 2 vols. Philadelphia: Jewish Publication Society, 1971, 1978.

Bode, Jenifer A., Harry M. Jol, Philip Reeder, Richard A. Freund, Paul Bauman, and Christeen Nahas. "GPR Investigation of the Nuestra Señora de la Blanca Church Site, Burgos, Spain." Proceedings of the Eleventh International Conference on Ground-Penetrating Radar, Columbus, Ohio, June 19–22, 2006, 307–15.

Leviant, Curt. *Masterpieces of Hebrew Literature*. Philadelphia: Jewish Publication Society, 2008.

Singerman, Robert. *The Jews of Spain and Portugal: A Bibliography*. New York: Garland Publishing, 1975.

———. *Spanish and Portuguese Jewry: A Classified Bibliography*. Westport, CT: Greenwood Press, 1993.

Sobibor and the Holocaust

Arad, Yitzhak. *Belzec, Sobibor, Treblinka: The Operation Reinhard Death Camps*. Bloomington: Indiana University Press, 1987.

Blatt, Thomas Toivi. *From the Ashes of Sobibor*. Evanston, IL: Northwestern University Press, 1997.

Browning, Christopher. *The Origins of the Final Solution: The Evolution of Nazi Jewish Policy, September 1939–March 1942*. Lincoln: University of Nebraska Press, 2004.

———. *Remembering Survival: Inside a Nazi Slave Labor Camp*. New York: Norton, 2010.

Dawidowicz, Lucy S., ed. *The Golden Tradition: Jewish Life and Thought in Eastern Europe*. New York: Holt, Rinehart and Winston, 1967.

———. *The War against the Jews, 1933–1945*. New York: Bantam, 1976.

Engel, Selma. Interview by Avinoam Patt and Sarah Rutman, September 26, 2008. University of Hartford Sobibor Documentation Project; written account available at www.holocaustresearchproject.org/survivor/selma%20engel.html.

Gilead, I., Yoram Haimi, and Wojciech Mazurek. "Excavating Nazi Extermination Centres." *Present Pasts: Journal of the Institute of Archaeology Heritages Studies Section* 1 (2009): 10–39.

Hilberg, Raul. *The Destruction of the European Jews*. New Haven, CT: Yale University Press, 2003.

Kola, Andrzej. *Bełżec: The Nazi Camp for Jews in the Light of Archaeological Sources: Excavations 1997–1999*. Washington, DC: United States Holocaust Museum, 2000.

Langer, Lawrence. *The Holocaust and the Literary Imagination*. New Haven, CT: Yale University Press, 1977.

———. *Holocaust Testimonies: The Ruins of Memory*. New Haven, CT: Yale University Press, 1991.

Mosse, George L. *The Crisis of German Ideology: Intellectual Origins of the Third Reich*. New York: Schocken, 1981.

———. *Toward the Final Solution: A History of European Racism*. New York: Howard Fertig, 1978.

O'Neil, Robin. "Belzec—The 'Forgotten' Death Camp." *East European Jewish Affairs* 28, no. 2 (1998): 49–62.

Parkes, James. *Anti-Semitism*. Chicago: Quadrangle Books, 1969.

Raab, Esther Turner. Interview by Sarah Rutman, August 27, 2008, University of Hartford Sobibor Documentation Project.

Rashke, Richard. *Dear Esther*. Lincoln, NE: Morris, 2000.

———. *Escape from Sobibor*. Urbana: University of Illinois Press, 1995.

Roiter, Howard, and Kalmen Wewryk. *To Sobibor and Back: An Eyewitness Account*, vol. 1 of *Memories of Holocaust Survivors in Canada*. Montreal: Concordia University Chair in Canadian Jewish Studies and the Montreal Institute for Genocide and Human Rights, 1999.

Trachtenberg, Joshua. *The Devil and the Jews: The Medieval Conception of the Jew and Its Relation to Modern Anti-Semitism*. New Haven, CT: Yale University Press, 1943.

Zielinski, Andrew. *Conversations with Regina*. Chelm, Poland: Muzeum Pojezierza Łęczyńsko-Włodawsiego, 2008.

Index

Note: Page numbers in italics refer to figures